ABOUT THE AUTHORS

JAMES O. PROCHASKA, Ph.D., is a professor of psychology and director of the Cancer Prevention Research Center at the University of Rhode Island. JOHN C. NORCROSS, Ph.D., is professor and former chair of psychology at the University of Scranton. CARLO C. DiCLEMENTE, Ph.D., is professor and chair of the department of psychology at the University of Maryland, Baltimore County. Their model for self-change has atttracted attention worldwide and has been applied in programs sponsored by such organizations as the National Cancer Institute and the National Institute of Drug Abuse.

CHANGING FOR GOOD

JAMES O. PROCHASKA, PH.D.
JOHN C. NORCROSS, PH.D.
CARLO C. DICLEMENTE, PH.D.

WILLIAM MORROW
An Imprint of HarperCollins*Publishers*

Writing contributions from Mark Beitman and Brian Crawley.

A hardcover edition of this book was published in 1994 by William Morrow.

HarperCollins books may be purchased for educational, business, or sales promotional use. For information, please e-mail the Special Markets Department at SPsales@harpercollins.com.

First Avon Books edition published 1995.

Reprinted in Quill 2002.

FIRST COLLINS PAPERBACK EDITION PUBLISHED 2006

The Library of Congress has catalogued a previous edition as follows:
Prochaska, James O.
    Changing for good / James O. Prochaska, John C. Norcross, Carlo C. DiClemente.
       p. cm.
       1. Behavior modification. 2. Change (Psychology). I. DiClemente, Carlo C. II. Norcross, John C., 1957. III. Title.
BF637.B4P65   1994
158'.1—dc20   93-44897
                                                                                 CIP
ISBN: 978-0-38-072572-4 (pbk.)
ISBN-10: 0-380-72572-X (pbk.)

15   FOLIO/RRD   50 49 48 47 46 45

To Our Children,
who have changed our lives
in so many good ways

Jason and Jodi

Rebecca and Jonathon

Cara and Anna

Acknowledgments

OUR COLLECTIVE fifty years of clinical and research experience behind *Changing for Good* have indebted us to our funding sources, students, clients, and colleagues. We gratefully acknowledge the financial support over the years of the National Institutes of Health, the University of Rhode Island, the University of Scranton, the University of Texas Medical School, and the University of Houston. We appreciate our students, too numerous to thank individually here, for their persistent inquisitiveness and research contributions. We cherish the courage and sharing of our research participants and psychotherapy clients, who have proven to be the ultimate teachers of self-change.

The development of the transtheoretical approach has been a collaborative effort involving many dedicated individuals who have made invaluable contributions. These include Drs. Wayne Velicer, Joseph Rossi, David Abrams, Ellie McConnaughy, Diane Grimley, Unto Pallonen, Joseph Fava, Colleen Redding, Michael Goldstein, William Rakowski, Raymond Niaura, Bess Marcus, Geoff Greene, Robert Laforge, Laurie Ruggiero, Susan Rossi, Karen Emmons, Gabrielle Reed, and many more. Others making special contributions include Elaine Taylor, Gabrielle Riley, Guy Natelli, and the entire staff of the Cancer Prevention Research

Consortium. Collaborating investigators in Houston included Drs. Jack Gordon, Joseph Carbonari, Michael Gibertini, Nancy Brandenburg, Sheryl Hughes, Chris Lovato, Michael Eriksen, Patricia Mullen, and Mary Velasquez.

Maria Guarnaschelli, our editor, committed her creativity and vitality to help transform our vision into a reality. We treasure her mission of reducing the distance between professionals and the public. The assistance of the William Morrow staff was particularly appreciated by the three of us—all novices in the process of publishing a book for the public.

Our families are the foundation for creative inspiration and personal support. Each of our spouses, Jan Prochaska, ACSW, Nancy Caldwell-Norcross, ACSW, and Lynn Dahlquist, Ph.D., are dedicated professionals, parents, and partners. Experiencing unconditional caring is a hallmark of successful self-change, and our spouses are remarkably good models of such consummate care. We dedicate *Changing for Good* to our children, who have changed our lives in so many good ways.

Contents

A Scientific Revolution

WELCOME OR NOT, change is un-avoidable. Life itself is change, as the Greek philosopher Heraclitus observed over 2,500 years ago. Each moment is different from every other. Nothing remains static for an instant, from a planetary to a molecular level. Few of the changes we experience are under our control: When we watch the often tragic history of the world unfold, just as when we face our personal tragedies, we may feel helpless, or at least limited as to what we can do. Even the unexpected rain on a summer vacation is frustratingly out of our control. And, of course, we have no say over the passage of time.

Although we cannot intentionally change many aspects of ourselves or our world, we can exert some power over the courses of our own lives. We can work to improve our economic situations, our family ties, and the condition of our homes. There are other kinds of changes we can make by ourselves—of our behaviors, thoughts, and feelings— and these are the kinds of changes that concern us here.

For over twelve years now, my colleagues and I have dedicated our efforts to discovering how people intentionally change. We have been searching for an underlying structure of change, one that might be common to both self-administered and therapeutic courses of treatment for addictive behaviors. People do successfully reverse complex problems and addictions, with and without psychotherapy. We wanted to know if there were some basic principles that reveal the structure of change.

We now have compelling evidence to suggest that there are. The three of us, John Norcross, Carlo DiClemente, and I, are practicing clinical psychologists, university professors, research collaborators, and self-change enthusiasts. We have conducted more than fifty different studies on thousands of individuals to discover how people overcome problems of smoking and alcohol abuse, emotional distress, weight control, as well as others. Our model—which draws on the essential tenets of many diverse theories of psychotherapy—has been tested, revised, and improved through scores of empirical studies, and is currently in use by professionals around the world. We never expected to produce a revolution in the science of behavior change—but that is just what our esteemed colleagues are claiming we have done.

Dr. Barbara Rimer, director of the Cancer Prevention Research Unit at Duke University, was one of the first to suggest that our work was precipitating a paradigm shift in how health professionals understand and change high-risk behaviors. Dr. Howard Schaefer, director of Harvard's Addictions Treatment Center, believes that we have provided an intellectual framework for a modern reformation in the approach to changing addictive behaviors. And Dr. William Saunders of Criton University in Australia reports that it is hard to remember how health professionals used to understand behavior change before our model emerged. Health establishments that use our model include the Centers for Disease Control and the National Cancer Institute, in the United States, the National Health Service of Great Britain, and Johnson & Johnson, worldwide.

Our novel approach to change belies the old action paradigm, wherein change was assumed to occur dramatically and discretely. This action paradigm has dominated behavior change programs for the past three or four decades. Following this model, clients are enrolled in relatively brief programs designed to conquer smoking, weight, alcohol, or other problems; within weeks they are expected to take action and adopt healthier lifestyles. If they fail to take or maintain action, the clients themselves are blamed for a lack of willpower or motivation.

We were the first to consider that it is this model of behavior change that is inadequate, and not those who wish to change. Successful self-changing individuals follow a powerful and, perhaps most important, controllable and predictable course. Along this course are various stages, each calling for particular and different approaches to change. The action stage is simply one of six stages—following precontemplation, contemplation, and preparation, and preceding maintenance and termination. No one stage is any more or less important than another. We have found, in a representative sample across more than fifteen high-risk behaviors, that fewer than 20 percent of a problem population are prepared for action at any given time. And yet, more than 90 percent of behavior change programs are designed with this 20 percent in mind.

Our scientific approach to self-change requires that you know what stage you are in for the problem you want to overcome. The key to success is the appropriately timed use of a variety of coping skills. During our studies, we have found much that is encouraging, including the fact that even people who are not ready to act can set the change process into motion. Our model can benefit individuals in any stage of a problematic behavior, from those who don't want to change to those who have spent years hoping to change . . . someday.

The model is being applied by researchers to help understand how people change in a remarkable range of circumstances. The stages of change are employed in rehabilitation programs designed for delinquent adolescents, cocaine and heroin addicts, and patients with brain injury; in therapeutic courses for clients suffering from interpersonal problems or depression, and for alcoholics and alcohol abusers; and in clinical trials of psychotropic medications for patients with anxiety and panic disorders. The model has also been used to change behaviors of sedentary people and people with high-fat diets, people who allow themselves to be overexposed to the sun, adolescent and adult smokers, and dozens of other groups.

Up until now, only a minority of psychotherapists were intuitively aware of how to guide self-changers through the different stages. This explains why so few people with problems go to excellent action-oriented treatment programs; fewer than 5 percent of smokers, 10 percent of alcoholics or obese individuals, and 25 percent of people with mental health disorders ever seek psychotherapy. It also helps to explain why over 45 percent of clients drop out of psychotherapy prematurely, since treatments too often don't match the stage clients are in.

Contrary to what many people believe, self-changers are just as successful in their efforts to change as those individuals who choose to enter therapy or join a professionally run program. The vast majority of people who change never visit a mental health professional or participate in an organized program. They cope with their difficulties themselves, using their own capacities and resources, drawing on others for support, and developing strategies based on hard experience. After years of ongoing work, we have gathered and evaluated data from thousands of these successful self-changers. And it is their experience upon which we have based our book, rather than on academic theory or "expert opinion."

Although psychotherapy can provide an excellent environment for change, there are fewer differences between therapy-changers and self-changers than was once believed, and many more similarities. In fact, it can be argued that all change is self-change, and that therapy is simply professionally coached self-change. Even when seeing a therapist, a client does all the work in the 99 percent of the week that he or she is not in the consulting room. Certainly many people need assistance in order to change, but that help can come from within, from nonprofessionals, or from a book such as this one; the key is always to use the right strategy at the right time.

Too many people look for easy solutions in the wrong places. There are no magic pills, magic pins, or magic plans. People progress through the same stages of change whether they are overcoming problems with substance abuse, anxiety, depression, or weight control. The result is that the principles that address one particular problem can be transferred to many other problems. In these pages, we will show you exactly what those stages of change are, and which processes you need to work your way through each stage.

Our system is simple to understand; indeed, it makes so much sense that most people grasp it immediately. This book will help to introduce our work to those therapists and health professionals who wish to know more about our model of self-change. It will be especially helpful to those of you (psychotherapists included!) who have a problem you would like to change.

Following the example set by successful self-changers, you can learn new skills, draw upon your inner strength, enhance your self-sufficiency, and avoid becoming dependent on others for solutions, thus building your self-confidence for the future. As behavioral psychologist B. F. Skinner once remarked, one thing wrong with the Western world is that we too often help those who can help themselves.

Though not all self-change is successful, very often failure is due to a lack of guidance. Most self-changers are so busy reinventing the wheel—discovering the passage through change by themselves—that they become exhausted during the course of their struggle. This book will help you to avoid repeating the errors others have made before you. We will chart the path that successful self-changers have followed. We cannot take you down it, of course, but we can provide you with the explicit directions you need.

To begin to be effective, the process described in these pages requires only that you be open and willing to learn. You will eventually make change a top priority. Armed with understanding and newly developed skills, you will have the best possible chance of success when the time comes for you to take action. Just as professional therapy can provide you with an hour a week to concentrate on change, this book provides you with a structure you can use to stimulate, guide, reflect upon and evaluate your progress. All you need do is make a commitment to read it.

—JAMES O. PROCHASKA, PH.D.
University of Rhode Island
Kingston, R.I.

Part One

THE SCIENCE

For every complex problem there is an
easy answer, and it is wrong.

—H. L. MENCKEN

CHAPTER I

How You Change

IF ONE SYSTEM of psychotherapy had ever demonstrated clear superiority over the others in helping humans shed undesirable behavior, the name of that system would be a household word by now. But until recently, change has remained enigmatic, and none of the several hundred different existing therapies can effectively explain just how it occurs. Furthermore, no therapy is any more successful than the change strategies that determined, persistent, and hardworking individuals develop for themselves.

My colleagues and I have made it our life's work to investigate how people change on their own, without the benefit of psychotherapy. This is work that began, for me, with a terrific frustration at my inability to help a certain man overcome the depression and alcoholism that were killing him. Because this man distrusted psychotherapy, and denied that his depression and addiction were problems, it fell to his loved ones to help him. And although we tried to help, nothing worked.

The man was my father. After he died, in my junior year of college, I began to study psychology in earnest in an effort to make sense of what had happened. I wondered if there wasn't some better way to help people like my father change themselves. Too few people with addictions or other

self-destructive problems either can or will seek out professional help. I wanted to find some way to bring the wonderful insights of psychology to the mass of people who
don't ordinarily benefit from them, those people who are
self-changers. As I studied, I was confronted—just as the
layperson seeking therapy is confronted today—with a be-
wildering array of psychotherapeutic systems from which
to choose.

Therapy is a complex topic: Think of the range of possibilities you confront when you combine an individual client, with one or more complicated problems, with a
therapist schooled in a particular theory. A relationship develops between the two, unlike any other relationship even
this therapist has with other clients. He or she may employ
one of any number of treatment techniques, and must continually decide what to do and when and how to do it. No
single system of therapy adequately addresses all of these
variables.

As often happens when a complex subject remains inadequately explained, new theories are developed. When
my colleagues and I began our work, the field of psychotherapy was becoming fragmented. In the 1950s, it was es-
timated that there were some thirty-six distinct systems of
psychotherapy; today, there are more than four hundred!
Many of these approaches are narrow. Each has its own
dogma, with its own saints and heretics along with its more
or less faithful followers. Too often these followers are blind
to the considerable affinities between their own theories
and the theories that issue from other systems. They see
only the differences. These differences command, it seems
to me, far too much attention.

As I continued my studies, I became terrifically frustrated
again. Now the frustration came from the feeling that I was
spending all my time doing other people's research. And
why was so much of this research aimed at bolstering one
theory at the expense of another? I had to remember my

basic reason for studying psychology in the first place—I wanted to learn what kinds of ways there were to help people change themselves. Could it be, I wondered, that the hundreds of extant theories reflected the existence of hundreds of unique processes of change, some more valuable than others?

It seemed more likely that no single approach could be clinically adequate for all problems, patients, and situations. And in 1975, Lester Luborsky, a psychologist from the University of Pennsylvania, declared the grand psychotherapy sweepstakes a tie, citing the Dodo's verdict in *Alice in Wonderland:* "*Everyone* has won and *all* must have prizes!" Subsequent studies have supported Luborsky's conclusion that all legitimate psychological therapies produce favorable and nearly equivalent outcomes.

Psychotherapy works. When they have finished with a course of therapy, clients are better off than 80 percent of people with the same problems who are on a waiting list for therapy. However, no one has ever demonstrated that one therapeutic approach is consistently superior to another.

THE TRANSTHEORETICAL APPROACH

The lack of an overall guiding theory, the search for the underlying principles, the growing acknowledgment that no single therapy is more "correct" than any other, the proliferation of new therapies, and a general dissatisfaction with their often limited approaches, led many thoughtful psychologists to call for an integrated approach to therapy. Struck by Luborsky's findings, and finally out of school and practicing, I decided to pursue my own research. Was there, I wondered, a way to combine the profound insights of psychoanalysis, the powerful techniques of behaviorism, the experiential methods of cognitive therapies, the liberating philosophy of existential analysis, and the humane relationships of humanism? Was there a way to exploit fully the essential forces of psychotherapy? Naturally, a few theorists insisted that such integration was philosophically impossible.

Still, it seemed intolerable that no one understood the process of human change. As the psychotherapist Paul Watzlawick put it, "If that little green man from Mars arrived and asked us to explain our techniques for effecting human change, and if we then told him, would he not scratch his head (or its equivalent) in disbelief and ask us why we have arrived at such complicated, abstruse, and far-fetched theories, rather than first of all investigating how human change comes about naturally, spontaneously, and on an everyday basis?" Rather than shaping the therapy to the needs of the individual client, most therapists assume that the client's issues will fit into a particular mold—that, for example, all his or her problems will eventually lead to conflicts over sex, or aggression, or whatever.

I set out to find the common components of the major therapies. The first step was to master the masters. I did what amounted to a "cross-cultural" study of the different schools of psychology, with an eye toward integrating them. I tried to isolate the principles and processes of change that each system advocated and practiced. There was a lot of information available about the origins and theories of the different systems, but comparatively little on how they actually helped people to change.

After working for some time gathering data, I ended up with what was basically a shopping list of the processes of change available in the different therapies. The data were disorganized and made little sense. I think it is worthwhile to demystify the scientific process somewhat. Too often we fetishize scientific discoveries, offering blind faith to ideas we find difficult to inquire into or understand. Many of us regard science as a definite body of knowledge—as if it were a place whose boundary and geography were well known and easily ascertained. In fact, it is a province whose vast unknown territories are filled in only a little at a time. Guesses are made, conclusions drawn, and regions penciled in accordingly, only to be erased or written over later. Scientists rely as much on creative intuition as any artist does—the difference is that the scientist willfully attempts to disprove or validate his or her insight by the most stringent tests imaginable.

Eventually I left off trying to make sense of my data, and went to spend a brief weekend's vacation with my wife, Jan, on Cape Cod. The first morning there, I suddenly received an inspiration, a kind of graphic idea that led to an organizing chart of the data. On my paper mat at the breakfast table I sketched the diagram that had occurred to me. I was able finally to see the connections among the different major theories of psychology. Because of a hunch, and a great deal of work, I had discovered processes that could account for change across all psychotherapies. This led to my first book, *Systems of Psychotherapy* (1979).

Very early on in the work, I discovered an irony: Although the major therapies usually disagree about what a client needs to change, and certainly they battle over why a client has a given problem, there is more agreement, albeit unwitting, about how change is effected. All of the hundreds of theories of therapy can be summarized by a few essential principles I call the "processes of change." These processes can be defined simply: Any activity that you initiate to help modify your thinking, feeling, or behavior is a change process. As you can see from Table 1, not all of the processes are used by all therapies. But all the four hundred or more psychotherapies produce change by applying two

TABLE I. SUMMARY OF THE
PRINCIPAL THEORIES OF PSYCHOTHERAPY*

Theory	Notable Figures	Primary Processes of Change	Representative Techniques[†]
Psycho-analytic	Sigmund Freud Carl Jung	Consciousness-raising Emotional arousal	Analysis of resistance Free association Dream interpretation
Humanistic/ Existential	Carl Rogers Rollo May	Social Liberation Commitment Helping Relationships	Clarification and reflection Empathy and warmth Free experiencing
Gestalt/ Experiential	Fritz Perls Arthur Janov	Self-Reevaluation Emotional Arousal	Choosing and feedback Confrontation Focusing
Cognitive	Albert Ellis Aaron Beck	Countering Self-Reevaluation	Education Identifying dysfunctional thoughts Cognitive restructuring
Behavioral	B. F. Skinner Joseph Wolpe	Environment Control Reward Countering	Assertion Relaxation training Managing reinforcements Self-control training

*Each theory of psychotherapy has its own sphere of excellence. Psychoanalysis, for example, is the preferred approach for raising awareness of both conscious and unconscious motivations, or consciousness-raising. Behaviorism, on the other hand, is demonstrably the most effective approach for modifying discrete problem behaviors.

As you can see, each system is especially useful at one or two stages of change. The transtheoretical model, which builds on the respective strengths of these systems, integrates the best of each into a coherent whole.

†These techniques are included here for the informed reader, although they are not explored in the text.

or more of these processes. As a self-changer, you have the advantage of being able to choose from among all the processes. You aren't limited to one theory of therapy.

THE PROCESSES OF CHANGE

In change, as in many other aspects of life, timing is everything. You will apply different processes to your problems at different stages of change. These stages will be introduced in the next chapter, and far greater detail will be provided as to how the processes of change work within the stages. First, here is a summary of the nine major processes of change.

Consciousness-raising

The most widely used change process, *consciousness-raising*, was first described by Sigmund Freud, who said that the basic objective of psychoanalysis was "to make the unconscious conscious." Today, almost all major therapies begin by trying to raise your level of awareness, increasing the amount of information available to you, and thus improving the likelihood of your making intelligent decisions concerning your problem.

Consciousness-raising is not, however, limited to uncovering hidden thoughts and feelings. Any increased knowledge about yourself or the nature of your problem, regardless of the source, raises your consciousness. If, for example, you are trying to lose weight but are unaware that your body can adjust quickly to dieting by lowering its basal metabolism—which in turn leads to burning fewer calories—then you may be baffled when your diet doesn't work immediately. Your elevated consciousness may help you to make adjustments in your approach to weight loss.

Social liberation

This process involves any new alternatives that the external environment can give you to begin or continue your change efforts. No-smoking areas, an alternative atmosphere for nonsmokers—and those struggling to become nonsmokers—are an obvious example of *social liberation*. Low-fat menu items in fancy restaurants are another.

Because social liberation is an external force, you will perceive it · quite differently depending on the stage of change you are in. Some people resist and resent no-smoking areas. Others struggle to create them. Any individual can act as an advocate for his or her own rights, striving to alter the social environment in ways that can help others change themselves. Advocacy organizations, such as mental health associations, gay and lesbian alliances, or women's rights groups, all lend support to personally empowering behaviors. Social liberation not only makes more actions possible, but it can also increase self-esteem as practitioners come to believe in their own power and ability to change.

Emotional arousal

This important tool, which forms the basis of so many therapies, can enable you to become aware of your defenses against change. *Emotional arousal* parallels consciousness-raising, but works on a deeper, feeling level and is equally important in the early stages of change. Known also as *dramatic release*—or, more traditionally, *catharsis*—emotional arousal is a significant, often sudden emotional experience related to the problem at hand. It is an extremely powerful process.

Emotional arousal sometimes results from real-life tragedies. Carlo DiClemente's brother was a cigarette smoker who had occasionally considered quitting but had made no definite plans. When his sister was diagnosed with ovarian cancer and asked him to give up smoking, he was so moved and so concerned about her and her illness that he finally did quit. Similar stories can be told of driving accidents involving one drunken family member that have stimulated an end to the drinking problem of another.

Obviously, it is preferable to generate emotional arousal through films, dramatic public-education spots, and fear-arousal methods. Psychodrama is a useful technique that attempts to portray events or relationships in a dramatic setting. The goal of all these techniques is to increase awareness and depth of feeling and to move individuals toward action.

Self-reevaluation

This process requires you to give a thoughtful and emotional reappraisal of your problem, and an assessment of the kind of person you might be once you have conquered it. *Self-reevaluation* enables you to see when and how your problem behavior conflicts with your personal values. The result is that you come not only to believe but truly to feel that life would be significantly better without the problem. How do you perceive yourself as a gambler, a drinker, or a sedentary person? How do you see yourself if you change your behavior? What will be the cost of that change, in time, energy, pleasure, stress, or image? What, overall, are the pros and cons of trying to overcome your problem? These are the emotional and rational questions people ask themselves when applying self-reevaluation.

Commitment

Once you choose to change, you accept responsibility for changing. This responsibility is the burden of *commitment*, sometimes called "self-liberation." It is an acknowledgment that you are the only one who is able to respond, speak, and act for yourself.

The first step of commitment is private, telling yourself

you are choosing to change. The second step involves going public—announcing to others that you have made a firm decision to change. This amounts to a self-applied pressure to stick with your program, because if you do not succeed in changing, you may feel ashamed or guilty in front of those with whom you have shared your decision. You may prefer to keep your commitment private, so others won't know if you fail. Although this protects you from embarrassment, it also weakens your will; public commitments are much more powerful than private ones.

Countering

The technical term for substituting healthy responses for unhealthy ones is *countering,* or counterconditioning. All of our behavior is conditional: We are more likely to overeat when dining out than when eating at home, to abuse alcohol when anxious than when relaxed, to smoke when bored than when active, or to feel emotionally distressed when alone than when with friends.

Almost any healthy activity can be an effective countering technique. For example, a drug user may choose to go jogging to counter the urge to get high, or a sedentary person may seek out a family member to spend time with instead of disappearing into the couch. There are many different good countering activities—the trick lies in finding the ones that will work for you.

Environment control

Like countering, *environment control* is action oriented. In this instance, however, you do not seek to control internal reactions but to restructure your environment so that the probability of a problem-causing event is reduced. (Technically, countering adjusts an individual's responses to certain stimuli; environment control regulates the stimuli.) Environment-control techniques can be as simple as removing narcotics or alcohol from your home. A positive reminder, such as a NO SMOKING sign or a warning on the refrigerator door, is another technique.

Rewards

Punishment and *rewards* are opposite sides of the same coin: You can punish problem behavior or reward desirable behavior. Punishment is rarely used by successful self-changers or therapists. Not only is it ethically questionable, it tends to suppress problem behavior temporarily rather than lead to lasting change.

Rewards, on the other hand, are often successfully used to change behavior. Self-praise is one simple form of reward. A present would be another, one that you give yourself upon reaching a certain goal, or that you purchase with the money you would otherwise have spent on the problem. Rewards can also be under the control of other people: Your family may shower you with praise for losing weight, or you may win a bet with a friend when you quit smoking.

Here in New England we have frequently encountered a negative reaction to rewards, perhaps reflecting the region's historical legacy. Too many puritanical people believe that they have no right to be rewarded for modifying behaviors that they should never have acquired, such as abusing alcohol, food, or tobacco. These people deprive themselves of reinforcements for progressing along positive paths. If you are such a person, check your responses against the perspectives of those who are close to you as you work with the next change process.

Helping relationships

Self-change refers to your own attempts to modify your behavior without professional assistance. It does not, repeat *not*, refer to refusing care, support, or other forms of assistance from significant people in your life. This clarification avoids the age-old misconception of self-change as "going it alone." Throughout the cycle of change, others can be enlisted to assist you. While we cannot control how our friends and family members act toward us, we can certainly request their support, offer them our preferences, and educate them about our experiences. This is what we mean by "enlisting" or "eliciting" *helping relationships.*

The helping relationship is the most frequently enlisted change process in psychotherapy, and it is also of critical importance to self-changers. Whether you turn to a professional, friend, member of the family, or the clergy, the helping relationship provides support, caring, understanding, and acceptance.

Unfortunately, many people are inadequately trained in even the simplest helping skills, such as listening and reflecting. Helping is not always easy. Many of us are uncomfortable relating to loved ones when they are in emotional pain. But because helping relationships are of such primary value to self-changers, this book includes in the first five chapters of Part Two detailed information intended specifically for helpers.

Processes versus techniques

Do not make the mistake of confusing these nine processes of change with techniques of change. Each process involves a broad strategy that may employ any number of techniques. For each process, there are dozens, even hundreds of techniques. We found that a group of self-changers who were quitting smoking, for example, relied on more than 130 different techniques to quit permanently. Table 2 outlines a few techniques used by psychotherapists to apply each process.

The following anecdote from a smoking cessation group run by John Norcross illustrates the distinction between process and technique: Group members were discussing successful ways to resist urges to overeat. One elderly woman said that when she earnestly played the piano, her temptations vanished. A young man reported that jogging

TABLE 2. SUMMARY OF SOME CHANGE
PROCESS TECHNIQUES

Process	Goals	Techniques*
Consciousness-Raising	Increasing information about self and problem	Observations, confrontations, interpretations, bibliotherapy
Social Liberation	Increasing social alternatives for behaviors that are not problematic	Advocating for rights of repressed, empowering, policy interventions
Emotional Arousal	Experiencing and expressing feelings about one's problems and solutions	Psychodrama, grieving losses, role playing
Self-Reevaluation	Assessing feelings and thoughts about self with respect to a problem	Value clarification, imagery, corrective emotional experience
Commitment	Choosing and commiting to act, or belief in ability to change	Decision-making therapy, New Year's resolutions, logotherapy
Countering	Substituting alternatives for problem behaviors	Relaxation, desensitization, assertion, positive self-statements
Environment Control	Avoiding stimuli that elicit problem behaviors	Environmental restructuring (e.g., removing alcohol or fattening foods), avoiding high-risk cues
Reward	Rewarding self, or being rewarded by others, for making changes	Contingency contracts, overt and covert reinforcement
Helping Relationships	Enlisting the help of someone who cares	Therapeutic alliance, social support, self-help groups

*These are primarily professional techniques used by psychotherapists. Throughout Part II you will learn the most creative and effective techniques that self-changers use to apply each process.

reduced his urges. Upon hearing this, a middle-aged woman in the group cried out in frustration, "Well, what the hell am I going to do? I don't play the piano or jog!" She had confused two techniques, piano playing and jogging, with their corresponding process, countering. However, countering is one of the broadest processes of change. It incorporates an almost infinite variety of techniques—relaxing, studying, gardening, walking, working, swimming, and so on.

The number of change processes, however, is quite limited. There are a few more, but the nine discussed here are the most common and powerful approaches to change used by professionals and successful self-changers. To maximize your ability to use these processes, the coming chapters will describe at least three of the most effective techniques for applying each change process. Research suggests that people are more likely to be successful in their change attempts when they are given two choices of how to pursue change rather than one; the success rate increases with three or more choices. Your motivation to change increases, your commitment becomes stronger, and you become more able to free yourself from your problem.

As shown in the table on page 26, all the processes have their origins in very diverse systems of psychotherapy. A weakness of many therapies is that they rely on a select two or three techniques for each process, and don't give clients adequate alternatives. Some changers prefer to be told by an authority that there is a single superior technique. The research my colleagues and I have done makes it clear that many methods can be effective for applying each change process, and that individuals who believe that they have the autonomy to change their lives are more likely to act successfully than those who are given limited choice.

As soon as I arranged these therapeutic processes of change in a coherent and meaningful fashion, I wanted to know how they figured in the efforts of self-changers. Did they have processes of their own that bore no relation to the processes developed by psychologists? Or were the same processes used by both groups? There was only one way to find out, and that was to study the self-changers them-selves. I expected that they would have something to teach me, but I did not expect the teaching to be as profound as it turned out to be.

CHAPTER 2

When You Change

FROM A COMPARATIVE analysis of
the major systems of psychotherapy, I isolated the most
powerful processes of change that psychotherapy had to offer. Once having done this, I interested a doctoral student
of mine, Carlo DiClemente, in working with me to determine how frequently people used each of the different processes when struggling to change on their own.

First, we had to find a large enough sample of self-
changers to study. The unguided efforts of all self-changers
with any kind of problem fail at about the same rate. Because there is a much larger percentage of smokers in our
population than drug or alcohol abusers or overeaters, there
is a correspondingly larger sample of smokers who have
successfully quit smoking. This practical consideration led
us to begin with these changes. Not too long ago, almost 50
percent of adult Americans smoked; that figure is down to
about 25 percent. Approximately thirty million smokers
have successfully quit on their own, almost twenty times as
many as those who did so following a treatment program.

We interviewed two hundred people who had tried to
quit smoking, mostly without professional help. The individuals we interviewed varied from impoverished farmers
living in trailers in the rural areas of Rhode Island to busi-
nessmen working in downtown offices. I remember in par-

ticular one middle-aged woman. She lived among the people whom we at the university called "swamp yan-kees"—indeed, she called herself one. She said she had never before met a professor from "Idiot Hill," which I was surprised and amused to find was the locals' name for our campus. Yet she was eager to share with me her struggles with smoking. This woman was convinced that quitting smoking was one of the greatest achievements of her life. She also felt that by quitting smoking she had lost her hus-band—he had refused to quit, and she had refused to go back to her habit.

I asked her how often she used each of the different change processes. She answered, "That depends on when you're talking about. There were times when I used one in particular and times when I didn't use it at all." This was the most direct statement of what many of our other sub-jects were hinting at. Listening with the therapist's third ear, Carlo and I began to hear what this woman and others like her were trying to tell us. They were teaching us something that was not part of any major system of psychotherapy or behavior change. They were teaching us that change un-folds through a series of stages.

I realized immediately that we had a major discovery on our hands. At certain moments in history, there are indi-viduals whose minds are prepared to recognize the impor-tance of things that unprepared minds ignore or throw away. Freud's recognition of the importance of repressed sexuality to human psychology depended, to some extent, on the relaxing mores of *fin de siècle* Viennese society. The pieces of Darwin's theory of natural selection fell into place after he read an essay by a statistical economist who had been writing on capitalistic competition. The historical mo-ment was right for their discoveries; had Freud or Darwin failed to formulate their ideas, others would probably have come up with something similar.

Our discovery depended on the discoveries of psychology's first one hundred years—principally of the various processes of change—and also on the historical moment. Because of the four hundred-some different therapies currently being practiced, other researchers were also intent on reconciling all the competing dogmas. We happened to be the first to make this integration in a comprehensive way. Intuition told me that the concept of stages was the key to relating all the various change processes from theoretically incompatible systems of psychotherapy in a coherent fashion.

Remarkably, this discovery was not based on sophisticated statistics or complex analyses. It resulted from paying attention to the common experiences of ordinary people struggling to be free of a deadly habit. I was reminded of what I had been taught by a renegade professor in graduate school—that science is the radical search for knowledge, no holds barred. Idiot Hill psychologists interviewing swamp yankee citizens were taught a fundamental lesson of change that had eluded most of the great thinkers in the field of psychology and psychotherapy.

THE STAGES OF CHANGE

My original research concerned how people changed; I was trying to identify what tools people used as they struggled toward their goal. But the truly surprising discovery was that successful changers used these tools only at specific times, choosing a different one whenever the situation demanded a new approach. And these specific times were constant from one person to the next, regardless of what their problem was. We named these times "the stages of change."

If you think about a specific problem that you have resolved, chances are you will recognize immediately that its resolution did not happen all at once, but rather that the solution took time and changed over time. Perhaps for a while you ignored the problem; then you considered tackling it; after that, you may have made definite plans to change. Then, once you had garnered your forces—mental, physical, and social—you acted and began to struggle with the problem. If you succeeded, you worked at maintaining your new self. If you failed, you probably gave up for a time, then went back to the drawing board.

Each of these experiences is a predictable, well-defined stage; it takes place in a period of time and entails a series of tasks that need to be completed before progressing to the next stage. Each stage does not inevitably lead to the next— it is possible to become stuck at one stage or another. However, by understanding these stages and the processes that are most useful within each one, you can gain control over the cycle of change and move through it more quickly and efficiently, and with less pain.

There are six well-defined stages of change:

- Precontemplation
- Contemplation
- Preparation
- Action
- Maintenance
- Termination

If this book helps you to progress just one stage through the cycle, it will greatly improve the chances that you will take effective action on your problem. A key to successful change is in knowing what stage you are in for the problem at hand. Our research has consistently shown that people who try to accomplish changes they are not ready for set themselves up for failure. Similarly, if you spend too much time working on tasks you have already mastered—such as understanding your problem—you may delay acting upon it indefinitely. Matching your challenges to your stage of change will help maximize your problem-solving efforts.

Although nearly all change begins with precontemplation, only the most successful ends in termination. But you
cannot skip stages. Most successful self-changers follow the
same road for every problem. You may be at different stages
of change for different problems; this book can help you
work on problems regardless of what stage you are in.

Precontemplation

The writer G. K. Chesterton might have been describing
precontemplators when he said, "It isn't that they can't see
the solution. It is that they can't see the problem." People
at this stage usually have no intention of changing their
behavior, and typically deny having a problem. Although
their families, friends, neighbors, doctors, or co-workers can
see the problem quite clearly, the typical precontemplator
can't.

Take the case of the fifty-five-year-old manager of a man-
ufacturing plant who fell asleep early each evening in front
of the television, even when company came over. Usually
irritable and tense, he had lost interest in all activities—
including sex—except for his work. He couldn't understand
why anyone was worried about him; he could not see that
the fact that he had checked out of life was a problem. All
he wanted to change was the incessant criticisms he received from his family and friends.

Most precontemplators don't want to change themselves,
just the people around them. Precontemplators usually
show up in therapy because of pressures from others—a
spouse who threatens to leave them, an employer who
threatens to fire them, parents who threaten to disown
them, or judges who threaten to punish them. When coerced into therapy, their first focus is often something like,
"How can I get others to quit nagging me?" When this fails,
precontemplators may change, but only as long as there is
great and constant external pressure. Once the pressure is
relieved, they quickly return to their old ways.

Precontemplators, in short, resist change. When their problem comes up in the conversation, they shift the subject; when newspaper articles reveal new information about it, they turn the page. They lack information about their problem, and they intend to maintain ignorant bliss at all costs. In the United States, nearly thirty years after the Surgeon General's report on smoking, there remain ten million smokers who refuse to believe that smoking leads to premature death. And we all have met troubled drinkers who deny that they have a drinking problem. Denial is characteristic of precontemplators, who place the responsibility for their problems on factors such as genetic makeup, addiction, family, society, or "destiny," all of which they see as being out of their control.

Precontemplators are often demoralized as well. They don't want to think, talk, or read about their problem because they feel the situation is hopeless. There is a certain comfort in recognizing that demoralization is a natural feeling that accompanies the precontemplation stage—and in realizing that if you take yourself systematically through the stages of change, you *can* change. Many professionals tell us one of the wonderful features of our program is that it helps counter the demoralization experienced by both patients and professionals.

At the end of Chapter 4 we shall tackle the paradox of helping people change who don't intend to change. The answer is in the approach; even precontemplators will progress toward change if they are given the proper tools at the proper times. Chances are good that you are in the precontemplation stage with at least one behavior that may be self-defeating or damaging.

Contemplation

"I want to stop feeling so stuck." Those simple words are typical of contemplators. In the contemplation stage, people acknowledge that they have a problem and begin to think seriously about solving it. Contemplators struggle to understand their problem, to see its causes, and to wonder about possible solutions. Many contemplators have indefinite plans to take action within the next six months or so.

Contemplators, however, may be far from actually making a commitment to action. They are much like the pedestrian encountered one evening by the psychotherapist Alfred Benjamin. As Benjamin was walking home, a stranger approached and asked directions to a certain street. Benjamin provided them and, after clearly understanding and accepting the instructions, the stranger began to walk in the opposite direction from the one Benjamin had indicated. The therapist yelled after him: "You are headed in the wrong direction." To which the stranger replied, "Yes, I know. I am not quite ready yet."

That is often the nature of contemplation: You know your destination, and even how to get there, but you are not quite ready to go yet. Many people remain stuck in the contemplation stage for a very long time. Self-changing smokers whom we studied typically spent two years in contemplation before taking action.

It is not unusual for self-changers to spend years telling themselves that some day they are going to change. Fear of failure can keep them searching for a more complete understanding of their problem, or a more sensational solution. This stalling can be interminable, as it was in the case of a thirty-seven-year-old director of a data analysis department who had been thinking about quitting smoking. Since she worked at an insurance company, she was well aware of the risks heavy smokers like herself faced. But she also knew that smoking cessation programs failed with a majority of smokers. So she kept on reading the latest books and articles on the subject, telling herself she would quit once the perfect program was developed.

People in psychotherapy can get stuck as well. Recently the cover of *New York* magazine featured a client behind bars yelling, "Help, I'm being held captive in long-term therapy!" Match a therapist who likes to contemplate with a client who likes to contemplate, and therapy can go on forever.

People who eternally substitute thinking for action can be called chronic contemplators. When contemplators begin the transition to the preparation stage, their thinking is clearly marked by two changes. First, they begin to focus on the solution rather than the problem. Then they begin to think more about the future than the past. The end of the contemplation stage is a time of anticipation, activity, anxiety, and excitement.

Preparation

Most people in the preparation stage are planning to take action within the very next month, and are making the final adjustments before they begin to change their behavior. An important step now is to make public your intended change, announcing, for example, "I will stop overeating Monday." But although those in the preparation stage are committed to action, and may appear to be ready for action, they have not necessarily resolved their ambivalence. They may still need to convince themselves that taking action is what's best for them.

This last-minute resolution is necessary and appropriate. People in the preparation stage may already have instituted a number of small behavioral changes, such as cutting their cigarette intake or counting calories. Awareness is high, and anticipation is palpable. People who cut short the preparation stage, for example, those who wake up one morning and decide to quit smoking cold turkey, lower their ultimate chances of success. You can make better use of this time by planning carefully, developing a firm, detailed scheme for action, and making sure that you have learned the change processes you need to carry you through to maintenance and termination.

Action

The action stage is the one in which people most overtly modify their behavior and their surroundings. They stop smoking cigarettes, remove all desserts from the house, pour the last beer down the drain, or confront their fears. In short, they make the move for which they have been preparing.

Action is the most obviously busy period, and the one that requires the greatest commitment of time and energy. Changes made during the action stage are more visible to others than those made during other stages, and therefore receive the greatest recognition. The danger in this is that many people, including professional therapists, often erroneously equate action with change, overlooking not only the critical work that prepares people for successful action but the equally important (and often more challenging) efforts to maintain the changes following action. The sometimes devastating result is that encouragement is scarce for those who are in the stages that precede and follow the action stage. Support for changers dwindles when they need it most, during the precontemplation and contemplation stages, and during the crucial stages following action.

Professionals who equate change with action design terrific action-oriented change programs, and are bitterly disappointed when sign-up rates are minuscule, or when a large number of participants drop out of the program after a brief stay. As you will see, successful programs designed to help precontemplators are vastly different from those designed for people in the action stage. Programs must be geared to the different stages they are in, not just to action.

Remember that the action stage is not the only time you can make progress toward overcoming your problem. Although modifying your behavior is the most visible form of change, it is far from the only one; you can also change your level of awareness, your emotions, your self-image, your thinking, and so on. And many of those changes take place in the stages that precede action.

Furthermore, any movement from one stage of change to the next represents considerable progress. If, after years of avoiding a problem, you consciously begin to acknowledge it exists, and think seriously about changing it, the transition from precontemplation to contemplation is no less significant than from preparation to action. As you will soon see, action, as important as it is, is neither the first nor the last stop in the cycle of change.

Maintenance

There are great challenges at every stage, and the maintenance stage is no exception. For it is during maintenance that you must work to consolidate the gains you attained during the action and other stages, and struggle to prevent lapses and relapse. Change never ends with action. Although traditional therapy sees maintenance as a static stage, in fact it is a critically important continuation that can last from as little as six months to as long as a lifetime.

Without a strong commitment to maintenance, there will surely be relapse, usually to the precontemplation or contemplation stage. I know a thirty-nine-year-old single parent who, after years of abusing alcohol and marijuana, had remained sober for more than a year. However, she knew she was at continued risk of relapse, so she consciously provided herself with distractions to lower her temptation to drink when she felt distressed; she practiced an active and intelligent maintenance. Another recently reformed drinker I treated kept a bottle of booze in his desk drawer, to "remind" himself, he claimed, and to "test his willpower." It wasn't long, of course, before his willpower knuckled under to temptation.

Programs that promise easy "change"—through crash diets, one-day smoking cessation sessions, or whatever—usually fail to acknowledge that maintenance is a long, ongoing process. Millions of people have lost many pounds through various trendy diets, but regain the original weight (and often more) over the next few months. We all know someone like our middle-aged friend, who enrolled in a weight-control program and summarized: "It's easy to lose weight. I started out at 155 pounds, and have lost 160 pounds in the past four years!" Her failure to consolidate the benefits of the action stage is typical of participants in change programs that ignore the importance of maintenance.

Termination

The termination stage is the ultimate goal for all changers. Here, your former addiction or problem will no longer present any temptation or threat; your behavior will never return, and you will have complete confidence that you can cope without fear of relapse. In the termination stage, all of this holds true without any continuing effort on your part. You will have exited the cycle of change and won your struggle.

There is a lively debate about termination. Some experts believe that certain problems cannot be terminated but only kept at bay through a life of decreasingly wary maintenance. Certainly one can terminate cigarette smoking. There are people who smoked heavily for much of their lives and stopped, eventually feeling absolutely no temptation. On the other hand, there are people who remain in maintenance, craving cigarettes fifteen years after they quit smoking. We shall explore which types of problems can be terminated and which types require a lifetime of maintenance.

THE SPIRAL MODEL
OF CHANGE

When Carlo and I first identified the stages of change, we believed that self-changers moved consistently from one stage to the next. Our plan was straightforward and linear:

Precontemplation → Contemplation → Preparation →
Action → Maintenance → Termination

But things did not turn out so simply.

Linear progression is a possible but relatively rare phenomenon. In fact, people who initiate change begin by proceeding from contemplation to preparation to action to maintenance. Most, however, slip up at some point, returning to the contemplation, or sometimes even the precontemplation stage, before renewing their efforts. The average successful self-changer recycles several times. Most people who quit smoking, for example, report three or four serious attempts before they succeed; New Year's resolutions are typically made for five consecutive years or more before resolute changers achieve the maintenance stage.

Don't be discouraged; read on and you will see how those who keep trying do finally succeed. Completing the challenging journey from contemplation through to termination requires ongoing work, the development of a relapse prevention plan, and continuing application of the appropriate processes of change.

The plan outlined in this book represents what we believe to be the best method to bring about the desired changes in yourself. However, despite everyone's best efforts, relapse remains the rule rather than the exception when it comes to solving most common problems. The feelings relapse evokes are not pleasant. You may feel as though you have failed completely; you are probably embarrassed, ashamed, and guilty. You may feel that all of your hard efforts at change have been wasted. Demoralization sets in, and you may want to give up on changing entirely; you may slide back all the way to precontemplation.

Several such setbacks may make you feel as though you are going around in circles rather than solving your problem. And, to some extent, that is the case, but the good news is that the circles are spiraling upward. A successful self-change is like climbing the Leaning Tower of Pisa: First, you walk up, but as you approach the lower part of each floor, you begin to head down. A few steps later you resume your ascent.

On page 49 is a graphic representation of the pattern of change; most successful self-changers go through the stages three or four times before they make it to the top and finally exit the cycle.

The vast majority of people struggle for years to find effective solutions to their problems. They try not to become demoralized by failure, although sometimes they feel they will never change. They are embarrassed or frustrated when someone comes along and tells them, "I quit smoking years ago. It was easy." In our studies, we did locate some people who were able to change with no false starts, no failures, and no relapses. But they are rare. Of the contemplators we followed for two years, only 5 percent made it through the cycle of change without at least one setback.

The vast majority of relapsers—85 percent of smokers, for example—do not go back all the way to precontemplation, but return instead to the contemplation stage. Very soon, they begin to make plans for the next action attempt, internalizing the lessons they have learned from their recent efforts. That is why we prefer the term *recycle* to *relapse*. The return to contemplation can be an auspicious, even an inspired time for continuing to change. Recycling gives us opportunities to learn. Action followed by relapse is far better

FIGURE 1. The Spiral of Change

than no action at all. People who take action and fail in the next month are twice as likely to succeed over the next six months than those who don't take any action at all.

As soon as we had good data on the stages of change, and the processes that bring it about, we were ready to ask the big question: Was every process equally useful at every stage, or were some processes more effective at one stage than at another? Although we weren't sure what the answer to our question would be, we did know that the answer would be interesting and valuable to everyone in the field.

CHAPTER 3

Making Changes

CARLO AND I solicited subjects for our first round of interviews by advertising in the local newspapers. As luck would have it, a psychology professor at Brown University, Rhode Island (a man not known to us), saw the ad. He called us to ask if we knew that the National Institutes of Health (NIH) was looking to fund exactly the kind of research we had already begun to do.

Smoking is a costly national problem. Heavy smokers are at great risk of developing emphysema, lung cancer, and various cardiovascular diseases. The cost of the medical care these individuals must eventually receive is a national burden. The NIH wanted ultimately to discover why most professional smoking cessation programs do not work, so that they might institute programs that *do* work. It made sense for the NIH, therefore, to encourage researchers to find out how people were able to quit smoking on their own; it was hoped that the data would lead to a useful model of change that others could emulate. And this is exactly what happened.

We obtained from the NIH a copy of its announcement seeking to fund research on self-change approaches to smoking cessation. Their requirements were tailor-made for our project. Even though the necessary applications were due in two weeks, we managed to produce a proposal of

160 pages! The NIH scored us very highly, on the strength of a study we ran on two hundred people who had tried to quit smoking, and funded five of the several projects we suggested.

By this time Carlo was practicing in Texas. John Norcross joined us (when still a doctoral student) in our efforts to follow, over a two-year period, one thousand people who were trying to stop smoking by themselves—five hundred in Texas, and five hundred in Rhode Island. Simultaneously, we collected data from eight hundred people who were attempting to lose weight, some by themselves, some by enrolling in weight-control programs.

We had progressed from primitive interviews to sophisticated studies and complex data sets. When eventually we fed all the reports through our mainframe computer, the result was a chaotic table of numbers. The numbers told us clearly that there were highly significant differences in how frequently people use the various processes at particular stages of change. There was less than a one in ten thousand chance that these differences were random.

The differences made no sense. I couldn't detect any meaningful relationships among the ten processes we had measured, and the five different stages under consideration. Imagine a table with five stages times ten processes: fifty different scores with no predictable pattern. Processes I expected to be used in the contemplation stage were used just as much by relapsers, who also used processes I thought were exclusive to the action stage. My data analyst announced that the study was a bust. He said that my belief that I could use the stages of change to integrate the powerful change processes from competing systems of psychotherapy was not supported by the numbers.

For months I felt lost, like one of my clients facing the wilderness of change and having no idea how to proceed. Maybe change truly was a random affair. Maybe trying to find a predictable pattern to human behavior was like trying to play the stock market scientifically and systematically, when the evidence proves that throwing darts at the stock page is likely to be just as profitable.

Night after night I studied the silent numbers, willing them to talk to me. I remembered how Freud had once complained about his brain not being big enough. I was reminded of my first research project in graduate school. Day after day I glared at my results, unable to interpret them, much less write them up.

In grad school I knew my data were garbage, based on a study that was hopelessly confounded. But now I was not faced with a fouled-up semester assignment. I no longer had to satisfy a dreaded authority figure. There was only myself to face—and the feeling that my life's work had been fundamentally unsound. Just when I was ready to despair I had an idea. About 1:00 one morning, I decided to remove the group of relapsers from the data. Relapse had not been part of our stage model. Maybe relapse was messing up our results the way it so often messes up people's efforts to change.

Once I removed the relapsers everything became clear. Just as I had hoped and believed, there were systematic relationships among the stages and the processes of change. Table 3 represents the integration occurring among the processes most often used by successful self-changers at different stages. I woke Jan up at 2:00 A.M. to share these exciting results with her. Her sleepy response was, "Jim, I'm happy for you. Now get to bed."

I'm not sure what happened that night. Empiricists would insist that I had discovered relationships that were inherent in the results. Constructivists would argue that I had created the patterns myself and superimposed them on the results. From this perspective, other patterns could just as readily have been constructed. After ten years I still don't know whether I discovered these relationships or constructed them. I also don't know if it makes any difference. If the

TABLE 3. STAGES OF CHANGE IN WHICH PARTICULAR
CHANGE PROCESSES ARE MOST USEFUL

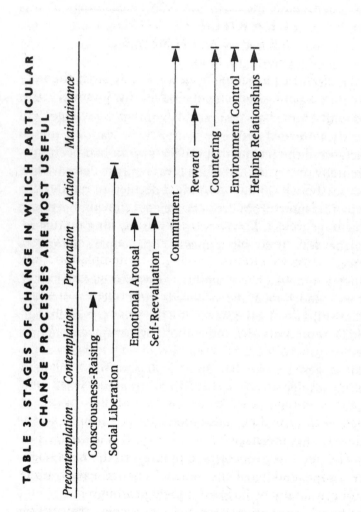

TABLE 3. STAGES OF CHANGE IN WHICH PARTICULAR CHANGE PROCESSES ARE MOST USEFUL

Precontemplation	Contemplation	Preparation	Action	Maintainance
Consciousness-Raising				
Social Liberation				
	Emotional Arousal			
	Self-Reevaluation			
		Commitment		
			Reward	
			Countering	
			Environment Control	
			Helping Relationships	

pattern holds, as this one has, across a wide range of data on self-changers, then who cares where the pattern comes from? It has provided a model of change that thousands of individuals have found useful. That's enough for me.

LEARNING FROM SELF-CHANGERS

Self-changers, never having been limited by strict theoretical or philosophical arguments, have always sought the change processes that work, and have been remarkably effective in discovering and using all of them.

Once we had evidence that the processes were at their most useful during specific stages of change, we went on to test this new linkage. The results clearly confirmed that the successful completion of certain stages was linked to the use of certain processes. Consciousness-raising, for example, is heavily relied upon by contemplators, as is emotional arousal. Self-reevaluation begins in the contemplation stage and becomes critically important in bridging movement from contemplation to action during the preparation stage. Each stage is best served by certain processes. Figure 2 shows the importance of several processes as measured during one group's progress through the different stages.

This discovery has enormous implications. The wisdom of successful self-changers has finally been understood, and can now serve as a field guide for anyone who wants to change, with or without professional help. For once an individual knows the stage he or she is in, this is the time to apply the necessary processes to progress to the next stage. Some understanding of the cycle of change exists; some control can finally be had over moving through it.

The matching of process and stage is one key strategy this book gives to the dedicated self-changer. You do not need

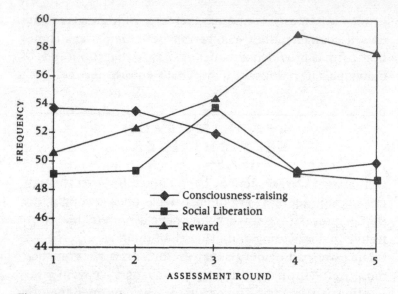

Figure 2. A group of smokers' use of three different change processes as they progressed from the contemplation stage to the maintenance stage. Notice how consciousness-raising is used most at the onset of change, whereas social liberation is more prevalent in the middle, and reward at the end of change.

to learn a new series of techniques every time you want to change a behavior. You do not need three self-help books, three therapists, or three programs to solve three problems. In fact, there is some evidence that it may be more efficient to apply the processes to more than one problem at a time, rather than to try to change problem behaviors one by one. We are in the process of gathering more data on whether simultaneous or sequential change is more beneficial.

Undesirable behaviors, it seems, travel in packs and nourish each other. The single most frequent reason cited for relapse to alcohol, food, or tobacco abuse is emotional distress; former smokers who drink double their chances of renewing their habit; and weight gain is one of the most frequently cited results of quitting smoking (and one of the primary reasons women give for returning to smoking). Many successful change efforts focus on a group of behaviors rather than isolating one at a time—which bodes well for anyone who wants to stop smoking but fears gaining weight, for those who want to stop drinking but do not want to increase their dependence on tobacco, and so forth.

At first, the simplicity of our model was seen as a weakness. In truth, even we were surprised to find that the integration of stages and processes described all kinds of change, not just one or two. Experts continue to tell us, "It's a very nice model, but it will never work for my special problem." (This comment is also frequently made by skeptical self-changers. You may, in fact, be feeling that way right now. Please read on.)

Our response has been to test our model of change—and to allow others to test it—in all types of situations. It has always held up. More than one thousand people suffering from emotional distress (a combination of anxiety, depression, and lowered self-esteem) reported to us on their attempts to change with and without therapy. Our studies of one thousand psychotherapists investigated how these well-trained experts tried to solve their own problems with psychological distress, alcohol abuse, and cigarette smoking. An equal number of therapists told us how they attempt to help their clients overcome similar problems. All told, our studies on change have involved more than thirty thousand people. (The Bibliography provides full references for most of these studies.)

At this writing, our model is being used by the National Institutes for Alcoholism and Alcohol Abuse; the National Cancer Institute (in a telephone hotline set up for smokers attempting to quit); the Centers for Disease Control (in several projects aimed at HIV/AIDS prevention); Johnson & Johnson worldwide; the American Lung Association; and the American Cancer Society. In Great

Britain, the National Health Service is training its employees to use the model to help smokers, drinkers, and drug abusers to quit, and to help people to improve poor eating habits. The World Health Organization is also considering adopting the model. It is part of ongoing projects in Finland, Sweden, Australia, Poland, and Spain. It is also being applied to encourage exercise, and to reduce drug, tobacco, and alcohol abuse, emotional distress, overeating, and more. (Appendix B outlines other applications and advantages of this "new paradigm" of behavior change. In all of these projects, the model holds up so well that its simplicity is now seen as its strength.

Our model also addresses a disturbing and little-known fact that therapists have come to regard as natural and unavoidable. Fully 45 percent of people who make an appointment with a professional therapist drop out of therapy after only a few sessions. They often don't show up in the data sets of success and failure rates of different therapeutic approaches. The thinking has been that since these people never really *tried* the therapy, they should not be counted— and this isn't a wholly indefensible idea. What is indefensible is that therapists often vilify the dropouts, labeling them "unmotivated," "resistant," or "not ready for psychotherapy," and give up trying to understand them.

We wondered if there might be a connection between drop-out rates and mismatched stages and processes. We wanted to test whether our model could predict the rate at which people would drop out of certain therapies. By this we hoped to demonstrate that people most often quit therapy, not when they are unmotivated but when the therapy fails to meet their stage-specific needs.

Our results were astonishing. Our model was 93 percent predictive of which clients would drop out. This predictive percentage provides strong evidence for the need to match therapeutic treatments to the stages clients are in.

INTEGRATIVE CONCLUSIONS

Efficient self-change depends on doing the right things at the right times. A person's stage of change provides proscriptive as well as prescriptive information as to which treatment to use. Treatments that are quite effective in one stage may be ineffective or detrimental in another.

We have found two frequent mismatches. Some self-changers rely primarily on those processes that are best adapted for the early stages—consciousness-raising and self-reevaluation—while they are moving into the action stage. They try to modify behaviors by becoming more aware of them. This reminds me of what many critics of the psychoanalytic method say about it: Insight alone does not bring about behavior change. Other self-changers begin with change processes that are most effective in the action stage—reward, countering, environment control—without having first gained awareness and readiness in the early stages. They try to modify behavior without awareness. This echoes a common criticism of behaviorism: Overt action without insight is likely to lead to temporary change.

In professional therapeutic situations, experienced clinicians may make stage assessments intuitively. If they do, they rarely write about it—prior to our work in this field, we found few references on the topic in the literature. However, when we asked a group of psychotherapists how they went about changing *themselves*, they told us they were very adept at using change processes from other traditions to suit the stages of change they were in. For this reason, we imagine that many therapists may be more heterodox in the consulting room than is apparent from the literature. It is my belief that one of the cardinal virtues of our work is that it will encourage therapists in their heterodoxy. It just makes good sense to use every strategy available out there, as the occasion demands.

Competing systems of psychotherapy have developed apparently rival processes of change. But these ostensibly contradictory processes can be complementary when intelligently applied according to the stages of change. Change processes traditionally associated with the experiential, cognitive, and psychoanalytic persuasions are most useful during the precontemplation and contemplation stages. Those processes associated with the existential and behavioral traditions, by contrast, are most useful during action and maintenance. People who change problem behaviors with and without therapy can be remarkably resourceful in integrating the change processes, even if psychotherapy theorists have been historically unwilling or unable to do so.

Where to go from here

Self-changers are readily able to assess their stages of change, but without guidance may have trouble determining the processes they need to use. A vague notion of the importance of willpower can dominate their perspective on self-change. Still, self-change is a wise and powerful investment of energy. If we can bring reasonable and positive expectations to the cycle of change, our chances of success will be increased. The first step is to grapple with myths that keep us from freeing ourselves from self-defeating behaviors. We will describe and debunk those myths before going any further.

Myth 1: Self-change is simple   Self-change is not simple. We all wish it was easier. We try not to become demoralized by our most recent failures, though we are tempted to believe that we can't really change. We are embarrassed or frustrated when someone tells us how easy it was to quit their habit.

There are, in fact, a privileged few who seem to have a

remarkably easy time of changing. Such dramatic recoveries receive undue attention, since most people have to struggle to find effective solutions to their problems. But once you begin to consider stopping smoking or drinking, to conquer your fears or anxieties, to eat moderately, to begin exercising, your options become clear.

Myth 2: It just takes willpower When we ask successful changers, "How did you do it?" the universal answer is, "Willpower." Our research seemed to confirm what everybody already knew. When we examine what "willpower" means to people, however, two different definitions are given. The first is technical: a belief in our abilities to change behavior, and the decision to act on that belief.

The second, sweeping definition is that willpower represents every single technique, every effort under the sun, one can use in order to change. If this is so, then it is inevitable that it takes willpower to change. This is a classic case of circular reasoning.

Self-changers do indeed use willpower in the first, true sense of the word, but it is only one of nine change processes, the one we call commitment. People who rely solely upon willpower set themselves up for failure. If you believe willpower is all it takes, then you try to change and fail, it seems reasonable to conclude that you don't have enough willpower. This may lead you to give up. But failure to change when relying only on willpower just means that willpower alone is not enough.

Myth 3: I've tried everything—nothing works! As you learn more about the processes of change—the activities that help us understand and overcome problems—you may say, "I already tried that." The key question is not whether you used a particular process, but whether you used it frequently enough, and at the right times.

The effectiveness of change processes is dependent on the

method and timing of their application. If a profoundly depressed person tells me that an antidepressant medication doesn't work, I do not immediately reject the medication. Rather, I ask, "How much are you taking? How long did you take it? Were you taking other drugs at the same time?" Any physician knows how much the dosage, the length of the trial, and the other drugs a patient may be taking can affect the efficacy of a given drug. Psychological change efforts are similarly affected by such considerations. Determining precise measures of how much, how long, and when each process needs to be used to be effective is one aim of our continuing research.

Myth 4: People don't really change Our work simply blows this myth out of the water. We have studied thousands of successful self-changers. Nonetheless, Dr. Tracy Orleans (1986), a health psychologist at the Fox Chase Cancer Control Center in Philadelphia, discovered that two thirds of physicians were pessimistic about their patients' ability to change. This pessimism is the single biggest obstacle to getting physicians to help their patients with their health problems. Yet studies show that if doctors take preventive medicine more seriously—spending just one or two minutes to counsel their patients about quitting smoking, for example—they can double the number of patients who are not smoking at the end of a year.

If all physicians acted similarly, it could save literally millions of lives. With such power, why are doctors so pessimistic? First, successful self-changers usually do not seek professional help. This means that professionals see primarily those individuals who are unwilling or unable to change on their own, and whose problems may seem intractable. They then mistakenly generalize from the failures of these people.

Second, as a nation we seek formal, expert solutions to our problems (the first stage in almost any big project is a study by experts). Self-change, by comparison, is a commonsense approach. The prominent psychiatrist Aaron Beck has commented on the ways in which many psychotherapists gloss over their clients' attempts to define problems in their own terms and use their own rationality to solve them. By doing so, these therapists denigrate the often accurate ideas and effective practices of self-changers, dismissing them as shallow and unsubstantial. This can erode a client's confidence in everyday methods of coping with difficulties. So, although some therapists in practice acknowledge the importance of their clients' efforts, others are inhibited by their theories from encouraging and aiding them to draw on their own resources.

Third, although society only looks at a single self-change attempt, most triumphant self-changers take more than one crack at a problem before they are finished with it. Success can only be achieved over the long haul, and through hard work. And finally, the self-esteem, legal mandate, and economic survival of many therapists depends on their unique and somewhat mythical ability to help people change. The convincing evidence of a self-changer's success threatens them and is thus frequently dismissed.

This does not mean that we oppose professional therapy, of course; we are, after all, practicing psychologists. In fact, our work can be valuable even to those changers who attend weekly sessions; self-changers and therapy-changers have much in common. Reading about the stages and processes of change while in therapy can have a synergistic effect. This is the reason why the majority of psychologists prescribe reading self-help books to their clients, and why approximately 70 percent of those clients report being "really helped" by them.

Although we predict that many self-changers will be successful if they follow the advice contained in these pages, no self-help book can benefit everyone. Self-help books have definite limitations. No book can help you if you have a severe mental disorder. Emotional problems that seriously interfere with your energy level, thinking ability, or experience of reality usually require direct professional help. This book is not a substitute for such help. Chapter 9 presents guidelines on when and how to seek professional guidance.

KNOWING YOUR STAGE

The first step along the journey of change is to know the stage you are in. You can learn this by completing the self-assessment on page 68. Although you may think you already know what stage you are in, a thorough self-assessment is important for accuracy. The processes of change are stage-dependent; where you enter the cycle of change determines what processes you must use to move upward. An incorrect assessment will result in a misapplication of processes, which may in turn slow your movement through the cycle of change.

Self-assessments are an integral part of our program, and you will find them throughout this book. Stage of change predicts the likelihood of success in people's change attempts with more accuracy than anything else about them. This assessment applies to behavior patterns over the next eighteen months. In an extensive study of smokers, we examined the relationship between a person's stage at the start of an action-based treatment and the progress made over the course of treatment; the findings were nothing short of remarkable.

Figure 3 shows the relationship between a specific stage of change before treatment, and successful maintenance over eighteen months. As you can see, the stages are wonderful predictors of which self-changers will be successful. Only 6 percent of those who jumped from precontemplation to the action stage were abstinent at eighteen months,

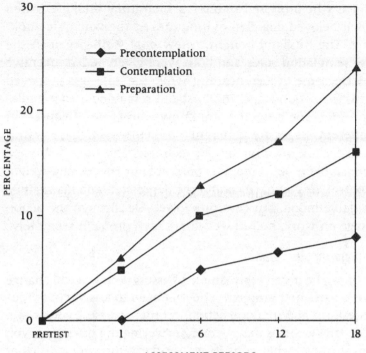

Figure 3. Percentage of smokers who became abstinent over 18 months, classified according to the precontemplation, contemplation, and preparation stages at the start of the study.

compared with the 15 percent who began in contemplation, and the 24 percent who began in the preparation stage. There is no variable that relates as directly to treatment success as the stage of change. Similar effects have been discovered in studies of Mexican-American smokers, smokers with cardiovascular disease, smokers with cancer, middle-aged Finnish male smokers, patients with anxiety and panic disorders, patients recovering from brain injuries, and clients undergoing different therapies.

Sometimes family members with identical problems are at quite different stages in the cycle of change. One of our self-change studies included an elderly married couple in

Texas who professed an interest in quitting smoking. When their beloved dog died of lung cancer, the wife quit smoking. The husband bought a new dog! Both began in the contemplation stage and both were given added incentive by the same occurrence. But while the wife was propelled into the action stage, the husband remained a contemplator. So, don't assume you know your stage. If you are at different stages for different problems—you have terminated work on smoking, for example, and have become a nonsmoker, but remain a contemplator concerning weight control, or you have conquered depression and maintained a stable mood, but continue to recycle through the action stage on workaholism—evaluate each problem separately.

Assessing your stage

It can be deceivingly simple to assess your stage of change for a particular problem. You will need to answer only four questions about taking action in order to assess your stage. The tricky part is that, before answering the questions, you must know what constitutes recovery for your particular problem.

Many people believe that by simply improving a problem, they are taking sufficient action. All of our research is geared toward discovering how people can become *free* from their problems. Our hope and goal for you is that you take action to *solve* your problem, not just improve it. It is not enough to switch to low-tar-and-nicotine cigarettes, or even to cut your number of cigarettes in half; solving this problem means quitting—period.

A problem behavior can be considered solved once you attain the criteria that health professionals agree place you at zero or minimal risk from the particular behavior. The "risk" includes both the health risks your problem poses and that of relapse, if your solution is less than complete. Cutting in half the number of cigarettes you smoke reduces the risk, but does not minimize it. Table 4 presents the ac-

TABLE 4. ACTION CRITERIA FOR
15 PROBLEM BEHAVIORS

Problem Behavior	Action Criteria
Smoking	Abstinence
Drug abuse	Abstinence
Gambling	Abstinence
Alcoholism	Abstinence
Troubled drinking	Abstinence, at times; or no more than 14 drinks per week, with no more than 5 drinks ever at any sitting
Sex (high risk)	Always use condoms
Depression	No more than 2 days of the blues at any time
Panic attacks	No panic attacks in any normal situation
Physical abuse	Never hit anyone and never be hit
Obesity (health criteria)	Less than 20% over standard weight tables
Diet (high fat)	Less than 30% of calories from fat
Sedentary life	Minimal: physical activity 3 times weekly, 20 minutes at a time Optimal: vigorous exercise 3 times weekly, 20 minutes at a time
Dental hygiene	Brush twice a day and floss each tooth
Procrastinating	Never put off anything that hurts you or others
Sun exposure	Always use sunscreens when exposed for more than 15 minutes

tion criteria for fifteen of the most important and most prevalent problem behaviors.

If your problem behavior is included in Table 4, you will see what recovery requires of you. We recognize that some people have to settle for a less than total solution. If significant improvement is the best you can do for now, then that is still something worth doing. But don't set your goals too low. Aim for full freedom from your problem.

With some problem behaviors, unfortunately, either there is no agreement among professionals on the criteria for recovery, or there is no easy or adequate measure for assessing recovery. If your problem behavior is not included in Table 4, then you will have to imagine what it will mean to be free from your problem. Usually it means never engaging in a high risk or troubling behavior, such as never engaging in high-risk sex, or it means consistently practicing a preventive behavior, such as always wearing seat belts.

Once you have a fairly clear idea of what action you need to take, respond to the following four simple statements to assess the stage you are in for a particular problem behavior.

1. I solved my problem more than six months ago.
2. I have taken action on my problem within the past six months.
3. I am intending to take action in the next month.
4. I am intending to take action in the next six months.

If you answered no to all statements, you are in the pre-contemplation stage. Contemplators will have answered yes to statement 4 and no to all the others. Those in the preparation stage will have answered yes to statements 3 and 4, and no to the others. If you answered yes to statement 2 and no to statement 1, you are in the action stage. You've reached the maintenance stage when you can answer yes truthfully to statement 1.

Now that you know your stage of change, based on the self-assessment above, and you have a basic understanding of the processes of change, you can begin to apply this knowledge, moving gradually from stage to stage. After completing your self-assessment, read through the rest of the book. Please avoid the temptation to skip a chapter or two and proceed immediately to that part of the book you feel is most appropriate for you. We believe that it will be most beneficial to read the book thoroughly, completing the work of every stage before proceeding to the next. You may feel ready for action, but you may not have completed all the preparation you need. Acquaint yourself with the chapters about precontemplation, contemplation, and preparation. They will be helpful to you, and may give you more confidence to move full speed ahead. Furthermore, a complete understanding of the processes will be invaluable as you tackle other problems in your life.

Part Two

THE APPLICATIONS

We would rather be ruined than changed;
We would rather die in our dread
Than climb the cross of the moment
And let our illusions die.

—W. H. Auden

CHAPTER 4

Precontemplation— Resisting Change

WHEN GEORGE FIRST CAME to see me, he was an unhappy, overweight, forty-year-old alcoholic. He began psychotherapy while in a miserable marriage filled with hurt, hatred, and betrayal; he fled after just a few sessions. There were more than a few factors contributing to his misery. His mother had failed to give him love or respect; his passive father had abandoned him emotionally, escaping into a series of extramarital affairs; and his belligerent older brother had mocked George's inadequacies. George's wife, Vera, cheated on him, making him feel still more foolish. To top it all off, his boss's business was collapsing, which left him entirely unsympathetic to George's problems.

Yet George had no visible desire to stop drinking, lose weight, mend his marriage, or change in any way. He blamed others for all of his faults and failures, and felt he had no reason to change. Like most precontemplators, he wanted everyone else to change. George wouldn't have minded turning his angry, egocentric wife into the loving and accepting mother he had never known. But until Vera changed, George preferred to sit in the local bar, commiserating with his drinking buddies. When George started to get anxious, angry, or depressed, his buddies knew exactly how to cheer him up—by bringing him another drink.

There was certainly no way I could cheer George up. His

marriage, career, and life were a mess. So I didn't pull any
punches. I told George and Vera that there was little chance
their marriage could be saved; still, if they were willing to
try, I would give them all the help I could. I also told George
that if he wanted to save himself, he would have to quit
drinking. Instead, he quit therapy.

Experts like to call alcoholism the disease of denial. But
this applies to most any problem: When we are mired in
the precontemplation stage, it is denial that holds us there.
If we are accused of doing something wrong, one of the
ways we learn to avoid punishment is to deny responsibility. This is especially true if we take pleasure in our mis-
behavior. Another step we take is to admit but justify our
behavior, creating good reasons for our bad actions. This is
one of the reasons we so often defend our right to defeat
ourselves.

What is it that is appealing about the precontemplation
stage that so many people struggle to stay in it? For one
thing, it feels safe. You can't fail there. It frees you from the
demands of time—you can change some other day, not
now. It also frees you of guilt. If you can avoid thinking
about bad habits, then how can you begin to feel guilty
about them? Precontemplators are free, finally, from social
pressures. You need only create a few awkward scenes in
order to convince those who care about you that you are
not open to talking about your problems.

I wish I could report that I exerted a magical influence
over George, that my strong statements moved him and
Vera to transform themselves and their marriage into something better. But this is a book about self-change, not miracles. George entered therapy in the precontemplation
stage, and he was still in it when he left.

I did find out years later that I had helped to raise some
questions in his mind. George had expected his perspective
to be validated, but discovered instead that he was partici-
pating in his problems. He began to recognize that although

his early background and his relationship with his wife posed legitimate problems, he was using these as an excuse to avoid facing his own issues. There was a small crack in his defenses, and increased awareness was beginning to slip in. There were other forces and factors assembling to help George move out of the precontemplation stage. When he was able not to fight these forces—as he fought any person who confronted him—he was able to move forward.

THE ATTITUDES OF PRECONTEMPLATORS

Precontemplation indicates in many cases an active resistance to change. The irony is that most precontemplators are doomed to remain trapped in the precontemplation stage without help from others. As people become more aware of their problems, they become more receptive to help. At any other stage of change, the issue is not whether help should be offered, but what type of help is best. With precontemplators, the question often arises whether help is even a possibility.

Some precontemplators are so demoralized that they are resigned to remaining in a situation they consider their "fate." They may have tried to solve their problems in the past, and failed. They believe that even to think about change is to risk failing again. They have admitted defeat and given up on changing.

Marie was five feet two, and had seen her weight climb steadily to over two hundred pounds. But she didn't care anymore: Her marriage was over and her career was going nowhere. Marie felt that she had seen the best of her life already, and now would do what she damned well pleased—even if it destroyed her.

When people abandon change altogether, they give up on themselves. They accept one of the several self-change myths: "I've tried everything," "I don't have enough will-power," "People don't really change." They exercise even less restraint than they did before their failure. Their drinking becomes excessive, their weight increases, their bad moods occur more frequently and last longer. By giving up on themselves they give in to their problems, which in turn become more dominant. Like Marie, they feel that life has passed them by.

I felt that way when I graduated from high school. At the time I was convinced that everything would be downhill from then on, and I became anxious, depressed, and cynical. When I finally overcame my psychological distress, I felt fortunate that I had not given up on life.

However, I did not learn my lesson well enough. After graduating from college, I chose a graduate school that turned out to be the wrong one for me. My feelings of despair returned. I began drinking too much, eating too much, and sleeping too much. I was training to become a clinical psychologist, and became nervous that my peers and professors would find out about my behavior. So I closed myself off from outside help, which made me even more distressed and demoralized.

Fortunately, I was able to enroll in a university located near my friends and family. When I finally overcame this second period of distress, I felt foolish for not having learned more from the first episode. Only after three or four times of experiencing life as peaking and passing me by did I finally learn that life only passes you by when you give up on your abilities to change.

Problem or preference?

Is a certain behavior pattern a problem or a preference? Can people have problems if they are not aware of them? Who decides what a problem is? Is it ethical to try to help someone change if he or she doesn't want to change?

There are those who would have us wait to intervene with precontemplators until their problems become truly intolerable. This school of thought perpetuates the myth that alcoholics, overeaters, or drug addicts will not be ready to change until they bottom out. This approach presents several difficulties, not the least of which is that it is painful to watch others, especially loved ones, deteriorate until they develop a host of ancillary problems that also need attention.

Alcoholics may eventually lose their families, friends, jobs, money, and physical and mental health. By the time they hit bottom they may be so demoralized and physically debilitated that they do not care about changing. They don't know where, much less have the ability, to begin.

Waiting for precontemplators to hit bottom is not only painful and inefficient, it is risky. We would not consider this approach with purely physical disorders. If someone shows signs of heart disease or cancer, we would not wait to do something until the disease was undeniable. When people exhibit symptoms of an impending heart attack, even if they refuse to see a physician, their loved ones usually force the issue. Research shows that problems are almost always treated more effectively when they are less rather than more severe, and when they are of shorter rather than longer duration. The longer people wait to change, the more difficult change becomes.

There are, of course, value judgments involved in evaluating psychological problems. Is heavy drinking a problem or a preferred lifestyle? Is smoking a problem or a valid choice? Who decides? And how do you decide whether you are in the precontemplation stage of changing a problem, or whether you have freely chosen behaviors that are your right?

Answer the following three questions truthfully, and you will begin to see the distinction between problem behaviors and lifestyle choices:

Do you discuss your behavior pattern? Precontemplators are usually defensive about their problem behaviors. Do you tell people to mind their own business, or do you appreciate their concern? People who are not in the precontemplation stage do not usually become defensive. They see the feedback from others as signs of caring rather than attempts to control them.

Are you well informed about your behavior? Precontemplators avoid learning about their problems. Do you turn the page or change the channel when you see an article or program about your behavior? Or do you read the article or watch the program with interest? If you drink and you are willing to learn the signs of troubled drinking, or if you smoke and you acknowledge that smoking is harmful to your health, you are well on your way to becoming a contemplator.

Are you willing to take responsibility for the consequences of your behavior? Precontemplators are uncomfortable with vividly imagining these consequences. Are you aware of the short- and long-term results of your behavior? Can you know how people are likely to feel forty-eight hours after drinking six beers? Have you any idea what impact suppressed anger has on your heart? Can you imagine developing lung cancer and feeling pleased and proud that you smoke? If you have frequent outbursts of anger, are you comfortable knowing your children live in fear of you? Will previous years of drinking seem wise when you have lost much of what you once cared for?

Precontemplators rarely take responsibility for the negative consequences of their actions. If your chosen behavior eventually kills you, would you consider this outcome natural? We can now say with certainty that most of the leading killers in the United States, including heart disease and many types of cancer, are partly caused by lifestyle factors. If you are dying prematurely from lung cancer or heart disease, will you regret not having changed high-risk behaviors like smoking or alcohol abuse?

Your responses to these three questions will give you a good sense of whether a particular behavior is a problem or preference. If you can honestly say that you are not defensive but are well-informed, aware of the consequences of and responsible for the long-term effects of your behavior, then perhaps it is a preference. If, however—like most of us—you answered no to one or more of the questions, you are probably in the precontemplation stage.

Developmental and environmental pressures

How can defensive, demoralized people become unstuck? There are things we can do to help precontemplators, about which we will go into detail later on. Sometimes, however, movement out of this stage occurs without anybody's help. This is unintentional change. Some common causes of movement from precontemplation to contemplation are developmental and environmental forces over which we have little or no control.

The developmental forces that move us from one stage of life to another can also help us to contemplate changing certain aspects of our lives. The advent of the fortieth birthday, with its accompanying increase in the awareness of mortality, is a powerful force for change in our society. Many smokers, for example, begin to contemplate seriously quitting as they approach forty. It is no coincidence that our research shows that the most successful self-changers who set out to quit smoking take action at a mean age of thirty-nine.

Age milestones are not our only developmental opportunities. Marriage, childbirth, promotions, illnesses, retirement, and other supermeaningful events often provide the needed push to move us from one stage of change into the next. For instance, before he became a father, John Norcross routinely brought home stacks of work for the class he taught and for his clinical practice, despite his awareness that he was a borderline workaholic, and despite repeated pledges to his wife that he would cut back. Only after the birth of his son—a high mark of adulthood—was John able to translate this awareness into action.

Changes in the external environment can be equally compelling. One of the couples we interviewed in the course of our research asked their soon-to-be twenty-one-year-old son what present he wanted for this special birthday. He said that the most important thing they could do for him would be to quit smoking. The request immediately moved them to contemplate giving up tobacco. Such stories are not uncommon.

Even without direct requests, people may realize that their environment no longer supports their lifestyle as it once did; suddenly, they are punished rather than rewarded for their habits. People now experience escalating social pressures to lose weight, get in shape, reduce stress, control their drinking, eat healthfully, and quit smoking, and each of these pressures can have an effect.

Sometimes coercive environmental changes can lead to unintentional change. Bill, a forty-year-old speech pathologist recovering from alcohol abuse, went through a long period of coerced participation in alcohol programs. Bill had been assigned to an alcohol education program in the army after wrecking a car; he took part in a hospital rehabilitation program in order to regain his driver's license after a DWI conviction; and he "dropped in and out of A.A. meetings" for years.

After several years and many different programs, Bill finally achieved an increased awareness that helped him to tackle change on his own. "I resisted all attempts to help me," Bill now says, "but some good stuff must have sunk into my brain." After being "locked up for drunken behavior, I got the message: Getting drunk got me in trouble."

Bill had once hoped to be a police officer himself, and this time his shame at being incarcerated finally tipped the balance of his awareness.

Precontemplators can advance more freely into the contemplation stage if they can identify with the developmental or environmental forces that are urging them to change. Take aging. People often have trouble identifying with the aging process, even though it comes from within. Whether we look at aging as a life crisis or an opportunity for growth depends on whether we see it as a natural process or an imposition. Many of us look forward to becoming twenty-one, which our society marks as the beginning of adulthood. Turning forty or fifty can in contrast feel like an imposition, especially since our society idealizes youth.

Some people can experience the developmental force of aging as liberating. A widow with four children, who had smoked heavily for forty years, told us she finally left the precontemplation stage when she became a grandmother. For her, smoking didn't jibe with her new identity as a grandmother, or with the increased sense of dignity she felt as a senior citizen.

Unfortunately, there are countless examples of the self-defeating ways in which precontemplators resist the effects of aging. They may deny new health problems so they needn't contemplate changing their drinking habits. They turn to cocaine or other stimulants to regain the energy of youth; they then turn to barbiturates to help them sleep. They indulge in meaningless affairs to deny any slight decrease in their sexual drives.

We are at our healthiest when we balance our need for control with an openness to external influences, when we satisfy our need for autonomy within a community and our personal lives within a family. Most of this chapter will focus on the realization of that goal, using the first three change processes—consciousness-raising, helping relationships, and social liberation—that can help move you toward the contemplation stage. First, however, we must examine a major stumbling block for precontemplators: defenses.

THE DEFENSES OF PRECONTEMPLATORS

We are all born without defenses; we develop them as we get older. It's a good thing that we do. Without the protection of these "mental shields" we would be bombarded constantly by undesirable feelings and external threats, both real and imagined. Defensive reactions allow us to avoid, temporarily at least, what we cannot confront, and let us get on with our lives.

Valuable as they are, we pay a price for these necessary psychic protectors. They alleviate pain but distort and disguise our experiences. Because defenses do not resolve problems, although they may help us feel better in the short run, they can damage us in the long run. And defenses can prevent precontemplators from seeing their problems. Defenses, generally, serve to distract us from the difficult and uncomfortable task of self-analysis.

The very act of noticing this distraction is the first step in breaking down defenses. Out of the more than twenty-five defenses we have at our disposal, there are seven that precontemplators specialize in, and they come in four main varieties. Let's look at these individually, so you can see whether any seem especially familiar.

Making the least of it: Denial and minimization

Probably the most common defensive reaction, denial allows us to protect ourselves by refusing to acknowledge unpleasant occurrences. From time to time, we all pretend that disagreeable realities, such as pain or danger, simply do not exist.

I had one client, Harold, who went through so much money he was nearly bankrupt. To make matters worse, he was on the verge of losing his job for the third time in four years. His violent temper terrified his children, who no longer wanted to be around him. His wife was considering leaving him. Yet, convinced that life was fine, he continued to pour all of his energy into his skiing club and none into his work or his family. As far Harold was concerned, "I'm coping perfectly well with all the stresses in my life. It's my wife who can't cope." He felt she was trying to take away his freedom and his fun.

Precontemplators love denial. Despite all evidence to the contrary, they can't admit to their problems. Alcoholics are especially well known for denial. I have encountered people faced with physical evidence of their intoxication, who still swear that they have not touched a drop. Problem drinkers also minimize, a form of denial: "Maybe I do drink a little too much, but I can handle it," they say, despite the fact that the incidence of job loss, liver disease, and divorce among alcoholics proves the opposite.

Denial filters out information that might help these people change. As a result, they are often surprisingly uninformed about the behaviors that others consider problematic. A thirty-seven-year-old nurse named Carol, who had smoked for twenty years, refused to believe that cigarettes could kill her. Even though she was in the health field, Carol truly did not know that smoking is the most preventable cause of death in the United States, one that claims 400,000 lives a year. "I just always insisted," she says, five years after quitting, "that the medical experts were still debating the effects of smoking."

"Good excuses": Rationalization

When we rationalize, we offer plausible explanations for our behavior. Even if that behavior is immature or irrational, we justify it in rational, adult terms. Our rationalizations may appear sound to us, but they are full of holes.

Every evening, Maureen spent more than an hour getting her eight-year-old daughter ready for bed; in the middle of the night, she allowed the child to crawl into bed between her and her husband. She drove her daughter to and from school every day instead of letting her take the bus with the other children. When friends and family members expressed their concern about Maureen's doting, she coolly told them to mind their own business.

Maureen's rationale for giving in to her daughter's every demand was, "My mother was much too severe, and never indulged any of my needs when I was a child." An overly restrictive mother does not provide a good reason for erring in the opposite direction with one's own child.

Nonetheless, rationalization is extremely common. The phenomenon is best expressed by this amusing conversation from the movie *The Big Chill:*

"Don't knock rationalization. Where would we be without it? I don't know anyone who'd get through the day without two or three juicy rationalizations. It's more important than sex."

"Oh, come on. Nothing is more important than sex."

"Oh yeah? Have you ever gone a week without rationalization?"

Rationalization's cousin, intellectualization, refers to the use of abstract analysis to rob events of personal significance. The intellectualizer is able to avoid emotional reactions to and painful awareness of his or her problem. Most of the reasons people give for remaining addicted to nicotine and alcohol are intellectualizations: "I need one vice, so it's cigarettes," say some smokers, although, of course, no one "needs" a life-threatening behavior. "My uncle drank a pint of whiskey a day and lived to be ninety!" say some heavy drinkers, although, in general, alcoholics shorten their average life span by twelve years. "That cancer stuff has only been proven in rats smoking the equivalent of eighty packs a day"—such ideas are disseminated by the tobacco industry, which interprets quite convincing studies in a shamelessly misleading style.

Turning outward: Projection and displacement

When we are unable or afraid to display our feelings toward the true source of our problems, we may redirect them against someone or something else. This defense involves transferring the source or object of pain to anything other than the self. "The best defense is a good offense" is the slogan of people who turn outward.

Carl had been abusing alcohol and drugs for a dozen years. His third wife, Beth, confronted him early in their marriage about his problems, but he didn't want to hear about them. So he began to criticize Beth. She had grown up with a hypercritical mother, and had always striven to be perfect; she couldn't stand the criticism. Carl tied Beth up in knots, making her face one imaginary problem after another while losing sight of his own problem. Meanwhile, Carl continued to drink and use drugs, free from interference.

Carl's systematic attack on Beth is an example of displacement. Also known as scapegoating, displacement is a form of turning outward, in which we take out our anger, depression, or frustration on a substitute object or person, one that is available and safe to attack. Another form of displacement, known as projection, occurs when we diagnose in someone else those problems that we carry ourselves.

Turning inward: Internalization

We can also turn feelings inward, believing not that others caused us pain, but that we ourselves created the problem. By turning inward consistently and failing to express negative feelings appropriately, we begin to internalize, or "swallow," these feelings. The result is habitual self-accusation, self-blame, low self-esteem, and sometimes depression.

Irene had this habit. After dating for five years without, as she put it, "a success" (getting married), she began to view herself as "a hopeless old spinster," even though she had just turned twenty-five! Frustrated with the dating game, Irene was internalizing the blame, beginning to feel and act hopeless. Thus began a vicious cycle: Irene didn't feel wanted, so she acted as though no one would want her, which decreased the chances of anyone expressing serious interest.

Resigned, demoralized precontemplators, who are aware of a problem but have given up doing anything about it, frequently turn inward. They say, "I can't do it." Their feelings of inevitable failure protect them from trying to change, and as long as they cling to their belief that they can't change, they probably won't. The defense works like a charm, but an unlucky one indeed.

HELPING PRECONTEMPLATORS

Part of the problem of keeping a program of research moving in a field that lacks consensus is that there is no agreement as to what should be studied next. Sometimes our sponsors pressured us to implement programs before we felt ready. The National Cancer Institute was so intrigued by our early studies of self-changing smokers that they requested we develop applications as we went along with our research, rather than waiting for all our data to come in.

Their request was sensible—500,000,000 people alive in the world today will die ten years before their time, on average, because of tobacco use. And other self-change programs have limited impact. We believed then (and have since demonstrated) that this is because such programs do not take into account the stages of change. For example, more than 70 percent of eligible smokers in a major West Coast health maintenance organization (HMO) claimed that they would participate in an upcoming home-based self-help program. However, when an excellent action-oriented program was developed and publicized, only 4 percent of the smokers signed up for it.

Even if the program had been successful with a third of its participants (which is an overgenerous estimate) its impact on the population of smokers in the HMO was paltry.

So we were asked to develop a program that would do better, that *did* take the stages of change into account. Because we did not yet have all the data we needed, there would be some kinks to iron out as we went along, but anything we could do to get a stage-matched program up and working would be valuable. How, we wondered, would we ever lure precontemplators, the people who by definition resist change? How could we reach people who were unaware of or defensive about their problems?

We found that a newspaper advertisement worded to appeal to those in the contemplation stage drew two hundred calls for our self-help materials. Different ads generated responses from about the same number of people in the action and preparation stages. We had to experiment with the precontemplators. We ran an ad asking for participants in a self-help program for "smokers who do not wish to change." Surprisingly, this advertisement—exactly the same size as the others—drew four hundred precontemplators.

And compare our program's success rate. In a stage-matched program at the largest HMO in New England, designed to meet the needs of all smokers—even those not yet ready to change or only just getting ready—we got a participation rate of approximately 85 percent. If this program had only a 20 percent success rate (the study is still in progress, but this estimate seems to be low), it means it had a 15 percent impact rate on the population, or one thousand to five thousand times greater than that achieved by traditional programs.

No one wanted to look at impact rates before because participation rates were so low. This is not surprising, considering that the vast majority of programs are designed to help only that small minority of people who are ready to take action. According to data from representative samples, fewer than 20 percent of any problem population are prepared to take action at a given time.

At one western HMO, when administrators discovered subscribers were avoiding the action-oriented program they had developed, they decided to go all out to persuade smokers to participate. Their doctors showed smokers a videotape detailing the horrors of smoking and the glories of quitting. The HMO nurses spent an unusually long time telling smokers what good medicine for them quitting would be. They followed up with telephone counseling calls pressuring smokers to sign up for the program. Thirty-five percent of their precontemplators did sign up, but 3 percent actually showed up, and only 2 percent finished.

As Abraham Maslow once said, if the only tool you have is a hammer, then you have to treat everything as if it were a nail. Although we hadn't expected to be developing treatment programs so quickly, we couldn't help but be pleased at how successful they were. And our programs were successful precisely because we first took the trouble to ascertain what tools were needed. In one sense these tools (the processes of change) were already in the toolbox, but till now nobody had known when exactly to use them. Let's take a look at some of the tools that precontemplators find most helpful.

CONSCIOUSNESS-RAISING

The first step in fostering intentional change is to become conscious of the self-defeating defenses that get in our way. Knowledge is power. Freud was the first to recognize that to overcome our compulsions we must begin by analyzing our resistance to change. We must acknowledge our defenses before we can defeat or circumvent them.

Increased consciousness, whether it comes from within or without, is invaluable. Many precontemplators lack the information to perceive their problems clearly. Like a flashlight in a dark library, consciousness-raising makes that information available. As is the case with all the processes of change, there are many different techniques that can be used to increase consciousness. You can gather information by reading, or by watching an informative program on television. You can explore the interpretations of your behaviors that friends or therapists suggest.

Sometimes awareness of a problem comes quickly. Ellen, a fifty-year-old fashion designer, had been obese all her life, carrying some two hundred pounds over her ideal weight. She had made a few halfhearted attempts to lose weight, but never really saw her obesity as a problem. "My husband always made me feel attractive," she reported. "And because I had my own business, other people did things for me, so I didn't have to move around much."

A visit to her doctor made all the difference. "When my doctor said, 'I don't want to scare you, but. . .' that was it." His words confirmed her escalating fears: "I could see I was dying; my sugar level and blood pressure were sky high, and my ankles were enormous." Within weeks, Ellen had decided to lose all of her weight, and two years later she had achieved her goal.

Some consciousness-raising techniques can be used in

everyday life. Once, when teaching a class of three hundred students, I developed a habit of ending sentences with the phrase "on it," in much the same way some people say "you know." I would say things like "Freud is the second most famous psychologist of all time, on it, and Skinner is now the most famous, on it." I was unaware of the problem until a freshman had the nerve to confront me about it. I tried to interpret what "on it" meant to me, but could not discover any deeper meaning. Without increased awareness, however, I could do nothing about this irritating habit. Eventually, I asked my class to raise their hands whenever I said "on it." With three hundred hands making me fully conscious of this habit, I changed in record time.

Becoming aware of defenses

Although consciousness-raising does not usually result so quickly in change, becoming aware of a problem behavior remains the first step in changing it. Accordingly, the first step in countering defenses is becoming conscious of what they are and how they operate. Below are a few examples that should help reveal which defenses you use most frequently. Try and pick out which responses represent which defenses commonly used by precontemplators.*

Situation: You are waiting for a bus on a city corner. The streets are wet and muddy after the previous night's rainstorm. Suddenly a taxicab sweeps through a puddle in front of you, splashing your clothes with mud. Possible responses:

1. I wipe myself off with a smile as though it didn't really happen.
2. I just shrug it off. After all, things like that are unavoidable in the city.
3. I yell curses at the taxi driver.

*Adapted from the Defense Mechanism Inventory (Gleser & Ihilevich, 1969).

4. I scold myself for not having worn a raincoat and protecting myself.
5. I let the driver know that I don't really mind, it was no big deal.
6. I let the driver know that bystanders have their rights too.
7. I begin to chase after the taxi, throwing whatever objects I can find.
8. I mentally kick myself for standing too close to the edge of the street.

Responses 1 ("it didn't really happen") and 5 ("no big deal") illustrate denial and minimization. Responses 2 ("these things happen") and 6 ("bystanders have rights too") are examples of rationalization and intellectualization; these answers circumvent emotional hurt by intellectually justifying the situation. Responses 3 (yelling curses) and 7 (chasing and throwing objects) clearly show turning outward against the object. Responses 4 ("I'd scold myself") and 8 ("I mentally kick myself") exemplify turning inward.

Checking our defenses

Although no one relies on one personal defense forever, we tend to be consistent. John Norcross, for example, is a wonderful intellectualizer, always ready with explanations to justify problematic behaviors. Here is a typical conversation between himself and a friend:

FRIEND: Hey, John, I notice you're putting on weight.
JOHN: Yeah, not enough exercise. I've been too busy writing.

This response sounds plausible enough, but does not directly address the problem (putting on weight), instead shifting the blame to something else (writing). If we look a little more closely at John's life, we see that he uses this defense in a variety of situations:

> NANCY (John's wife): John, I notice that you're spending an awful lot of time in the office and less with us.
>
> JOHN: Yeah, not enough time. I've been too busy writing and seeing patients.

By examining his own defenses, John made an important step in moving toward contemplation in changing his problems with weight control and overwork. After all, we are not completely governed by our defenses, merely guided by them. Simple awareness of our "mental tricks" helps us to gain a measure of control over them.

In fact, all maladaptive defenses can be transformed into positive behaviors with awareness and practice. Throughout the course of this book, you will learn techniques to transform defenses into coping mechanisms. Table 5 gives a few examples of these transformations.

Consciousness-raising self-assessment

For each process of change, we will provide you with a brief self-assessment. These checkpoints are powerful tools for information and self-correction. The information these assessments yield can dramatically increase your chances of moving into the next stage and thus successfully reaching termination. We emphatically recommend that you take these self-assessments, and take them seriously. Be honest and realistic. You must engage in these processes to move forward; if you mislead yourself, you will impede your progress.

Fill in the number that most closely reflects how frequently you have used the method in the past week to combat your problem.

1 = Never, 2 = Seldom, 3 = Occasionally, 4 = Often, 5 = Repeatedly

FREQUENCY:

_____ I look for information related to my problem behavior.

_____ I think about information from articles and books on how to overcome my problem.

_____ I read about people who have successfully changed.

_____ I recall information people have personally given me about the benefits of changing my problem.

_____ = Score

TABLE 5. TRANSFORMING DEFENSES INTO COPING

Defense	Coping
Denial: refusing to face painful feelings or thoughts; ignoring painful and dangerous feelings	Concentration: setting aside painful thoughts or feelings in order to stick to the task at hand; returning to those feelings at a more appropriate moment
Rationalization and Intellectualization: "explaining away" problem behaviors; retreating, with words and abstractions, from painful emotions	Logical Analysis: thoughtfully and carefully analyzing problem behaviors without becoming overwhelmed by emotion
Projection: unrealistically attributing objectionable feelings or thoughts to another person	Empathy: seeing a situation through another's eyes; imagining how others feel
Displacement: "taking out" negative feelings on another person	Sublimation: releasing negative emotions through alternative, socially acceptable channels. Exercise, chores, sports, art, and music can be forms of creative aggression.
Internalization: blaming oneself for all problems	Self-determination: motivating positive actions. Attributing painful thoughts and feelings appropriately, to the environment, other people, or oneself—when justified

Your score is the sum of the four numbers under Frequency. The cutoff scores provided for each self-assessment are general guidelines based on many problems, not specific absolutes for any one problem. These scores, derived from our research with thousands of self-changers, should be regarded as rules of thumb, not strict laws.

On this self-assessment, precontemplators usually get a score less than 10; people who have successfully passed into the contemplation stage usually score 10 or more. However, self-changers struggling with certain problems—such as weight control—often obtain scores of 12 or more. There is so much information on obesity in our society that even precontemplators have trouble avoiding it.

This, and the other change-process self-assessments that follow, have direct implications for your progress. When your score is low, we advise that you spend more time with the process in question. The importance of timing cannot be overstated. A haphazard, trial-and-error application of the processes leads to ineffective movement through the change cycle. It is always better to make certain that you have made full use of a process than it is to advance to the next stage inadequately prepared.

HELPING RELATIONSHIPS DURING PRECONTEMPLATION

A solid helping relationship is as important to most self-changers as the relationship to a therapist is to those who change in therapy. The helping relationship provides you with a supportive context within which you can process developmental or environmental events, and see yourself as others do. This, in turn, allows you to ease up on your defenses and to contemplate making intentional changes.

Our defenses rarely fool others, especially those close to us. That is why our spouses, children, parents, friends, and others who know us well are usually aware of our problems long before we are. Our defenses, however, not only serve to keep us in the dark about our problems, they often get in the way of those relationships that could be most helpful in solving them. Intimate relationships can be seen as either a threat or a special source of support, depending on whether or not we welcome help.

Because the helping relationship is so critical to self-changers, we will review helping skills as we discuss every stage of change, for the benefit of people who care for and are close to self-changers. Here, however, we examine the role of the helping relationship in breaking down defenses and helping you move toward contemplation.

Examples of the potent influence of helping relationships abound. You undoubtedly have had several accepting people who valued you enough to help you through troubled times—a soothing parent, a best friend, a special teacher, a trusted confidante, a loving mate. Sometimes the simple, nonjudgmental presence of an intimate friend or mate is enough. The dramatic rise of self-help support groups also attests to the efficacy of helping relationships.

Mike, a media personality, was anxious about a big Memorial Day party he and his wife were planning. Mike feared that his alcoholic brother, Tom, would spoil the party and embarrass the family. But he didn't dare say anything to Tom—his brother didn't admit to his drinking problem. This continued a family pattern: Mike's father died from alcoholism, but no one ever said anything to him about his problem. Tom was defended not only by his own denial but also by an unwritten family law.

Mike wanted to break this defensive law and help his brother, his family, and himself, but he doubted that he would be able to do so. All he could think of to say to Tom was that he needed to quit drinking. This is one of the common mistakes people make in trying to help precontemplators—they rush them toward action. Tom was in no way ready for action. His likely response would have been, "Quit trying to control me, big brother!"

I advised Mike to try to inspire Tom to begin thinking about his drinking as a potential problem rather than pushing him immediately to do something about it. We agreed that approaches like "Tom, let's talk about your drinking. I'm concerned that it is becoming a problem," or "Tom, what could I do to help you with your drinking?" would be appropriate. But Mike was still afraid to say anything. In his family, as in so many others, intervening is seen as interfering. Precontemplators defend their right to damage, defeat, or destroy themselves. How then can we help precontemplators? How can we be our brother's helpers without becoming their keepers?

First, we must recognize that precontemplators are powerless to change without assistance. We can help by lending our eyes, ears, and hearts. We must see for those who are partially blinded by their defenses, hear for those who are too embarrassed to speak, care for those who are too demoralized to care. Gently, we must encourage the precontemplators we love to move into the contemplation stage so that they can open themselves up to change.

Helping another person may seem a herculean task, requiring enormous effort, patience, and strength. Patience, however, can be acquired, and strength in this context is really the knowledge of what works and what doesn't. A helper's first task is to enable the precontemplator to consider his or her problem behavior. There are a number of mistakes helpers make in trying to aid the change process. Here is an overview of what *not* to do when trying to help another person:

Don't push someone into action   Remember, change does not equal action. The most common error is to push someone to take action too soon. A precontemplator is not ready to take action, but may be ready to consider changing. Encourage this inclination.

TABLE 6. DIFFERENCES BETWEEN ENABLERS AND HELPERS

Enablers	Helpers
Avoid discussions and confrontations.	Address specific disruptive and distressing behaviors.
Soften consequences by minimizing the import of events.	Ensure that each negative behavior is followed by a consistent consequence.
Make excuses, cover for, and even defend problem behaviors.	Insist that precontemplators accept responsibility for actions.
Indirectly or rarely recommend behavior change.	Directly and frequently recommend behavior change.

Don't nag   Repetitive, insistent comments usually backfire. Worse yet, they weaken the helper's special relationship with the changer. "It got to the point where I wanted to divorce my wife rather than lose weight," one self-changer told me.

Don't give up   A precontemplator may mistake a helper's apathy as a sign that a problem behavior is really not serious after all. To a precontemplator apathy looks like approval of the behavior.

Don't enable   Enabling begins naturally enough, when the helper cares about the precontemplator and wants to understand his or her concerns. However, the enabler is actually colluding in the precontemplator's denial and minimization. Denial is strengthened rather than diminished by well-meaning attempts to soften the damage. Enabling continues when the helper fears that any challenge to the precontemplator's problem behavior will risk a break in the relationship. If the problem is ever to be resolved, however, it will be because the helper dares to intervene.

Using helping relationships

As a precontemplator, you can take advantage of people who care about you by letting them help you. Acknowledge that loved ones can see you as you cannot, and allow them to assist you to enter the cycle of change.

Ask others to identify your defenses   Ask someone you trust to describe, clearly and directly, how you defend yourself and what it is you defend. This is not easy to do, since normally people do not want to confront others' defenses; in fact, they are supposed to "go along" with your defenses. This is where therapists traditionally are helpful. They tell you what your best friends won't.

Convince your helper that you are serious, and be prepared for impressive results. If your helper knows you well, this will not be as difficult a task as you might imagine. He or she knows what your problems are, and whether you tend to deny them, rationalize them, or blame them on others or yourself. Encourage your helper to let you know when he or she senses that you are becoming defensive.

This open discussion is a major step in not allowing those defenses to defeat you. And it serves another critical purpose—you will have enlisted a helper in your struggle.

Become aware of your defenses   As you realize that your defenses do not fool others, you will become less invested in fooling yourself. After all, if your friends are already on to your act, what do you have to hide? It may be embarrassing to discover that you are the last to know about your problems, but is it not a relief to realize that your friends and family have decided not to reject you? And, as you become less defensive and more open about your frailties, they will probably come to care even more about you. Remember, it is hard to live with a saint—especially a self-righteous, defensive saint.

Begin to guard against your defenses. Let your helper know when and why you are feeling defensive. You might say, for example, "I notice I'm becoming uncomfortable about talking about smoking because I don't want to admit to myself that it is a problem." Or "I realize I changed the topic because I get self-conscious when the subject of obesity comes up." These simple statements identify defenses and help defeat them.

At first you will be aware that you are becoming defensive; but try to acknowledge your defenses as soon as possible. You will quickly begin to notice them, and will reach the point where you can say, "I'm starting to get defensive and I really don't want to." This means you have attained some control over your defenses, and they will stop controlling you. Don't expect, however, that you will be able to shut them down entirely; they are powerful forces that will continue to win out at least some of the time. Keep working on developing openness and awareness, and your chances of successful change will increase.

Help others to help you Most people assume that the best way to help is to push you to take action. Taking action before you are ready for it is usually a mistake. When helpers try to rush you into doing something, they are actually diminishing the effectiveness of their help, since you will become resistant to the pressure.

Tell your helpers that you are trying to be more open and less defensive, but that you are not ready for action. You need to talk, get feedback, and feel cared for; criticisms or personal attacks will only serve to increase your defensiveness.

Helping relationships self-assessment

This self-assessment will allow you to measure your progress in using helping relationships. Be honest and realistic. Fill in the number that most closely reflects how frequently you have used the method in the past week to combat your problem.

1 = Never, 2 = Seldom, 3 = Occasionally, 4 = Often, 5 = Repeatedly

FREQUENCY:

_____ I have someone who listens when I need to talk about my problem.

_____ I can be open with at least one person about experiences related to my problem.

_____ I have someone on whom I can count when I'm having problems.

_____ I have someone who understands my problems.

_____ = Score

   The level of helping relationships should be high and sustained throughout the cycle of change. People in the precontemplation stage who are ready to move forward into contemplation generally achieve scores of 12 or higher. If your score is lower, review the techniques we have mentioned, and try to put them into practice within the boundaries of your relationships. Don't be unwilling or afraid to enlist the support of those who love you. Continued progress through the stages of change will depend on the sustained support from your helpers, so it is important that you establish good working habits with them now.

SOCIAL LIBERATION

The process of social liberation involves creating more alternatives and choices for individuals, providing more information about problem behaviors, and offering public support for people who want to change. No-smoking sections in airplanes, restaurants, and workplaces are well-known examples of change that are designed to free people from smoke or from the temptation to smoke. Community-sponsored post-prom parties provide a healthy alternative for high school students who do not want to drink or use drugs. Even the simple act of naming a "designated driver" is a form of social liberation.

Self-help groups are the most familiar social liberation activity in the United States. There are more than a million such groups, with 15,000,000 members, ranging from Alcoholics Anonymous, Overeaters Anonymous, and Neurotics Anonymous, to self-help groups for people with phobias and panic attacks and those for relatives of those with schizophrenia, to relatively new groups for AIDS sufferers. In addition to consciousness-raising inherent in such groups—in which the latest information about problems and their treatment are always an important focus—these groups provide a social environment in which people can maintain their dignity and feel they will not be stigmatized or ostracized.

Self-help groups send out a powerful message to isolated precontemplators who are embarrassed or ashamed to admit that they have personal problems. The very existence of these groups says, "You are not the only person in the world with this problem; we can help you to accept yourself as a person with a problem and to do the best that you can to change it."

That precontemplators experience the forces working for social liberation is inarguable. But just how do they experience these forces? This process can be extremely helpful to the ones who experience it positively; others see social liberation as just another coercive force. How precontemplators respond to social liberation can determine whether they will progress to the contemplation stage or remain stuck defending their troubled behavior.

There are huge struggles occurring in our society, between social forces seeking to liberate people from their problems and commercial forces that profit from them. The United States government spends $50 million a year, for example, trying to help people stop smoking. The tobacco industry spends ten times that amount to win new smokers and retain old ones.

Both sides in this battle target precontemplators. Public-health campaigns develop effective methods for getting their messages through the defenses of precontemplators. Witness, for example, the emotional depictions of car crashes involving young people who drink and drive, that seek to hammer home information about one of the dangers of drinking to an audience that is well defended against such information.

Meanwhile, advertising campaigns counter with messages designed to shore up defenses. The old slogan "I would rather fight than switch" is a blatant example, but others come along every year. Establishing no-smoking sections, alcohol-free parties, and self-help groups might not seem to be coercive approaches to change. Nonetheless, they are seen as threats not only by precontemplators, but by the commercial forces that profit by peddling the tools of self-destructive behavior.

The tobacco industry periodically funds advertising that portrays antismoking campaigns as antifreedom forces. In these ads, they claim that there are three types of people: smokers, nonsmokers, and antismokers. The first two groups, they say, are basically the same: freedom lovers who respect the right to smoke or not smoke. Conversely, anti-smokers, who want to limit people's rights to smoke, are depicted as being antidemocratic. Therefore, the message goes, antismoking activities should be resisted not only by precontemplators who want to smoke, but by freedom-loving people everywhere, even those who do not smoke or would like to quit smoking. This campaign is undoubtedly effective, especially with resistant precontemplators.

Appendix A outlines the differences between foolish freedom and responsible freedom. If you have difficulty distinguishing between the two, please review Appendix A before proceeding further in the cycle of change.

Using social liberation to help you change

How can social liberation work to your advantage? Here's an obvious example: It's great to be in a public no-smoking area when you have been thinking about quitting anyway.

Other instances are more complex. A husband of one of my clients called late one night, saying that his wife was falling apart. She had learned that she was going to be fired from her secretarial position, even though she had been doing her job well. Gossip had spread through the office about her being a former mental patient, and the most powerful secretary in the office did not want to work with her; the boss was succumbing to office politics.

We met at midnight. The woman wept over the anticipated loss of her job and, more important, of her lifelong dream of having a home of her own (the couple was about to buy a house with a mortgage based in part on her income). Anger threatened to make her irrational. She wanted to tear apart the manipulative secretary, but knew she couldn't. Together we developed a plan of action. She would go to her legal aid office in the morning and begin to assert her rights under the Handicapped Persons' Law, which prohibits firing anyone because of physical or mental handicaps. Her action worked: Not only did the boss change his decision, but the increase in self-esteem the woman felt left her in a significantly more powerful position.

To use the process of social liberation, you must be aware of alternatives such as these, resist the efforts of antichange forces, and see those alternatives as options for growth rather than as coercion. Here are three social liberation techniques that can facilitate intentional change and help you resist commercial advertisements.

Ask who is on your side   Look at the social forces that make it easier for you to change. Why are they trying to help you overcome your drinking, eating, smoking, gambling, stress, or other unwanted behavior? What do they gain if you and people like you change? Do they want to rob you of your freedom, or to create a healthier society and a healthier you? Do they want to control you, or just make it easier for you to control yourself?

Next, look at the forces that want you to continue your problem behavior. What is their motive? Do they want to create a healthier society and a healthier you, or do they want to profit by your habits and those of others? What will they lose if people like you change? Do they want to increase your control over problem behaviors, or keep you controlled by these behaviors?

Ask whose side you are on   If you could liberate people from smoking, overeating, and overdrinking, would you use this power? If you could keep people from smoking, overeating, and overdrinking, would you use that power? Would you rather make a donation to the National Cancer Society, American Heart Association, and American Lung Association, or to the American tobacco industry or the national liquor lobby? Even if you don't want to change your habits, would you rather provide moral support to groups that are trying to help change problem behaviors, or to those who seek to reinforce them?

Seek and welcome outside influences   It isn't necessary to be defensive and resist people who want to change you. Although you may like yourself and your lifestyle, you may have a sneaking suspicion that in fact you would be better off changing.

Surely if you knew all there was to know about your behavior and its consequences, you wouldn't need to be open to outside influences. But you don't know everything. So try to welcome input from people who may see your blind spots or inform you of them. Being encouraged to change by someone who knows more about a problem behavior than you do does not make you a lesser person. If you feel, however, that you are being manipulated, by all means tell the person to back off. But if you can identify with the motives or the message, let it move you. If you keep your defenses down, the liberating forces will be able to reach you—before it is too late.

Social liberation self-assessment

Here is a self-assessment to check your progress in using the process of social liberation. Fill in the number that most closely reflects how frequently you have used the method in the past week to combat your problem.

1 = Never, 2 = Seldom, 3 = Occasionally, 4 = Often, 5 = Repeatedly

FREQUENCY:

_____ I encounter social situations that are designed to help reduce my problem behavior.

_____ I find that society is changing in ways that make it easier for me to change.

_____ I notice that people with the same problem I have are asserting their rights.

_____ I read about people who have successfully changed themselves.

_____ = Score

Compare your score (the sum of your four answers) with the benchmark of 14, scored on this process by self-changers who had smoking and weight problems. Self-changers who believe that alcohol abuse, anxiety, and depression are problems should consider scores in the range of 9 to 10 as a sign that they are ready to enter the contemplation stage.

Lower scores mean also that you may be resisting social influences too much, or that you are not open enough to social cues and options that could ease your journey through the cycle of self-change. Try again to admit these cues and options before proceeding. Try also to incorporate responsible freedom and avoid foolish freedom, as defined in Appendix A, before moving forward into the contemplation stage.

GEORGE'S INCREASED CONSCIOUSNESS

Consciousness-raising played an important part in the progress of George, whom we met earlier. Although he left therapy in the precontemplation stage, the things we had talked about there had apparently shaken him up. The man whom I felt I had not helped began years later to refer patients with alcohol problems to me. I was curious enough to call him and find out the rest of his story.

George allowed himself to begin to change when he turned forty. When he was sober, the very word "forty" sounded like a combination of "fatty" and "baldy" to him. He was afraid that he had already missed the best part of his life. And if this was the best that life had to offer, he felt he might as well drink; at least it dulled the pain of disappointment.

Even drinking could not prevent him from worrying that he was suffering from the disease he called "terminal failure." His assurance that his problems were due to the failures of his family, his wife, and his boss was weakening. Perhaps that was partly true, he thought; but it was also partly a defense. He was failing himself, and that was becoming unacceptable.

One night, some friends invited George to a performance of Eugene O'Neill's *The Iceman Cometh*. Although he loved theater, George preferred comedies; he wanted to keep things light. But against his "better" judgment, he went along to *Iceman*, which he knew was about characters in a pub. Perhaps, he thought, it would just be a heavier version of *Cheers*, his favorite TV show; as it turned out, the play did not cheer him.

O'Neill's play is filled with characters trapped by their drinking and defenses, fooled by pipe dreams that someday they would change, someday they would act, someday they would face their futures directly rather than through the bottom of a beer bottle. George found himself crying for the characters—and himself. Then he went out and got drunk.

Soon thereafter, George discovered he wanted to learn more about the effects of alcohol. "After all," he joked, "I'm well versed in all my other pastimes. I should be more of an expert on drinking—there's nothing worse than a dumb drunk."

George was shocked to learn that he and his buddies typically drank three to four times more beer than was considered low risk. Even more upsetting was the knowledge that excessive alcohol kills brain cells. It was bad enough that his body was turning to fat; to imagine his brain being planted with fatty cells was downright alarming. George had a brilliant mind, and he prized it above any other part of himself.

At the same time, George started to become aware of and moved by special helping relationships—those with his children. He recalled the night when he first heard his young daughter plead, "Daddy, don't go out—we need you here." Although he still went out drinking, that night he felt guilty for the first time. His jokes didn't seem so funny, and he knew what it meant to be laughing on the outside and crying on the inside.

George continued to drink heavily. He got divorced. He was angry, striking out at others verbally and physically. But he was also seriously contemplating changing himself. He experienced the formidable truth about consciousness: Once you let your defenses down, and become aware of the facts about your behavior, it is difficult to reverse the process.

If you have identified your defenses, solidified a helping relationship by becoming open with yourself and others, especially about problem behavior, and have become receptive to the forces of social liberation, you are probably ready to move to the contemplation stage of change. However, even if you are not ready to change at this time, read on. You'll see what's ahead of you, and how rewarding it can be to contemplate tackling the problems of your life.

CHAPTER 5

Contemplation—Change
on the Horizon

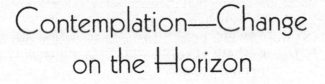

LARRY HAD BEEN immobilized in his reclining chair for seven years. It seemed as if it was the only place where he felt safe and secure. Lately though, things were changing. He remained self-conscious, anxious, and angry around people, but he was gaining insight into his passive-aggressive approach, and that excited him. He saw, for the first time, how his parents had undermined his trust of other people by sending him negative messages about them. He finally realized it was actually his parents who were negative! It was scary how much he had internalized their harsh words, and how that kept him trapped. When Larry began to talk about himself and his problems, his teenage children were shocked. But he knew he was getting ready to get out of his chair and back into life.

Larry is in the contemplation stage of change. He is aware of his problems with passivity and depression, is struggling to understand their causes and cures, and is seriously thinking about solving them. Excited about his new awareness, Larry is letting down his defenses and welcoming others into his life, and he is confident that he will act soon. He is in the strongest position possible in this stage, and will soon move on into preparation.

Others typically get stuck in the contemplation stage, sometimes for years. They fall into a major trap: chronic contemplation. Chronic contemplators substitute thinking for acting, promising that they are going to act "someday." Their motto is "When in doubt, don't change."

In Samuel Beckett's play *Waiting for Godot*, the two main characters defer all decisions until Godot arrives. Godot never comes. This is a perfect description of chronic contemplators—they seem always to be waiting for Godot. Conflicts and problems hang suspended; decisions are never finalized; action is avoided. Some believe that Godot represents God, and many chronic contemplators do seem to be waiting for divine intervention. On the other hand, *godot* is the French word for boot, and a swift kick from one is just what some chronic contemplators need to get them moving.

Regardless of their tendency to procrastinate, almost all people in the contemplation stage are eager to talk about themselves and their problems, searching for reassurance that their concerns can be understood and overcome. Unlike those in the precontemplation stage, contemplators are open to reading articles and books about psychology in general, and their problems in particular. But while they can actively read, think, and talk, they are not ready to prepare for action until they achieve a greater understanding of their behavior. As a result, consciousness-raising is just as important in the contemplation stage as it was during the earlier stage.

Contemplators want to change, but this desire exists simultaneously with an unwitting resistance to it. This ambivalence is understandable, since action brings with it a terrifying, even paralyzing fear of failure. Add to this the anxiety that contemplators feel about sacrificing the life with which they are familiar, and the fear of meeting the "new self" created by change, and you can easily see why so many contemplators become stuck. They prefer a familiar self to one that is better, thus postponing anxiety and avoiding failure.

Don't scoff at the anxiety attached to change. The prominent existential psychologist James Bugental called the fear of changing "a fate worse than death." Change threatens our very identity and asks us to relinquish our way of being. However healthy change may be, it threatens our security, and sometimes even self-defeating security feels better than none. An awareness of this ambivalence can prevent you from falling into one of the many traps that are the negative responses to contemplation. Here are some of them.

The search for absolute certainty   Alfred didn't think that he understood his problems well enough to know how—or even what—to change. An engineer, Alfred mistrusted psychology. It didn't seem a "real" science that could provide any solid information about his behavior. He explored it anyway, taking an engineer's exhaustive approach. He spent five years analyzing the factors that had made him so passive and shy. The farther he went back into his history, the more he found to analyze, and he concluded that his analysis would never come to an end. Alfred was getting lost in the mazes of his memory and his mind.

Certain people's personalities virtually guarantee that they will become bogged down in prolonged contemplation. Obsessive people like Alfred believe that they must explore every aspect of an issue until they achieve an absolute certainty as to its origin. Perhaps, they hope, the problem will go away while they are thinking about it, or perhaps they will find enough pieces of the puzzle to complete the picture and make change happen easily.

By substituting worrying for working, fearful obsessives can search for years, shifting from one therapist or book to another, always waiting until they are completely certain that their approach to change will be perfect. Not coincidentally, there are psychotherapists who decline to suggest action without an obsessive understanding of their clients' problems. Such practitioners unwittingly encourage chronic contemplation and place obstacles to their clients' growth.

The unfortunate truth is that we may never know enough about behavioral problems to be certain about their causes or cures. As we shall see in the next chapter, although there is always room to doubt our understanding, our intentions, and our actions, there comes a time when decisions must be made.

Waiting for the magic moment   Deborah talked about her marital troubles until her friends were sick of hearing about them. Deborah had been miserable for as long as they could remember. They all knew about her husband's drinking problems and his neurotic behavior, and they all advised Deborah to leave him. Deborah agreed, but always she found excuses for delaying action. Someday soon, she would get a divorce—but for now, all she did was talk.

Many people have an almost mystical belief that someday, somehow, there will be a magic moment that will be absolutely perfect for change. Like Deborah, chronic contemplators tell themselves that they will change "when the time is right." But when will the time be right? "When I'm good and ready," they declare. But when will they be ready? "When things slow down." Things, of course, never slow down.

Wishful thinking   This is probably the most common behavior that prevents people from progressing from contemplation to preparation and action. Wishful thinkers want to have their cake and eat it too, to go on living as they always have, but with different consequences. Here are a few examples of wishful thinking we have encountered; see how many of these wishes you make from time to time:

- I wish I could eat whatever I want and not gain weight.

- I wish I could drink as much as I like and not lose control.
- I wish I could work a seventy-hour week and spend lots of time with my children.
- I wish they would discover a cure for lung cancer.

It's easier to wish for change than to work toward it, just as it's easier to win the lottery than to work for a living. The passive approach, however, is rarely successful. Reflect on your own life experiences: How often have important, desirable changes occurred as a result of your wishing for them?

Prayer can be a kind of wishing or hoping, and the wisest of those who pray for divine intervention always remember that "God helps those who help themselves." This injunction underlines the subtle difference between wishing and hoping. Bernie Siegel, author of *Love, Medicine, and Miracles,* writes that wishful thinking is passive and external—"wishing on a star" for a miracle or magic. Hope, by contrast, is active and realistic. Hoping demands that you envision your success, and then work toward it. Those who hope put their personalities behind their desires, and thus have a more realistic opportunity to achieve them.

Premature action One of our workshop participants, a newly married middle-aged woman, implored her husband, Fred, to kick his fifteen-year-old cigar habit, and took every opportunity to remind him of the health dangers. Fred was just developing a contemplative interest in modifying his behavior, and he ignored this "constant bantering" until his wife's suggestions escalated into demands. Fred then reluctantly registered for a smoking cessation program, from which he dropped out after two meetings, telling her, "See, I told you I couldn't do it! I hope you're happy now!" He had taken premature action, knowing that by failing this time he could forestall, if not prevent, a next time. She had set her husband up for failure by pushing him too quickly into action.

We frequently see this self-defeating response in contemplators who are faced with threats from family or friends to "change or else." As an aggressive response to this implied or actual threat, the contemplator makes a halfhearted attempt to change. Naturally it fails—by unconscious design, so the contemplator can justify his or her continued resistance to change while simultaneously heaping guilt onto those who demanded the change.

Premature action frequently occurs on New Year's Day, Labor Day, birthdays, and other times when people feel pressured to take action. We are "supposed to change" on these dates, and may well jump into action, ready or not. The payoff for premature action is that it can relieve some guilt and social pressure. After the invariable failure, the implicit message is, "Now stay off my back about this change nonsense."

The search for absolute certainty, waiting for the magic moment, wishful thinking, and premature action are all "negative processes," delay tactics that retard movement through the cycle of change. Despite these traps of the contemplation stage, a period of contemplation prior to preparing for action is essential for lasting and meaningful self-change.

There is a certain level of awareness of both problem and solution that must precede action. Without it—and the accompanying commitment that takes place during the preparation stage—maintenance of change proves very difficult indeed. Many successful self-changers have informed us that awareness preceded action in their cases, and psychotherapy patients also express a definite preference for awareness and insight into their difficulties before modifying them. In a recent major clinical study in Sheffield, England, clients found the awareness–behavior change therapy sequence quite comfortable, whereas the behavior change–awareness sequence felt all wrong.

This helps explain not only the high rate of failures associated with premature action, but the problems inherent in those action-oriented programs that ignore awareness. It also explains why so many self-help books fail to assist people to develop an awareness of their problem before encouraging them to take action. Techniques without awareness behind them don't have a chance to make any real impact on our inner selves, and so have little lasting effect.

Awareness is developed during the contemplation stage, which need not involve ponderous study or intense psychoanalysis. As we shall see, it may require no more than a few weeks of honest self-appraisal, using the now familiar techniques of consciousness-raising. In addition, it can be helpful to use a little self-administered scare—the time-honored tradition of catharsis, or emotional arousal.

THE FOURTH PROCESS: EMOTIONAL AROUSAL

Emotional energy is a powerful force. You can harness it to give you the impetus and resolve you need to make the decision to change. As you know from life experience, the rational thing to do is not always what you want to do. Emotions, however, can provide a burst of energy that allows you to supersede procrastination, and determine what is really in your best interests. Used correctly, the stirring techniques of emotional arousal will get your adrenaline flowing and help move you from contemplation to preparation and action.

Although simple facts are sometimes all that are needed to change a problem behavior, more often it takes a dramatic, emotionally charged event to do so. Emotional arousal is not the same as fear arousal. In discussions of smoking cessation techniques, someone often suggests showing vivid pictures of diseased lungs to the smokers. This is an understandable concept, but it is rarely effective—fear arousal is easily diverted by defense mechanisms. "That could never happen to me," "This is an extreme case," "I did not smoke as long or as much as this person," are the kinds of comments that such photos provoke among smokers.

Contemplators who are already seriously considering changing can use emotional arousal effectively. Don't make the mistake of confusing emotions with change. Like blood in surgery, emotions in self-change are necessary and inevitable, they serve a cleansing function, and they must be respected, but they are not the object of the endeavor. Emotions must be related to all parts of the effort to change, and must be used as you move forward into more advanced stages of change.

There are a variety of emotional arousal techniques that can be useful. Here are three:

Go to the movies   From the patriotic propaganda movies of World War II to the three-hanky tearjerkers, films stir our emotions more readily than any other art form. They can be a wonderful way to arouse your emotions as you decide to change. There are many commercial films, documentaries, and television specials that dramatically portray the consequences of almost every problem there is.

The trick is to use these helpers nondefensively. Seek out films that focus on your problem. Although informational videos can be helpful, they most often offer advice and "how to" information. The riveting emotional messages that dramatic materials provide are preferable. Jack Lemmon's portrayal of an alcoholic in *Save the Tiger* cannot fail to move you, nor can Yul Brynner's final interview, in which he talks about lung cancer and cigarette smoking.

Similarly, a film like *Clean and Sober* portrays the denial, relapse, and recovery cycles typical among cocaine addicts.

Video rental stores will make your search a lot easier, as will local referral centers that can recommend and sometimes rent films about specific problems. Television stations can be persuaded to make news specials available, and there are self-help distributors that offer specialized videos and materials. There is plenty of material out there. If you make the effort to obtain, view, and consider dramatic video messages, they can help you make a firm decision to change.

Make your own propaganda   If you find that watching movies made by others does not get your adrenaline flowing, try creating your own scenario, one that arouses your disgust, disappointment, and distress. There are a number of ways in which you can do this.

We frequently sensitize smokers to the problems caused by cigarettes by taking a clean white handkerchief and blowing the smoke of one entire cigarette through it. If you do this, don't inhale; just puff and blow the smoke so that all the tar and residue ends up on the handkerchief. Examine the hanky and you'll see what goes in your mouth and lungs twenty, forty, or sixty times a day. Or try filling a jar with cigarette ashes and butts from a day's smoking—add a little water to the jar and keep it around to remind you just how filthy smoking is.

If you have a problem with alcohol, have a friend videotape you after you have been drinking. Nothing is more effective in capturing the slurred speech, the poor coordination, and the semicoherent conversations drinkers exhibit. Such a video invalidates the denial that people with alcohol problems so often demonstrate. Watch the video the morning after; a hangover will increase your emotional distress about your drinking.

Similar tactics can be used for most other addictive or behavioral problems. Overweight people, for example, can use mirrors to encourage them to change. It's no coincidence that most gyms and health and exercise facilities have mirrored walls.

There are two things you should be aware of before going ahead with this technique. First, remember the goal is to create helpful emotional arousal, not to overwhelm yourself with disgust and disappointment. You don't want to become discouraged, nor do you want to blame yourself for the problem. Second, be aware of timing. It is extremely helpful, even important, to focus on the negative aspects of your problem behavior during the contemplation stage. However, in the preparation and action stages, concentrating on the negatives seems to hold self-changers back, by keeping them concentrated on the problem rather than on the solution.

Use your imagination   If renting videos is impossible and creating your own home experiments seems too difficult, you can arouse your emotions simply by using your imagination. Make your own "mental movie." Concentrate on the negative aspects of your problem, and confront your defenses within the confines of your mind; allow yourself, even force yourself, to imagine distressing scenes and scenarios. This is the opposite of relaxation; the objective is to create negative images that will sensitize you to the dangers and the drawbacks of your problem behavior.

Fast forward through the years and visualize the consequences of not changing. Picture your high-fat diet clogging your arteries, shortening your breath, producing pain in the chest, and panic too, that the heart you failed is failing you. Imagine that your passive or depressive approach to life is leaving you isolated in your reclining chair. Your children stop coming around; your friends find more active associates; your spouse starts talking about leaving.

Construct a scene in which people who know you well are confronting you about how your constant need to control alienates them. Some are angry that you always have to have your way. Others resent your stubbornness and your sense that you're always right. Few want to get close lest they lose their right to choose. Feel yourself getting defensive, and rationalizing about the virtues of being so responsible. But also experience how inferior or inadequate you can make others feel when you treat them like children.

This is not a time for wishful thinking. This is not a time to let your defenses turn faults into virtues, problems into preferences. This is a time to picture in your mind's eye the troubling consequences that can come from waiting for the magic moment. You do not need a psychic to forecast where your unchecked negative behaviors will lead.

A critical barrier to changing many problem behaviors is that serious consequences seem too distant or long-term to matter. By using your imagination to bring the future into the present you can effectively overcome this barrier, and arouse your emotions to the point where you are ready to make a firm commitment to take action. This will be of critical importance during the preparation stage.

Emotional arousal self-assessment

Here is a self-assessment to check your progress in using the process of emotional arousal. Be honest and realistic. Fill in the number that most closely reflects how frequently you have used the method in the past week to combat your problem.

1 = Never, 2 = Seldom, 3 = Occasionally, 4 = Often, 5 = Repeatedly

FREQUENCY:

_____ Dramatic portrayals about my problem affect me emotionally.

_____ I react emotionally to warnings about the consequences of my problem.

_____ Remembering reports about illnesses caused by my problem upsets me.

_____ Warnings about hazards of my problem move me emotionally.

_____ = Score

Your score indicates the extent to which you are emotionally aroused by portrayals, warnings, and hazards connected with your problem. In this self-assessment, a score of 10 or more indicates that you are ready to begin moving forward to engage in the preparation stage. If your score is 9 or less, we recommend that you redouble your efforts at emotional arousal.

THE RETURN TO CONSCIOUSNESS

If you progressed from precontemplation to contemplation, through consciousness-raising you have already become aware of your defenses and resistances; this change process remains important now as you gain more knowledge about the problem you are defending. Since you are less defensive, you are freer to process information about your problem in general, and about how it affects you in particular.

Many people attempt to solve a problem when they have minimal information about it, and the results are predictably dismal. You would never try to fix a car without understanding how it works beyond that it starts when you put gas in the tank and turn the key; it equally makes no sense to tackle change if you know little more about your body than that you need to rest it at night and put food in it several times a day. When physical disorders arise, most people rely on physicians to help fix them. But when psychological disorders emerge, most rely on their own resources, without first gathering the necessary information.

Fortunately, there are several consciousness-raising techniques that can help us "fix" ourselves. These are especially useful to successful self-changers:

Ask the right questions   Albert Einstein said that the key to solving problems is asking the right questions. Emphasize asking the right questions in your search for powerful knowledge. Don't look for magic information or miracle cures, like the dieters who purchase an endless number of fad diet books, but ignore factual information about nutrition, calories, and exercise.

Here are a few sample questions that may help you get started on solving some problems. Use them as a guide for developing questions specifically geared to your situation, and remember to ask yourself these questions without getting defensive:

- How many calories does an average forty-year-old male (or female) need to consume in an average day?
- How long must you jog to lose one pound?
- How does your body adjust to dieting in order to conserve calories?
- What effects do nicotine and nicotine withdrawal have on your body and your behavior?
- How can you tell if you are addicted to nicotine?
- What type of mood changes are you likely to experience two days after drinking too much?
- How can you tell if you are a problem drinker?
- What effects does alcohol have on your brain and behavior?

The answers to these and similar questions can generate important information that will assist you in changing. Armed with this information, you will be better prepared to fight the battle of the bulge, the bottle, or anything else.

Define your own goals   Vague objectives, such as "I want to become a better person," or "I want to feel good," beget vague self-change attempts. Lewis Carroll summed it up nicely in *Alice in Wonderland:*

ALICE:	Would you tell me, please, which way I ought to go from here?
THE CHESHIRE CAT:	That depends a good deal on where you want to go.

One of the first steps in becoming more aware is to specify your goals. Ask yourself: Exactly what behavior(s) do I wish to change? How can I measure and track my progress? If you cannot think of a way to measure your progress, the chances are good that your goal is too vague.

Don't let others dictate what is important to you. This is a trap that everyone falls into from time to time. Your goal can relate to almost any behavior, even if it seems unimportant to others around you. For example, in one of our weekly research meetings a few years ago, when I was discussing difficulties in maintaining regular teeth flossing, John Norcross called these concerns "silly" and "insignificant." Shortly thereafter, John was informed by his dentist that he was in danger of losing his teeth to periodontal disease if he didn't floss. The lesson has stayed with us both: Define your own goals regardless of what others think or say.

Collect the right data   From contemplation right through the maintenance stage, monitoring your problem is critical. Most self-changers rely only on informal monitoring, such as estimating their intake of drinks or calories each day. It pays to be precise and constantly hone your awareness about your behavior. Informal monitoring can easily be misleading, especially with overeating, drinking, and smoking, since even well-intentioned people underestimate how much they consume.

For example, I counseled a sixty-two-year-old physician

who was certain that he only drank two martinis a day; that had been his pattern for years. When he monitored his drinking more formally, however, he was shocked to discover that his self-made martinis contained eight to ten ounces of gin, or the equivalent of six to eight regular-sized martinis a day. The moral: Don't assume you know your intake—measure it.

Monitoring yourself for a week or more not only gives you a baseline to assess your progress once you take action, it can also make you more aware of exactly what needs changing.

Different problems should be measured with different yardsticks. Consumption problems—overeating, drinking, smoking, or spending money—are usually best measured by the amount consumed or spent. Recording your daily food intake and counting calories, for example, is a more sensitive measure of change than a daily weigh-in. Although decreasing your calorie intake from 2,000 calories to 1,500 calories per day is a 25 percent improvement, it is unlikely to lead to a loss of more than 1 percent of your body weight during your first week or two of action. Despite a highly significant cut in intake, weigh-ins may not initially show you any improvement!

With emotional problems, measure the frequency, duration, and intensity of distress episodes. Take the case of the thirty-six-year-old golf pro who was trying to control his ugly and abusive rages against his wife. He focused primarily on changing the intensity of his outbursts. Several months after he had taken action to control his temper, he blew up just as intensely as ever, and immediately became discouraged about his progress, until he realized that the frequency of his rages had declined from several times a week to just once in the past two months.

With most problem behaviors, the frequency of the episodes changes before their intensity does. What we choose to monitor, then, can make a major difference in our feeling of progress. For some habits, like swearing, spitting, and nail biting, frequency can suffice. The general rule in behavioral research is that multiple measures are better than single measures. When in doubt, measure more rather than less.

Functional analysis: learn your ABC's In addition to monitoring, try to track the events that immediately precede and follow your problem behavior. Do you drink more when something makes you feel angry? Lonely? Happy? What happens right after an angry outburst? Does the other person give in? Do you have a drink? Or do you withdraw to be alone? What makes you crave a piece of cake? How does eating it make you feel?

This "functional analysis" can illuminate what is controlling the parts of your life that seem out of control. It is easy as A (antecedents) B (behavior) C (consequences). Antecedents can trigger a problem behavior, while the consequences reward or strengthen it, no matter how maladaptive it is. There is a psychological principle that states that every human behavior is goal-directed. Functional analysis helps you identify the goals of your problem behavior.

TABLE 7. SAMPLE FUNCTIONAL ANALYSIS

Antecedent ⟶	Behavior ⟶	Consequences
Stress		Satisfaction
Fatigue	Smoking	Relaxation
Social discomfort		Calm

An ABC functional analysis helped a forty-four-year-old teacher get to the bottom of his nicotine addiction. His craving always occurred when he was exhausted or stressed during a hectic day at work, or when he was uncomfortable at a social function. Once he discovered the true antecedents and consequences of his need for cigarettes, he became aware that he didn't smoke—as he had always claimed—because he "liked the taste." Rather, smoking functioned for him as a kind of sedative.

Try taking one of your problem behaviors and listing its typical antecedents and consequences. Table 7 presents a sample functional analysis for cigarette smoking. To be most helpful, your functional analysis should focus not only on the external events that precede and follow a behavior, but also the internal events that may be controlling it. Pay attention to what you tell yourself before engaging in an undesirable habit. Just before you ate that piece of cake, did you tell yourself, "This will make me feel better"? Before starting on a weekend binge, did you declare, "What else are weekends for?" Prior to getting depressed, did you ask yourself, "Am I some kind of idiot?" Are angry outbursts at your husband preceded by thoughts such as, "He's just like my father"?

These types of statements, which trigger problem behavior, may be so automatic or unconscious that you are not even aware of them. To increase your awareness, ask yourself, "What am I telling myself that leads to engaging in this problem behavior? Am I giving myself unconscious permission to indulge?"

Many people can control their problems at work, but their controls go to hell when they return home in the evening. They eat sensibly all day long, for example, but pig out at night. What self-statements help them to justify this lack of control?

- I'm home and I can do whatever I want.
- There's nothing I have to do for others now, so I can indulge myself.
- I just need to escape from reality.
- After all I've done today, I deserve this.

Make a written list of the statements you make to justify your problem behavior. You may be surprised, and you will certainly move toward taking action.

What is the payoff for indulgence? There is the pleasure

of gratification, of course. Look at all the other reinforcements that can be gained from a single act of self-indulgence
in a consumptive behavior. First, there is pleasure—*mmm,
mmm*, good! Then, there is often a very real reduction of
stress; letting go of ego controls can feel like a break from
the hassles of everyday life. Also, indulging a vice can feel
naughty but nice. And finally, there comes a feeling of freedom in doing what you want to do—and to hell with the
consequences!

How wonderful it would be if most problem behaviors
did not exact a heavy toll. One barely delayed consequence
of self-indulgence, however, is that often we end up saying,
"I shouldn't have eaten so much," "I shouldn't have wasted
so much money," "I shouldn't have smoked that cigarette,"
"I shouldn't have been so anxious." In short, "I shouldn't
let one part of me take over the whole of me. That part
becomes like a demon I can't control."

Functional analysis involves us in two long-standing psychological controversies: How deep should we search for the
unconscious antecedents and consequences of our behavior? And how far back in time should we go in analyzing
these triggers and payoffs? Psychoanalysts say we need to
go to the core of our unconscious, a journey that often takes
us to our earliest childhood experiences. Behaviorists, on
the other hand, say we should examine events in the immediate environments that precede and follow our problem
behavior.

What should a self-changer do? Unburdened by ideolo-
gies, successful self-changers tend to go as deep into unconscious events as they can on their own, and as far back in
time as they believe is relevant to their particular problem.
Sometimes, these explorations are far-ranging.

A forty-eight-year-old housewife was well aware that she
often responded to her husband as if he were her father. He
knew it too, and occasionally said, "I'm not your father.
Quit treating me like him." Over the years, she realized that

she was projecting some deep-seated resentments she felt toward her father onto her husband. Gradually, she began to accept that she needed to face the unresolved conflicts with her father in order to improve her marriage. She went to her father's grave and pounded her fists on the earth, expressing rage at his abandonment of her at a young age.

Most self-changers, however, focus simply on the events preceding and following their problem, and on their internal reactions to these events. For that reason, we encourage a functional analysis that stays primarily in the present. However, if you find that less conscious thoughts and feelings are accessible to you, you should certainly consider them.

Consciousness-raising, as you have seen, remains important throughout the contemplation stage. Your objectives should be to develop greater awareness of your problem behavior, to gain insight into how your thinking and feeling maintain the problem, and to begin to develop a personal conviction of the value of change. When you have completed these steps—more information, more awareness, more self-motivation—you will be ready for the preparation stage of change.

GEORGE'S CHANGING SELF-IMAGE

George took consciousness-raising so seriously that he began to joke that he knew more about alcohol than was good for him. Until he discovered that alcohol abuse was a factor in more than 50 percent of automobile accidents, George had always attributed his accidents to the people who got in his way. Until he read that the majority of violent encounters involved alcohol abuse, he had ascribed his violent behavior to others who got on his case. He learned, too, that drinking was often the root cause of divorce and job loss. All these insights, along with George's weakened defenses and keen intelligence, meant that he could no longer deny that he had the profile of a problem drinker.

He still resisted the label of "alcoholic." Alcoholics drank before noon—George could wait until lunch. Alcoholics drank until they blacked out—George never lost consciousness. Alcoholics drank hard liquor—George preferred beer. Alcoholics were addicted—George could go a day without drinking, and even thought he could last a week. Alcoholics had no control over their drinking—George accepted that he had a drinking problem, but he was convinced he could control it.

George's increased awareness about the consequences of alcohol abuse, however, was continually changing his attitudes toward drinking. Until this awareness, the pros of drinking had always outweighed the cons. Drinking was his favorite social activity, an important part of his Irish heritage, an instant stress reliever, a frequent family event, a way of doing business and sharing with friends, a part of his tough reputation, and a source of outrageous stories. Drinking was so natural to George, it was like air; but now he realized that his air was polluted.

Because of his love for his friendly pub he had lost his wife, his job, and his automobile insurance. His drinking had cost him brain and liver cells. His short-term stress relief was won at the price of his long-term stability. He had gone from a happy drunk to a bitter beer drinker, always ready for a fight. He knew from his readings that alcohol abuse leads to increased anxiety and depression. He mocked himself for treating his depression by drinking a depressant.

Through consciousness-raising and emotional arousal, George was changing his mind about drinking. It was not easy. "Damn this awareness," he cursed, more than once. He drowned the facts, the ambivalence, and the conflict with drink, but still had to face himself when sober. Worse still, he had to face his children. They were not proud of him, and who could blame them? He was wrecking his future and jeopardizing theirs. And George no longer had his wife, who had left him, or his boss, who had fired him, to blame.

George had clearly reached the point of being disgusted by his habit; he was growing sick and tired of being sick and tired. He was sick of himself as a substance abuser. He was tired of telling his children lies, and of having constantly to make excuses for his shortcomings as a father and a friend. George was getting ready to make a change. All he had still to do was a positive reappraisal, envisioning a new self after the change.

THE FIFTH PROCESS: SELF-REEVALUATION

There is another critical change process that you have to use to move through the contemplation into the preparation stage. This is self-reevaluation, or taking stock, an emotional and cognitive appraisal of your problem and your self. Self-reevaluation will reveal to you, once and for all, that your essential values are in fact in conflict with your problem behaviors. Successful self-reevaluation leaves you feeling, thinking, and believing that life would be substantially improved if you didn't have those behaviors.

Self-reevaluation follows naturally from consciousness-raising. Once you are well-informed about your behaviors and their consequences, you will begin to question seriously whether you can feel good about yourself while continuing with those behaviors. Self-reevaluators ask questions like "Can I consider myself to be rational if I continue to smoke?" "Can I feel responsible if I continue to drink too much?" "Will my self-esteem go up if my weight goes down?" "Can I feel like a family man if I work seventy hours a week?" "Can I become successful if I cannot cope with stress?"

These questions are some of the easier aspects of self-

reevaluation; we all would like to be more rational, responsible, successful, and healthy. There are tougher questions:
What will you lose by abandoning your problem behavior?
What time, energy, pleasures, or fantasies must you sacrifice in order to change?

If change brought only positive gains, few of us would
hesitate to make changes. After all, we can all engage in the
kind of wishful thinking described a few pages back: "I wish
I could change spontaneously, instantly, and effortlessly."
There are still people out there to feed those fantasies and
tell you that an hour of hypnosis—rather than weeks or
months of effort—will get you to stop smoking; that strap-
ping a gizmo around your thigh or belly will cause you to
lose weight; that listening to "miracle" tapes while you
sleep will help beat depression. Although buying devices is
easier than making an effort, it cannot help you make real
behavior changes. Any change that is worth anything will
cost something dearer than money.

Self-reevaluation, then, requires not only that you abandon all hope of finding an effortless route to change, but
that you confront some difficult questions: What are you
willing to sacrifice for the sake of your self? Giving up drinking may mean you will spend less time with your buddies.
Becoming assertive will be a shock to friends who are accustomed to your submissiveness. Less emotional distress
may mean that those friends who helped you when you
were down will be less focused on you.

Change may also threaten your self-image. I knew a
three-hundred-pound musician who looked like Shake-
speare's Falstaff onstage; when he moved through a crowd,
people made way. After he lost 130 pounds, however, he
was depressed to discover that his self-image had shrunk.
He had not adequately reevaluated his problems before taking action.

The techniques of self-reevaluation

From both self-changers and our psychotherapy clients, we have learned that there are two complementary forms of self-reevaluation. One is an evaluation of the present, a negative view of how depressed and controlled we are by a problem behavior, and how we fail ourselves by not changing. This sentiment is frequently expressed by how "disgusted" we are by our habit. On the flip side of the coin is positive reappraisal, a forward-looking assessment of our healthier, happier, freer changed selves.

The most effective self-reevaluation methods judiciously combine both approaches, and allow us to be pushed by our present, negative view of ourselves just as we are being pulled toward our future, positive selves. Leaning too much to either extreme can be self-defeating, and it is especially dangerous for those changers who picture themselves as disgusting, loathsome creatures. Such intense self-deprecation can easily slide into psychological distress or self-blame, either of which inhibits rather than stimulates change.

As with the other change processes, there are a number of techniques useful in self-evaluation. Here are three frequently used by contemplators who are making the transition to the preparation stage:

Think before you act   Especially effective in dealing with consumptive behaviors such as overeating, drinking, or smoking, this technique can also be adapted to other problems. The fact is that over time, almost any habitual behavior can become so unconscious that it is reflexive. You can drink, smoke, eat, spend, or become angry, scared, or depressed without ever reflecting on what you are doing or why you are doing it.

Stopping to think allows you to pause before the reflex, to begin to reevaluate just what your behavior means to you. Before eating something, for example, ask yourself,

"Why do I want to eat this? Am I really hungry?" After you recognize the reason, go ahead and eat it if you feel like it. But after just a week of stopping to reflect, rather than responding reflexively, you will gain a measure of control over your habit.

Although the questions you ask yourself vary from one problem to another, the intention remains the same. These are "why" questions: "Why do I want this cigarette?" "Why am I responding this way?" "Why do I think I need food?" The questions help you determine the reason for your immediate behavior or if you are acting out of sheer habit. You may find, for example, that you are acting for immediate gratification or trying to project an image of being cool, in control, or sociable. Even if you believe that the reason is physical—you crave a cigarette, a drink, or food—upon reflection, you will find that boredom, anxiety, or your current social situation account for your cravings far more often than you would think.

Create a new self-image   Manufacturers spend billions of dollars on advertising in order to create marvelous images for their products. Consumers spend even more billions to buy into these images. Images sell and persuade because they blend thoughts and feelings at varying degrees of consciousness, appealing directly to fantasies without considering reality. If you fantasize that you are a rugged male, free to roam the range, you know just what cigarette is the right one for you. If you want to be a sophisticated drinker, there is a scotch with your name on it. If you fancy yourself a sportsman, you'll work extra months, even years, to pay for the car that reflects your sporting image.

Advertisements project various images of drinkers as individuals—from those who work hard, play hard, and drink hard, to those who drink for relaxation. Similarly, advertisers create images of smokers as having fun, being cool, and acting sexily.

What advertisers ignore, not surprisingly, are the harsh realities of drinkers who crack up their cars, wreck their careers, mess up their marriages, and screw up their children. They also ignore the health effects of smoking. A few years ago, a nonprofit group created a realistic film of a smoking cowboy. It began with an idyllic western setting, from a familiar advertising campaign, through which rides a lean cowboy, a cigarette dangling from his mouth. As the cowboy comes into focus, it becomes apparent that he is not a rugged model of health. He has the cough and wheeze of a heavy smoker, and appears to be dying. Predictably, lawsuits have kept this film from being widely viewed.

You can create images for yourself just as easily as the mavens of Madison Avenue do. Try a scenario in which you don't change: Your health and other aspects of your life, depending on your problem behavior, deteriorate further. Then imagine how you would think and feel about yourself if you did change. Would you feel relieved? Freer? Healthier? Would you be a better role model for your children? Would you be pleased about the change? Would others feel pleased for you? Would you actually feel that you have grown? The answers to these questions are self-evident.

Make a decision   Decision making is at the heart of moving from contemplation to preparing for action. But the decision to take action sooner rather than later is usually preceded by an evaluation of the pros and cons of a problem behavior. An evaluation or decisional balance is best made using the following four basic categories:*

- Consequences of change to self
- Consequences of change to others
- Reactions of self as a result of change
- Reactions of others as a result of change

*The notion of decisional balance is discussed at length in the book *Decision Making*, by Irving Janis and Leon Mann (New York: Free Press, 1977).

TABLE 8. SAMPLE DECISIONAL BALANCE SCALE

	Pros	Cons
1. Consequences to self	Improved health Increased happiness More money More marital success	Loss of some friends Less time with extended family Loss of "mood medication" Have to find other things to do
2. Consequences to others	Children can trust me Husband will be happier Boss can count on me	Some friends, some family members will be threatened Family is not used to dealing with my moods, and will have to learn to do this
3. Reactions of self	See self as determined See self as more responsible See self as not needing a crutch	See self as less fun See self as moodier See self as a stranger See self as getting older
4. Reactions of others	Children will be proud of me Husband will be pleased too Others will see me as being trustworthy again	What will most friends say? Perhaps they will say I'm afraid to drink, I'm less social, I'm "different"

The positive and negative aspects of changing a problem behavior can be listed next to each of these four categories, as illustrated in Table 8, which provides a sample decisional balance scale that was completed by a woman who considered quitting drinking. Completing such a scale is an individualized matter requiring considerable self-examination and honesty.

In Table 8, Jane is considering how quitting drinking would bring greater health, happiness, and success, and how it could provide her with freedom and some self-esteem. At the same time, she is considering the positive impact it would have on her children, husband, and boss.

The possibility of freeing her family from her alcoholism is a major positive consideration for Jane as she contemplates quitting drinking.

But Jane's negative considerations are also substantial. The loss of certain friends, the loss of the social ease she experiences with her hard-drinking extended family, and the looming search for new things to do all factor against her decision to quit. And although the future happiness of her husband and children are positive elements, the reality of their having to deal with her mood swings may tip the balance against Jane's taking action at this time.

Some decisions follow the evidence and logic revealed by consciousness-raising; the decisional balance scale makes the right choice clear. Deciding to get divorced, for example, is not the correct choice for everyone who makes it to the contemplation stage, but quitting smoking is, and action is almost inevitable. The decision to take action can be made at this point (although this doesn't necessarily mean that it is the next logical step; commitment is still part of the process).

The decisional balance scale should be as comprehensive as possible. Avoid the mistake of focusing only on the negative side of things. Any problem has its positive aspects. If it had no benefits you would have abandoned it long ago. If you deny or fail to acknowledge these aspects, you will attempt an ill-timed or ill-prepared change. In the long run, you do not have to give up the ultimate rewards of a bad habit. Most problem behaviors represent elaborate and indirect means of achieving relaxation and assertion. During the action and maintenance stages you will learn how to substitute alternative, healthier ways of deriving the same benefits.

After you complete the decisional balance scale, weigh and reevaluate the assets and liabilities of your problem behavior. If the pros seem stronger than the cons, you are probably not ready to move to the preparation stage. Spend some time gathering more information and focusing on the cons of your problem behavior. The best position for preparing for action is to have the pros of changing slightly higher than the cons of changing. This tips the decision making toward action and readies you for commitment.

Self-reevaluation self-assessment

Here is a brief self-assessment to check your progress. Again, be honest and realistic. Fill in the number that most closely reflects how frequently you have used self-reevaluation in the past week to combat your problem.

1 = Never, 2 = Seldom, 3 = Occasionally, 4 = Often, 5 = Repeatedly

FREQUENCY:

_____ I consider that my family and friends would be better off without my problem behavior.

_____ My tendency to give in to my problem makes me feel disappointed in myself.

_____ I reassess the fact that being content with myself includes changing my problem behavior.

_____ I get upset when I think about giving in to my problem.

_____ = Score

Scores of 14 and higher indicate you have made sufficient use of self-reevaluation to be able to move from the contemplation stage to the preparation stage. Scores below 13 strongly suggest a need for a more cognitive and emotional reappraisal of your self in relation to your problem. If you attempt to continue on in the cycle of change without such a reappraisal, our research indicates that you are likely to relapse. Why not do your reappraisal now, instead of the second or third time you pass through this stage?

GAIL, THE DIET EXPERT

When Gail began to consider the pros and cons of losing weight, she was forty-six pounds overweight, and her thirtieth high school reunion was less than six months away. Hers is a story, like George's, which we will follow through several chapters. Facing fifty, this successful executive was convinced that she was doomed to follow her mother's example: Trim and attractive until Gail was born, her mother afterward fought the battle of the bulge for thirty years until she ended up defeated, depressed, and obese.

Gail had already attended two of the top commercial weight-control programs that "guaranteed" permanent weight loss. After five cycles of weight loss followed immediately by weight gain (she lost more than 220 pounds and gained back 240), she doubted whether the benefits of losing weight were worth the costs. She could appreciate why her mother had given up.

On the other hand, Gail knew she had a lot more going for her. She had a rewarding career as a vice president in a communications company, while her mother had been a housewife with little to do once the children were off to college. Gail was a good athlete, like her mother before her—both swam, skied, and played golf and tennis. But unlike her mother, Gail continued to pursue sports even while her two children were in school. Fortunately Dan, Gail's husband, proved to be a much more active partner in raising the children than her father had been.

Besides obesity, age brought Gail's mother menopause, the empty-nest syndrome, feelings of inadequacy, and a declining future. However, a fuller future was in store for Gail. She could become president of her company; she would certainly travel, for business and pleasure; she could look forward to years more of competitive tennis; she had a happy marriage, and lovely children with exciting futures.

She wished it were possible not to worry about her weight. Although she hadn't been overweight until she reached her thirties, she had been acutely sensitive to weight issues all her life. Growing up, she saw how poorly fat kids were regarded by other girls. She also knew that heavy girls were not popular with the boys. And her mother, because of her own problems, was painfully observant of the changes Gail's body underwent during puberty, during menstrual periods, and even during pregnancy.

Gail often felt that her preoccupation with her excess weight was self-centered—she called it "the vanity factor." But as a young woman she had taken pride in her lean legs and her trim torso (as had her husband). She used to say, "If you can't look yourself in the stomach, you're not living right."

Now her words returned to haunt her, and her high school reunion was approaching. Gail began thinking seriously about doing something dramatic to lose those extra pounds. She thought the fasting program at her local hospital might help. Gail charted the pros and cons of the program (Table 9); the results once again left her dejected.

Normally Gail was a positive person; it shocked her to see that her list of cons was twice as long as her list of pros. No wonder she didn't feel motivated to move ahead. Her decisional balance underscored her doubts about taking dramatic action to lose weight. Why not be a feminist and reject the anorexic ideal that advertising campaigns had foisted upon her? Why not face fifty by accepting the fact that her fat was a permanent part of her life? Why fight biology, and risk her health, by undergoing still another episode of drastically and uselessly cutting calories?

At this point, to raise her consciousness, Gail read several articles that I had written. She discovered that weight loss is not a behavior, it is an outcome. Counting calories and cutting calories are behaviors, and it is ques-

TABLE 9. GAIL'S FIRST DECISIONAL BALANCE SCALE

	Pros	Cons
1. Consequences to self	1. The vanity factor will finally be satisfied! 2. My health will be improved.	1. Losing and regaining weight endangers my health. 2. This new diet will be costly. 3. I can't fast forever.
2. Consequences to others		4. Can't eat out with others.
3. Reactions of self	3. I'll feel better about myself.	5. I'll be embarrassed if I fail. 6. I'm not really sure my weight is a health problem—maybe it's genetic? 7. I'll feel like a slave to the fashion media.
4. Reactions of others	4. Children won't have to be embarrassed of me. 5. Husband will think I'm sexier.	8. Feminists won't approve. 9. Family says they love me however I am. 10. Husband isn't willing to fast with me to get rid of his own tummy.

tionable whether their consequences are healthy or not. But there was a possible "no lose" solution open to Gail, if she worried less about the final outcome, and concentrated instead on choosing alternative behaviors that were unquestionably healthier than either unrelieved feasting or periodic fasting.

There is a clear consensus that certain behaviors are good for one's body. By committing herself to following a low-fat diet, a consistent exercise program, and to giving up binge eating, Gail was unlikely to start any fights with feminists. Besides, she would suffer no doubts about the health

TABLE 10. GAIL'S SECOND DECISIONAL BALANCE SCALE

	Pros of a Low-Fat Diet	Cons of a Low-Fat Diet
1. Consequences to self	1. Prevent breast cancer. 2. Prevent colon cancer. 3. Prevent osteoporosis. 4. Prevent heart attack. 5. Prevent strokes. 6. Lower cholesterol. 7. Lose weight. 8. Increase fiber.	1. Must give up some favorite foods. 2. Extra food preparation, for husband's meals.
2. Consequences to others	9. Can dine out with others. 10. Be more responsible.	
3. Reactions of self	11. Feel less sluggish. 12. Feel more modern.	3. I'll be embarrassed if I fail.
4. Reactions of others	13. Husband will be happy I'll be able to eat with him.	

	Pros of Exercising	Cons of Exercising
1. Consequences to self	1. Play better tennis. 2. Have more energy. 3. Have better moods. 4. Prevent cardio-vascular disease. 5. Prevent cancer. 6. Lose weight. 7. Maintain muscle mass.	1. Takes time. 2. Health club is costly.
2. Consequences to others	8. I'll be more responsible.	
3. Reactions of self	9. Increased self-esteem. 10. I'll feel younger. 11. I'll have lower stress.	3. I'll be embarrassed if I fail.
4. Reactions of others	12. They'll see me as healthier.	

benefits, no preoccupation with calorie count, and no need to feel guilt about personal vanity.

The pros on Gail's list grew longer and healthier, as shown on Table 10.

It became obvious that her decisional balance had shifted dramatically, from two to one against fasting, to four to one in favor of a low-fat diet and aerobic exercise. Gail had overcome her demoralization and doubts about the pros and cons of dieting. She was convinced that she was developing a "no lose" plan; although weight loss would not be a primary goal (indeed it accounted for only two of the twenty-four pros of her plan), she had good reason to hope that a healthier, happier self would lead to a trimmer self.

Gail imagined that aerobic exercise would reaffirm her active and athletic self. She would not end up a passive person like her mother. She was a modern woman, eating a contemporary diet. Eating too much fat has become the equivalent of smoking cigarettes: Experts unanimously agree that it is bad for you. Fat clogs your arteries, and causes cancer, cardiovascular disease, and other chronic conditions.

The more Gail read the more she liked what she contemplated becoming. She would end up more fit, with less fat in her body. Being active physically and socially is the best way for the elderly to maintain physical and mental health. Plus, physically active women stay more sexually active. The pros were winning so decisively that Gail felt ready to forge ahead and prepare for taking action.

HELPING RELATIONSHIPS DURING CONTEMPLATION

Successful self-changers report that they value their helping relationships most during the stages of contemplation, preparation, and action. The first two techniques given here, especially valuable during contemplation, were originally described by the renowned psychologist Carl Rogers, who dedicated much of his life to studying the interpersonal strategies of helping relationships.

Empathy   This is the ability to take another person's place emotionally and cognitively, to walk in his or her shoes. Most contemplators actively seek and readily accept this special understanding, and welcome the knowledge that others have experienced concerns similar to their own. It is especially valuable to know that ambivalence need not lead to paralysis, that one can simultaneously feel positive and negative about changing a problem, and that it is possible to move forward to action despite self-doubt.

To maximize the empathy you receive from helpers, it is important to let helpers know where you are in the change process. Although you have achieved heightened awareness and have moved past the precontemplation stage, helpers must be aware that you are not ready for action. They should also know that change and action are not synonymous, and that you are changing in your own way and at your own pace. Don't let overzealous helpers push you into premature action.

In addition, as in any relationship, it is your responsibility to inform helpers of your specific needs. Contemplators typically need support, listening, and feedback. Many helpers, however, are more apt to offer glib answers and quick solutions. It might, therefore, be necessary to tell helpers that you seek understanding and support, but not advice, at this time. Statements such as "I'd like someone to just listen now; I might benefit from your own change techniques in a few weeks, but first I'd like to understand myself and the problem," will guide your friends and family toward the type of support you need rather than the type they might automatically offer.

Warmth   Another relevant strategy for enhancing change is warmth, defined by Rogers as a nonpossessive caring and prizing of another person without imposing conditions. The lack of conditions is tricky, since we frequently tend to attach strings to our kindnesses. "I'd like to help you change, but I'm going to leave you if you don't," and "I'll help you after you stop [drinking, eating, smoking, arguing]," are two examples of conditional "support" that encourage premature action and discourage sensible change.

How does one ignite the real warmth of helpers during contemplation? Start by being as caring and warm as you can be: Warmth begets warmth. And since no one profits from insults and threats, ask your significant others to express their concerns as observations, rather than as confrontations. Instead of saying, "You're doing it again—you know I can't stand that," concern can be presented in a caring manner: "I know how hard it can be to alter your behavior immediately." We all respond more positively to the second kind of feedback.

Warmth should not manifest itself as uncritical praise or incessant compliments—phony platitudes are counterproductive. Instead, it should represent a genuine attitude of acceptance and caring. An early study on coping with stress found that the most supportive statements are along the lines of "I know you'll do the best you can. I'll like you no matter how well you do." By contrast, the most unhelpful statements indicated false confidence—"Of course you'll do it!"—which implies conditions of worth and creates performance anxiety.*

Solicit input One of the central tasks of precontemplation was recognizing and overcoming maladaptive defenses; you asked others to point out your self-defeating defenses. During contemplation, you should ask helpers to assist you in your quest for more information, more awareness, and more self-motivation.

Loved ones can dramatically increase your self-knowledge by calmly reporting their observations, their personal experiences, and any information about your

*Mechanic, 1962.

problem that they have gathered through reading, television programs, and so on. Family members are often able to report with great accuracy just what precedes and follows a problem. For example, John Norcross, who is battling a weight problem, is frequently asked by his wife to evaluate why he is overeating in order to have him think before he acts.

Although other people can be of great help in our becoming conscious of the causes and consequences of our problems, few of us are secure and open enough to solicit their input. Take the risk with your loved ones. The resulting awareness will help you to make the transition into the preparation stage, an exciting time filled with positive anticipation.

CHAPTER 6

Preparation—Getting Ready

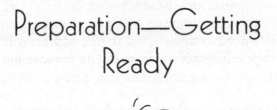

THE VALUE OF being prepared—as any Scout can tell you—is that it readies you both to take action and to handle unexpected challenges. It is unquestionably worthwhile to gain the skills and have the resources you need to manage the problems of life effectively. The success of most long-term projects is in large measure due to patient preparation; most successful self-change projects similarly rely on a sometimes brief but always thoughtful period of preparation.

People do not always heed calls for preparation. For those who live along the Gulf Coast, June marks the beginning of the hurricane season. The nightly news reports the early stages of the storms as they form as far away as the coast of Africa. When hurricanes become a real threat, newscasters exhort people to stock up on bottled water, canned food, batteries, flashlights, and radios.

Most people are rather casual about preparation until the warnings begin in earnest. Even then—when the storm's course is uncertain and its arrival is more than twenty-four hours away—many people ignore the warnings and do nothing. But as the storm gets closer and the probability of a direct hit increases, supermarkets and hardware stores become jammed with last-minute shoppers, many of whom find that necessary supplies are exhausted, leaving them quite unprepared for a deadly storm.

If, like those last-minute shoppers, you are betting that you won't need to prepare for action, you are setting your self-change efforts up for failure. The preparation stage is the cornerstone of effective action, and affords us an opportunity to make a solid commitment to behavior change. In fact, commitment is the most important change process available to you during the preparation stage. Any lingering ambivalence that undermines your determination must be resolved during this stage.

What is preparation like?

Preparation takes you from the decisions you make in the contemplation stage to the specific steps you take to solve the problem during the action stage. At the outset of our research, we did not separate the preparation stage from the contemplation stage; their differences are subtle. Our experience has since determined that proper preparation is vital to successful self-change. In the preparation stage, you will continue to reevaluate both yourself and your problem, but feel increasingly confident of your decision to change. Your personal reevaluation will look more toward your future self, and less to your problematic past. And instead of gathering information about the problem, as you did in contemplation, you will focus on finding the most suitable type of action to overcome it.

Rick's wife, Lana, did not appreciate his business dinners. He drank too much, she said, and came home soused, or tipsy, as he would have it. Rick always admitted that he had a few drinks—you had to socialize with clients or you couldn't do business—but at least he had them with a meal. He felt that Lana, who was raised as a Baptist, was too conservative and had a knee-jerk reaction against his drinking.

One night, driving home from a dinner meeting, Rick was stopped by the police. Confident that he was sober enough to drive, he agreed to a Breathalyzer test. The results showed a blood alcohol level of .18, almost twice the legal limit; Rick was arrested at once for driving while intoxicated. It was hard for him to rationalize this incident— maybe he had more of a problem than he had been willing to admit.

After his arrest, Rick's cockiness turned to concern, and he began to realize all that drinking had cost him. He also recognized, for the first time, that his father had had a drinking problem also. His twelve-year-old son and Lana were quite upset about the arrest. Rick saw it was time to break this cycle. He decided to use the mandatory DWI course and the court recommendations to help him take action.

Rick has entered the preparation stage of change. Over time, he has overcome the barriers he had to admitting his problem, and after evaluating his options, has decided to take action. His first prudent steps in implementing his decision involve careful planning, positive self-reevaluations, and commitment.

Preparation may also incorporate certain tasks that make up the first steps on the road to action. Rick's decision to go to the DWI classes is a good example of a preliminary task, as would be decisions to cut down on smoking, curtail spending, obtain the telephone number of a support service, or begin to substitute healthy activities for unhealthy ones. From the outside, much of the work of preparation looks like a rehearsal for action.

This stage can be tedious, at times, which often leads to problems. The end of contemplation, when we decide that a given problem is significant and needs to be changed, brings us to the edge of action. The work we have done up until preparation is hard, even courageous. But many of us wish that admitting a problem would be enough to make it change. We begin waiting for a magic moment, or we engage in wishful thinking and become stuck.

The desire to shortcut preparation and leap into action

prematurely—is another common problem. Being so close to action makes people antsy, but premature action usually leads to ineffectual change.

George's premature action

Day after day, George thought about controlling his drinking. And week after week he kept putting it off. Weeks turned to months as George waited for that magic moment. Finally becoming fed up with himself, he abruptly decided to act. He didn't want to go on merely contemplating a drink-free existence, like those haunting characters in O'Neill's play.

George announced to his kids that he was going to control but not cease his drinking. They were delighted. He imagined that controlled drinking would allow him to keep his friends, his principal social activity, his stress reducer, his tough image, his Irish heritage, and his style of life, while minimizing the consequences of alcohol abuse.

When George first began to use his personal computer to monitor his drinking, he was appalled to realize that he was consuming between fifty-five and seventy-five drinks a week. He was spending between $50 and $150 a week on booze. He had been living off a small inheritance, but that was dwindling. George had to get the new business he had started on a solid basis soon or he would be out on the street.

So he set a goal of having no more than three drinks a day, and developed a simple computer program to help him. He called the program DADD, Defenses Against Dangerous Drinking. He programmed his shopping list to print out alcohol-free beer as a substitute for his old brand. When he logged in his daily consumption at three drinks or less, his computer rewarded him with messages like "Good going, George," or "Atta boy, you can control it." When he drank more than three drinks, his computer told him, "George, you slipped yesterday, you need to get back on track," or

"Hey, George, you can't afford to mess up. Your kids are counting on you."

George also told bartenders to serve him low-alcohol beer, and to give him no-alcohol beers after he had had three. Because George had not told his friends about his change, he asked the bartenders to pour the substitute beers behind the bar. They looked the same, they smelled the same, and—after a couple, anyway—they tasted the same. Only the feel was different, and it felt good to be in control.

George sailed along smoothly for a few months. The biggest challenges he faced were from his friends and extended family. They soon knew what only his kids and his bartenders were supposed to know and began pushing real drinks on George, not those "sissy beers," as they called them. They weren't satisfied just to have George drink with them; they wanted him drunk with them.

Unfortunately, his friends and his extended family didn't care or were threatened by his decision to control his drinking. After all, if Big George could control his drinking, what excuse did they have to go on getting drunk every night? Eventually they won; George began drinking again. He had not prepared well enough for action.

CONTINUING
SELF-REEVALUATION

In the contemplation stage you learned how to reevaluate your self and your problem, and to see that resolving the problem, and re-creating yourself, agree with your current values. Self-reevaluation helps you make a firm decision to change. In the preparation stage, you can increase your chances of success by focusing on the future and your new self. The great motivator is a hopeful vision of what your life will be like once you have changed your behavior. Make a list of the benefits of the change, and keep it always in front of you.

Carlo saw how important this vision of a future self can be in a therapy group he ran for people addicted to cocaine. In the group there were individuals at different stages of recovery. Those who were in the contemplation stage delighted in recounting war stories of their drug-using days, complete with descriptions of the terrible things they did to get coke, as well as the terrible things coke did to them. Although there was a clear emphasis on the negative aspects of their addiction, these stories kept them in touch with the excitement and danger of drug use. Since they were still in a decision-making stage, this was appropriate for them.

However, those who were in the preparation and action stages found that the war stories were distracting them from the task at hand and even tempting them to return to drug use. These people fared much better when they were separated, and led to focus on the positive aspects of life without cocaine—how they would become closer to their spouses, spend more time with their children, function better at work, and feel pride and a sense of accomplishment at quitting. Focusing on their new selves energized them and reinforced their commitment to change.

Here are two frequently used techniques that are especially useful to self-reevaluators in the preparation stage:

Turn away from old behavior   Let go of the past and look toward the future, even though letting go may be difficult and the future uncertain. Imitate the trapeze artist, who lets go of one swing while trusting the partner on another. It can be scary to let go of old patterns of behavior, but your new self will be there to greet you.

Leaving the past behind may create disorientation. Our problem behaviors are established habits and integral parts of our lives. Just as positive habits would be hard to break— imagine trying to learn to stop brushing your teeth—so are problem behaviors. Remember, all problem behaviors offer benefits. Some women worry that if they shed weight, they will become sexual objects. Their unwanted weight has for years served to shield them from unwanted attention.

Creating new, functional images of your future self will help you let go of the past. Ask yourself: What is my potential if I change? What will it free me up to become? How will my life be enhanced?

Make change a priority   Since most of us lead busy lives, intentional self-change cannot happen unless it is given a prominent place on our list of goals. We have seen many individuals who make personal behavior change a goal, but a vague one. On their list of things to do, it is relegated to a place somewhere between getting a haircut and going shopping. Such shortsighted plans can hardly be adequate to making a major change in your life.

If you tend to try to accomplish too much, you undoubtedly put off the more difficult tasks, like personal change, in order to attend to the relatively simple, less challenging ones. If you let others set your agenda and goals for you, personal change will always take a backseat. If you hate making goals for yourself, you will have to wait until someone forces you to change.

At the end of the contemplation stage you decided to change your problem behavior. In the preparation stage you must concentrate on moving this change task to the top of your list of things to do. Change requires energy, effort, and attention. You will not be ready to move into the action stage until changing your behavior becomes your highest priority.

THE SIXTH PROCESS: COMMITMENT

Commitment includes not only a willingness to act, but also a belief in your ability to change, which in turn reinforces your will. People begin to use commitment during the preparation stage, and continue to apply its techniques well into the action and maintenance stages. Part of the commitment process is better known as willpower; believing in your will and acting upon that belief is a powerful experience.

Concerned about the effects of nicotine on her growing fetus, Rosemary did not smoke at all during her pregnancy. But the day after she stopped breast-feeding, she smoked a cigarette. Predictably, she was back to a pack a day within a week. She did not smoke around the baby, but found time to grab a cigarette or two periodically during the course of the day.

When Rosemary's daughter Monica was eighteen months old, she was quite a handful—quick but clumsy. Rosemary had to watch her every minute. One day, while Rosemary was smoking, Monica came running over and brushed her hand against the burning cigarette. Rosemary became upset and angry. Cigarettes were not good for her or her child. She had thought she would quit when Monica got older. Now she wanted to quit immediately.

Rosemary threw out her remaining cigarettes and removed all smoking paraphernalia from the house. She found the toll-free hotline number of a cancer center that offered materials and advice on smoking cessation, and decided to keep it handy in case she experienced any difficulty. Since her husband, Jeff, did not smoke, she could count on his support. Although she needed his help, she was also convinced that she could quit; after all, she had been smoke-free during pregnancy.

Accidentally burning her baby led Rosemary to make a powerful commitment to change. When you make such a commitment, it is an act of faith in yourself. Begin by having faith in all you accomplished during contemplation. You are now aware and informed about your problems, not groping in the dark. Have confidence in your evaluations of the pros and cons of changing, so that you honestly believe your life will be enhanced rather than diminished by the action you are about to take.

There are a number of stumbling blocks associated with commitment. You will need to work at strengthening and encouraging your will. People often weaken their wills by putting action off for too long; by relying exclusively on willpower, which puts too much pressure on this single process; by drinking alcohol, which reduces anxiety but also strength of mind; or by taking premature action, which can damage a personal belief in the ability to change. Let's look at how to deal with some of these concerns.

Make the tough choices

Sometimes there is enough information on a given problem that action becomes almost inevitable for anyone who makes it to the preparation stage. Research has left little doubt, for example, that the negative consequences of smoking always outweigh the benefits. Quitting is unquestionably the right course to take.

Regardless of the good work you have done in the contemplation stage, you may still feel ambivalent about the pros and cons of your particular problem. You may not have sufficient information for you to be absolutely certain of the choices you must make. If you are involved in a troubled marriage involving children, should you divorce or remain married? Just how troubled must a marriage be before divorce becomes the better alternative? With an issue like this, there is rarely "adequate" information. Making a choice is far more difficult, since you know that successful action is far from guaranteed, and it involves difficult commitments.

A student named Ann began having anxiety attacks after telling her parents she was pregnant. Despite the fact that she and her husband were joyful at the prospect of having a baby, her parents insisted that she get an abortion. They felt that her life would be ruined if she had a child at her

age. The young couple were students, and entirely dependent on Ann's wealthy parents for financial support; the
parents threatened to disinherit her if she went ahead with
the pregnancy. In twenty years, Ann had never openly dis-
agreed with her parents. Although she was controlled by
them, she had always felt protected by them. After a few
therapy sessions, Ann became aware that her anxiety attacks reflected a need to make a choice between herself and
feeling secure. She made the commitment to herself.

Fortunately, the very act of committing yourself to a
given alternative increases the likelihood of success. The
more entirely you throw yourself into a new way of behaving, the more likely you are to experience that way as being
the best path to follow. In any case, commitment requires
you to have faith in your ability to succeed at the action you
have chosen to take.

Commitment and anxiety

Your work during the contemplation stage will have determined whether change is possible. Your commitment
during the preparation stage makes success more likely. But
there are limits to the power of any commitment. The "se-
renity prayer," well known to all members of Alcoholics
Anonymous, acknowledges these limits. It asks for the "se-
renity to accept the things I cannot change; courage to
change the things I can; and wisdom to know the difference."

There are never any guarantees that change will be successful. You must accept the inevitable anxiety that accompanies the recognition that action may fail regardless of the
strength of your commitment. Almost everyone experiences anxiety when the time for action draws near. Change
can be threatening. Anxiety brings with it avoidance and
delay, a temptation to make excuses to wait until tomorrow
or some other "better time." Anxiety can make people hide
their actions, so that no one will know if they fail. Anxiety

also leads people to encourage themselves by doing things that weaken their will, such as drinking.

Anxiety cannot be conquered, but it can be understood and countered, and that is part of the work of the commitment process. Here are five commitment techniques that can help you to counter anxiety:

Take small steps   Just as it is wise to stock up early on necessities in preparing for a hurricane, so is gathering emotional and physical supplies an important part of the preparation for action. Preparation is filled with small but essential steps that lead to the leap into action. Don't underestimate their importance.

If you are going to follow a strict diet which measures portions, be sure you buy a scale. If you wish to avoid drinking at the company party, rehearse ordering sparkling water or ginger ale, and plan how to handle the heckling from your colleagues. To cut down on compulsive spending, it may be time to cut up your credit cards. These are all the first tentative steps on the road to action.

Set a date   Setting a time frame is critical for behavior change. Choosing a date to begin can help prevent both premature action and prolonged procrastination, and can help make your action as convenient as possible. The date should be realistic, but it should also be scheduled as soon as possible, so you can capitalize on your decision-making momentum. If you are truly ready for action, choose a date within the next month. Delaying your action date for much longer than that only risks unforeseen circumstances that can interfere with your plan. Deciding to delay the date is a good sign that you are still in the contemplation stage.

Once you commit yourself to an action date, guard against finding excuses or reasons to delay it, which can weaken your will. Plan to complete whatever preparations, and—rather than waiting for a magic moment—take re-

sponsibility for taking action on the date. Be realistic about
the nature of the tasks ahead. Underestimating the challenges of change can lead to cockiness and overconfidence.
Wishful thinking about the ease of change will lead to disappointment, which in turn may contribute to ineffective
action.

While there are no perfect times for action, some are unquestionably better than others. The summer months, like
the holidays, tend to be times for self-indulgence rather
than self-discipline. Deciding to change when the external
environment is most supportive—on New Year's Day or after a birthday—can be helpful. These are auspicious times
to reevaluate your life and take action to enhance it.

Go public Don't make the mistake of keeping your commitment secret. Going public with your intended change
increases anxiety, since you may feel embarrassed if you
fail. Public commitments are more powerful than private
pledges. When you go public, you enlist the sympathy of
others, and allow them to understand your behaviors as
they change.

Don't keep it in the family. Tell your colleagues and your
neighbors, write friends and relatives. Some people even
put a short advertisement in the newspaper, announcing
that on a certain date they will quit smoking or start losing
weight, and that they will not be responsible for their
moods.

It takes courage to go public, but remember: Courage is
not the absence of fear but the ability to act in the face of
fear.

Prepare for a major operation Many changes—quitting
smoking or drinking, losing weight, reducing stress, or becoming active—involve a psychic surgery that is as serious
as many life-saving operations. The date you set to make
your change is as important as one for coronary bypass sur-

gery or chemotherapy. Change is powerful and real. Throw yourself fully into overcoming your problem, and spend the time and emotional energy your recovery will require.

Preparing for psychic surgery means that you and those who support you put the operation first and everything else second. Changes in your mood, in your relationships, in your work performance, and in other areas should be accepted as consequences of the all-important work that will soon enhance your life. This much disruption may last for several weeks or more. Top priority must be given to recovering from your problem behavior; other areas of your life may suffer for a short while as a result.

Create your own plan of action   An effective plan of action, employing all the information obtained during the contemplation stage, can include helpful hints from others who have made a similar change. Listen to your friends' advice (but don't assume that their successful plans will work for you). Look also to books and other literature, and to support groups that deal with your problem. There is no dearth of action-oriented plans out there, and many of them contain valuable information. But to maximize commitment, the final plan must be yours.

Why is it so important to develop your own plan? Once I was in a drugstore waiting for a prescription to be filled. At the checkout counter there was a display of six different items offering "effective" ways to quit smoking. There was gum, a package of tablets with audio tapes, a series of nicotine-reducing filters, and so on. All the packaging featured testimonials from smokers who had quit successfully using that particular method. Were these people lying? Are all of these methods equally good?

The skeptic would say, "None of them is any good." Indeed, there are ineffective methods, offered by charlatans. But any program that is based on sound theory, research, and experience will produce successful change for some people. How each method works is not always clear. What is certain is that one key element for success is the confidence the individual has in the program he or she is using. To a large extent, success depends on using a plan that you believe works; if you create the plan yourself, that belief becomes much stronger.

Your plan for action may be lengthy or short, but it must be specific. At this point, you may already have completed the precontemplation and contemplation stages, and begun the work of this stage. Your plan should list a variety of techniques for coping with any expected barriers to change. Make sure to review your previous attempts to change: They hold valuable information about your own barriers. And pay attention to the external environment—which may indicate stress, too many activities, or problems at work—and your current internal state, which may reveal low self-confidence or negative thinking. Address these barriers to change and include techniques to overcome, avoid, or circumvent them.

Here is a rather simple example of an action plan: To quit smoking, a number of years ago, Carlo scheduled the date at the most convenient time possible, the end of the semester. He smoked more cigarettes than usual the week before quitting in order to increase his disgust with the habit, and he stocked up on gum and mints to help satisfy his oral cravings. His firm commitment to this simple but detailed plan, his understanding of the problem and his behavior, and his vision of himself as a nonsmoker helped make his attempt a success.

Chapter 10, which gives specific strategies for taking you through the cycle of change with three common problems, contains other more complex action plans. However, your own thoughtful action plan is the best one for you.

Commitment self-assessment

Here is a brief self-assessment to check your progress with commitment. Once again, be honest and realistic. Fill in the number that most closely reflects how frequently you have used the methods below in the past week to combat your problem.

1 = Never, 2 = Seldom, 3 = Occasionally, 4 = Often, 5 = Repeatedly

FREQUENCY:

_____ I tell myself that if I try hard enough I can change my problem.

_____ I make commitments against giving in to my problem.

_____ I use willpower to keep from engaging in my problem behavior.

_____ I tell myself I can choose to change or not.

_____ = Score

In order to be ready to take effective action, your score on this self-assessment should be 14 or higher. If your score is lower, you have more work to do on the commitment process before you can move forward successfully.

GAIL PREPARES

Preparing a plan for a new low-fat diet and aerobic exercise program was easy for Gail. Finding time to put the plan into action was not. But she knew she had to make a big commitment; she told herself that a halfhearted effort now would leave her with an unhealthy heart later. Opening up time in her schedule to accommodate the plan became her first priority, and her first chore.

There was an aerobics class that started at 6:30 A.M. at a local health club. First she considered taking out a monthly membership, but decided to take the initially more costly step of enrolling for a year. Gail enlisted Dan's help with the morning routine, which gave her the extra time she needed to take the class. Even so, she could only restructure her schedule enough to take two classes a week, but at least this got her started.

Gail began her diet by focusing on low-fat substitutes for some of her favorite foods. She also allowed herself to consume certain fattening foods at one meal a day. This way she didn't feel deprived. She asked Dan to hide his favorite junk foods, especially potato chips and blue corn chips, since these were the high-fat foods she turned to when looking for a fast fix. When the chips were no longer within easy reach, Gail found she could stop, think, and talk herself out of her cravings, where before she had automatically satisfied them.

Dan actively supported Gail's new lifestyle. At his request, she detailed the things that he could do to help her; in past efforts at dieting she had asked for his help, but then scolded him for nagging whenever she decided to break her commitment. He was wary of falling into these old patterns, and by clearly setting out what each expected of the other, Dan and Gail came up with some ground rules that both were comfortable with. He was willing to try some new, healthier restaurants that offered low-fat alternatives. He hid his most tempting junk food. Most important of all, he reinforced Gail in her morning aerobics classes and in her healthier eating habits.

Gail also went public with her commitment. She let her colleagues know she was committed to a healthier lifestyle, so that they would not offer her snacks during coffee breaks. When she and Dan hosted a dinner party for their friends, she prepared a selection of delicious, low-fat dishes, proving that her diet was no barrier to entertaining. Without pressuring them to follow her example, Gail also enlisted their friends' support for her dieting efforts.

HELPING RELATIONSHIPS
DURING PREPARATION

Whenever someone decides to change, the people close to that person are affected, sometimes greatly. Our partners, spouses, and other helpers can play an important role during the preparation stage. Since preparation usually involves noticeable changes, it is virtually impossible to disguise them from your spouse or close friends. So, if you have not yet enlisted them in your crusade, this is the time to do so.

You need support from others even if you decide against going public. Be assertive in asking others for their consideration, especially in those difficult situations when you need to overcome the barriers to change. If you are stressed and feeling overwhelmed, for example, ask for help. Set up your situation at work and home to free up your energy for change.

Going public makes things somewhat easier. When you announce your planned change to others, you also can advise them how they can be most helpful. People who love you are willing to help, but don't always know how. Don't depend on their reading your mind and understanding your needs. Offer them instead a comprehensive list of "dos and don'ts." For example:

- Don't keep asking how I am doing.
- Don't nag me.
- Offer to help when I look overwhelmed.
- Tell me how proud you are that I am doing this.

The first few days will be the most difficult as you begin to shift your routine and change your old ways of handling things. It is tempting, and in fact quite easy, to give up during those initial days or weeks. At this time, support from others can help tremendously. Prepare your helpers by letting them know when you are going to implement your action plan, and by asking them to be tolerant when you are on edge. Ask them directly for their attention and help during this time. When people know why you are being difficult, they can be much more understanding.

THE PRINCIPLES OF PROGRESS

One morning I was in my study revising a complex manuscript that contained fifteen profiles of smokers in four stages of change. A colleague, Wayne Velicer, the first author on this paper, was making a sophisticated case for there being three types of changers in each stage. Suddenly, it struck me that his sophisticated case could probably be reduced to a few fundamental principles for progressing across the stages.

Quickly, I took out a manuscript I had mailed to a scientific journal earlier. This manuscript contained the twelve graphs shown in Figure 4. These graphs involve the relationships between the pros and cons of changing and the stages of change for twelve different problem behaviors. The horizontal axis represents the five stages of change: PC = Precontemplation; C = Contemplation; P = Preparation; A = Action; and M = Maintenance. The vertical axis represents the importance of the pros and the cons for people at each stage of change for each problem behavior.

The graphs show that for all twelve problem behaviors, the cons of changing are more important than the pros for people in the precontemplation stage. The opposite is true for people in the action stage in eleven out of twelve problems.

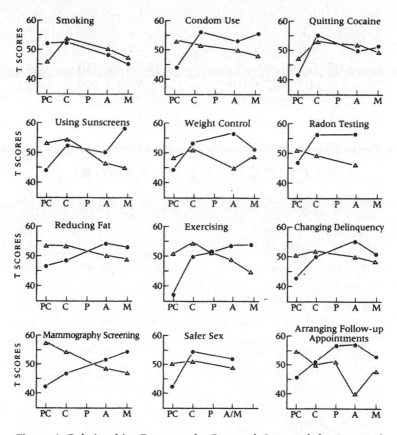

Figure 4. Relationships Between the Pros and Cons and the Stages of Change

That morning I had a feeling I had experienced only a few times before when I had explored something unknown and unexpected. I felt as if the back of my head had opened up and light was pouring in. My eyes felt as if they were on fire—with an intense glow enlightening the raw data in front of me.

First, I noticed that the pros of changing always increase

from precontemplation to contemplation. The first principle of progress is, therefore, that if you are to advance from precontemplation to contemplation, you must increase your perception of the pros of changing your problem behavior. Don't worry about the cons of changing at this stage. They come later.

Next, the cons of changing always decrease from contemplation to action. The second principle of progress states correspondingly that if you are to advance from contemplation to action, you must decrease your perception of the cons of changing your problem behavior. Don't worry about the pros of changing at this stage. They come earlier.

After these quick insights, I nevertheless suspected there might be more information to be had. After all, those graphs represented eighty thousand data points from over three thousand individuals from twelve different groups of self-changers. If there were generalizations to be made about human behavior change, these graphs were likely to hold the key.

What I noticed next was that the pros seemed to increase more than the cons decreased. I got out one of my high-technology tools—a ruler—and measured the maximum increase in the pros between precontemplation and action and the maximum decrease in the cons. To my amazement (and the amazement of every behavioral scientist who has seen these results), it became evident that two mathematical ratios underlie the two principles of progress mentioned earlier. I found that across the twelve problem behaviors, the pros increased an average of 10 T points. Across the twelve problem behaviors, the cons decreased an average of 4.96 T points.*

---

*A T point is a certain statistical unit of measure; you need not understand the unit it represents to understand these principles of progress.

My wife, Jan, was home reading in the living room. I ran in in a frenzy, shouting about the amazing discoveries I had just made. I couldn't believe it. It was too good to be true. Nothing like this had ever been found before. In her calm way, Jan communicated her concern that I might be getting a little manic. I must say I felt a little manic. I was having trouble believing my eyes or my mind.

But I was prepared to go back into my study and subject my precious principles of progress to the riskiest tests available. I was prepared to destroy in the afternoon what I had discovered in the morning. This is the terrible obligation of a scientist: You must be prepared to falsify what you most want to believe is true.

So, I took out an article we had published the previous year, containing data on 1464 smokers in the first 3 stages of change. I predicted that from precontemplation to preparation the pros of changing would increase 10 T points. They increased 9.6 points. I predicted the cons would decrease 5 T points. They decreased 5.6 points.

I felt I had just opened, like some latter-day Pandora, the lid that had kept two tremendously potent principles of behavior change hidden for centuries. I knew that the power of science can always be used for good or ill. I pictured the magnates in the tobacco industry being the first to organize ad campaigns around these principles to prepare kids for smoking.

But fears such as these can't stop science. When you're a scientist, you have to share whatever truths are revealed to you. I called a meeting at our research center and showed my colleagues what I had discovered. Words like "amazing," "incredible," and "thrilling" peppered their comments.

Early in this research, I had worried that self-destructive behaviors, and our attempts to be free of them, were as indeterminate as electrons, whose speed and location can never simultaneously be ascertained. Certainly it was possible that action based on personal freedom could follow some principles of indeterminacy. Maybe people made unpredictable "quantum leaps" from one stage of change to the next, and my hunch that there *was* some pattern to it was merely a reflection of my emotional need to help people. If change were unstructured, we could not have helped people get rid of unwanted problems. They would simply have had to rely on a roll of the dice—with which, in spite of what Einstein said, I once worried that maybe God was playing.

After a time it became apparent that self-change was neither indeterminate nor unstructured. With all our prior discoveries, nothing prepared us to recognize the degree to which self-change may be predicted.

Behavioral and social scientists are pleased as punch whenever they can predict which variables make a difference in human behaviors. But they have never been able to predict the *magnitude* of those variables. Predicting the magnitude of the differences on key variables has historically been the provenance of physics and other lawful sciences. As the director of the Addictions Center at the famous Maudely Hospital in London said when he saw our research, "Behavioral research has never behaved this way before."

To appreciate these two mathematical principles of progress, you need to know that on our tests, 10 T points equals 1 standard deviation. A standard deviation (S.D.) is a measure of how a given score varies or deviates from the average or mean of a population. With IQ tests, for example, the mean of a population is set at 100 and a S.D. is 15. People who vary 2 S.D.s above the mean (IQ = 130) are considered gifted, while those who vary 2 S.D.s below the mean (IQ = 70) have traditionally been considered mentally retarded. This gives some measure of the relative significance of a standard deviation. Raising your IQ 15 points would clearly make a major difference in your life. Keeping this in mind, let's examine our two principles.

The Strong Principle of Progress states that progression from precontemplation to action involves approximately a 1 S.D. increase in the pros of making a healthy behavior change. The formula is:

PC → A = 1 S.D. ↑ PROS

The Weak Principle of Progress states that progression from precontemplation to action involves approximately a .5 S.D. decrease in the cons of making a healthy behavior change.

PC → A = .5 S.D. ↓ CONS

What are some of the implications of these principles? First, if you are in the precontemplation stage with a particular problem, you are going to have to increase your perception of the pros by 1 S.D. in order to be adequately prepared to take effective action. This is like raising your behavior change IQ by 15 points. Fortunately, we are confident that by reading this book, the average person can raise his or her behavior-change IQ by at least 15 points. You may not be gifted when you're finished, but you may become a much brighter self-changer!

Second, you've always known that you have to be highly motivated if you're going to change a chronic problem behavior. But you've never known how high your motivation should be. The principles of progress will help you to assess your level of motivation, though we prefer the term "preparation." It's hard to imagine consciously and willfully increasing your motivation. It's much easier to imagine consciously and willfully improving your preparation. The assessments in this book are designed to give you feedback about your efforts at preparing for change.

Preparation lies in the balance between your perception of the pros and cons of changing. If you are currently in the precontemplation stage, you are likely to perceive the cons of changing as outweighing the pros. You will need to increase your pros of changing twice as much as you will need to decrease the cons. Furthermore, the processes of change applied in the early stages have the greatest impact on the pros. The processes you apply in the preparation and action stages have the greatest impact on the cons.

We have placed this section on the principles of progress here, immediately before the chapter on action, as a kind of Do Not Pass Go warning. By all means, read the book once through, to give yourself an overview of the stages. But once you're ready to embark on the journey of change, be sure to work methodically through the stages. Many people will be tempted to head straight for the action techniques before they are fully convinced of the pros and cons of changing. According to our model, if you bypass the contemplation and preparation stages, your change efforts are highly likely to fail. The preceding section gives you an example of the strong mathematical evidence that lies behind our model.

We use the metaphor of people who would like to run the Boston Marathon. Those who aren't prepared at all are probably in the precontemplation stage and don't intend to enter this year's race. Those who are more prepared and are in the contemplation stage may intend to enter this year's race, but because of ambivalence about the pros and cons of running, they sign up for the race but do not show up. Those who are adequately prepared are most likely to sign up, show up, and finish up the race. They will certainly find at times that they want to give up; some surely will give up, and save their energies for another day. However, those who are best prepared, who have increased their pros of changing by 1 S.D. and have decreased their cons of changing by .5 S.D., are most likely to keep going even when they hit the infamous Heartbreak Hill.

Let's evaluate your cons of changing, and see how much you have still to do to prepare yourself to finish your race the next time you start.

Decisional balance

Answer the following questions in terms of a problem behavior. Rate each item as to its importance in deciding to take action. Rate each item as accurately as you can. Fill in the number that most closely reflects the importance of each item.

PROS AND CONS OF CHANGING

1 = Not important, 2 = Slightly important, 3 = Somewhat important, 4 = Quite important, 5 = Extremely important

1. Some people would think less of me if I change   —
2. I would be healthier if I change   —
3. Changing takes a lot of time   —
4. Some people would feel better about me if I change   —
5. I'm concerned I might fail if I try to change   —
6. Changing would make me feel better about myself   —
7. Changing takes a lot of effort and energy   —
8. I would function better if I change   —
9. I would have to give up some things I enjoy   —
10. I would be happier if I change   —
11. I get some benefits from my current behavior   —

12. Some people could be better off if I change _____
13. Some people benefit from my current be-
    havior   _____
14. I would worry less if I change   _____
15. Some people would be uncomfortable if I
    change   _____
16. Some people would be happier if I change   _____

                                    PROS _____
                                    CONS   _____

Add up your scores on the odd-numbered items; this is your current score on the pros of changing. Add up your scores on the even items; this is your current score on the cons.

For people in the precontemplation stage the mean score on the pros of changing is approximately 21. One standard deviation on this test is 7. If your average score is 21, then you will need to raise your pros by approximately 7 points in order to become adequately prepared for action.

If your pros score is below the mean of 21, you will need to apply the processes of change at each stage even more diligently before you progress to the action stage. If your score is above the mean by less than 1 S.D., you will need to apply the processes of change but you will probably be prepared more quickly than many of your peers.

For people in the contemplation stage the mean score on the cons of changing is approximately 21. One standard deviation on this test is 8. If you have an average score of 21, then you will need to decrease your cons by approximately 4 points if you are to become adequately prepared for action.

If your cons score is above the mean of 21, you will need to apply the processes of change even more diligently before you progress. If your score is below the mean but less than 4 points, you will need to apply the processes but you will probably be prepared more quickly than most of your peers.

Only if you have scored both 1 S.D. or more above the mean on the pros (28 points) and .5 S.D. or more below the mean on the cons (17 points) are you ready for action. If you *are* ready for action, begin your change efforts with the techniques described in the next chapter.

CHAPTER 7

Action—Time to Move

WHEN GEORGE RELAPSED, he blamed his friends and family, just as he always had. He desperately wanted to deny any personal responsibility and return to the precontemplation stage, where he could drink without conflict and without controls. But George had become too sensitized to regress that much. He knew that his drinking would eventually destroy him and that sobriety was going to cost him more than he had expected. Originally, George had hoped to change his drinking habits without having to change the context in which they occurred. There are a few people who *can* change a problem behavior without restructuring their lives. Such changes are simple, and cost less than more extensive efforts; but for George this approach didn't work.

George realized he was going to have to give up his drinking buddies, for now at least. And he couldn't continue to be so close to his extended family, whose intimacies were largely dependent upon beer. George wept. He grieved for the losses he was facing, not only of his friends at his neighborhood bar, but of his personal chair there as well. He grieved too for his family—more for the one he wished he had than for the one with which he had to drink to be a part of. Most of all he grieved for the loss of his old persona, big bad George, who could raise hell and then walk away from it unscathed.

He devised a new computer program, and called it DAD.1 for Damn All Drinks (the number .1 is traditionally given to a new edition of an existing program). The new program paralleled his old one, rewarding him, for example, when he reached his goal for the day. But George was aiming now for total abstinence from alcohol, rather than for controlled drinking. Alcohol-free beer was still an item on his shopping list, but only for when he felt particularly tempted at home, and he stopped going to bars entirely.

George also reprogrammed his computer to reward him for the processes of change he applied. Going to the gym instead of his local bar brought kudos from the computer. Asserting himself at a family gathering by insisting that he would drink soda without any sauce was reinforced by DAD.1 messages: "Someday they will see the light, George." George's children would type in affirmations: "Do you realize you have been sober for 25 days? That's terrific!"

George also had DAD.1 suggest alternatives for his temptations to drink. Whenever he was at a loss, his computer spit out things like "Listen to [M. Scott] Peck's recording of *The Road Less Traveled*," "Talk to your children," "Go for a walk by the ocean," "Visit a friend," or "Call your sponsor."

Conscious that his old friends and family supported his alcohol abuse rather than his sobriety, George restructured his social life and sought out sober support. Alcoholics Anonymous offered alcohol-free social interactions and helping relationships. Going to A.A. meetings helped him not only at home but when business took him on the road. In the past being anonymous in strange cities had given George an excuse to act out. Now he could be anonymous with others who cared about staying sober and healthy.

These acts marked George's entrance into the action stage. He purposefully modified his life in order to alter his behavior. He made his strongest commitment ever to quitting drinking, and made sure his home and social environments supported his efforts.

Real, effective action begins with commitment. Once the commitment to change is made, it is time to move; in the action stage the focus is on the processes of control, countering, and reward, with a continuing emphasis on the importance of helping relationships. The use of these processes continues throughout the action stage, which usually lasts for months.

Even if you have done all the necessary preparation, there are no guarantees that your action will be successful. Awareness of the pitfalls will greatly increase your chance of success. The four following approaches to action all leave self-changers spinning their wheels, unable to proceed.

Taking preparation lightly People too often equate action with change. This attitude ignores the need for adequate preparation. After a day or weekend of eating, drinking, or fighting too much, people feel the need for emotional relief. To assuage their guilt and anxiety, they promise themselves to take action the next day. And quite often they do; the morning is rarely a time for indulgence anyway. So temporary, convenient action becomes the rule. More often than not, action without preparation lasts only a day or two. Without the necessary groundwork, the temptation to return to problem behavior is too strong.

Cheap change Some people are unwilling to make any sacrifices in order to change. Cheap change isn't worth much. Real change takes work, and the more effort you put into contemplation and preparation, the more likely it is that action will bring success. Quitting a habit can require not only an enormous sacrifice of energy, but the pain of others' disapproval of the anxiety and anger that self-changers can temporarily experience.

Kay, for example, had tried to quit smoking three times. She had been to Smokenders, a hypnotist, and a bioenergetic psychotherapist, but she still smoked heavily. Her husband and four adult children promised they would do anything to help her quit. Their promises were halfhearted: As soon as she became irritable, her family pressured Kay to return to her "regular" self. Since Kay used cigarettes to control her anxieties, of course her "regular" self included smoking.

Kay made a new vow to make quitting her top priority. This time, if her family did not like her aggressive feelings, she wasn't going to stifle her anger with cigarettes. Kay knew in advance that change would not be easy, or cheap, and she made her plans accordingly.

The myth of the "magic bullet" There are no simple solutions to complex behavioral problems. Yet people continue to fantasize that there is a "magic bullet," a single "right" technique, that will make it easy to change. Some are attracted to our work because they hope we have discovered just such a miracle cure. When members of the media call us, they often want us to reduce our findings to a single, pithy sentence. According to them, the public demands simple answers; people are used to thirty-second commercials promising lifelong change. "Can't we just tell them to use relaxation or willpower?" they ask.

We always answer, "No." Relying on any single technique during action makes no sense. The belief in the "magic bullet" leaves only one, defeating conclusion when success is not immediate: that you are not doing enough and must do more of the same.

More of the same This deceptively simple idea* leads to the stubborn retention of methods that may have been partially

*From the work of the renowned family therapist Paul Watzlawick.

successful in the past. Partial success, however, does not guarantee validity forever; situations change. Using "more of the same" techniques often leads to more of the same misery.

Of course, the techniques we apply to our problems make a difference. But by clinging to old methods, we fail to realize that other, perhaps better, techniques exist. Our research consistently demonstrates that no single method is so effective that its use guarantees success. In the action stage, as in all other stages, combining a variety of techniques at the proper time is more likely to bring the desired results. Let's look now at the different change processes that are especially useful in this stage.

THE SEVENTH PROCESS: COUNTERING

For decades, research has shown that countering—substituting healthy responses for problem behaviors—is one of the most powerful processes available to changers. Many undesirable behaviors have benefits, for example, helping people cope with emotional distress. When unprepared self-changers get rid of one problem, such as drug abuse, they replace it with another—often the very distress they began taking drugs to avoid. Now these self-changers find that they need to cope with renewed distress, and the easiest way to do that is to return to taking drugs.

When you remove troubled behaviors without providing healthy substitutes, the risk of returning to old patterns remains high. Countering finds preferable substitutes. Five effective countering techniques that self-changers often employ are:

Active diversion

The most common, healthy alternative for problem behaviors is called "active diversion." Our patients call it
"keeping busy," or "refocusing energy." Whatever the label, the technique remains the same: Finding an activity
that precludes a problem behavior.

The possibilities for active diversion are endless. They include cooking, piano playing, cleaning, doing crossword
puzzles, knitting, walking, reading a book, having sex, even
calling a friend. In selecting your own diversion, your priority should be one that is enjoyable, healthy, and incompatible with your problem. Watching television obviously
does little to prevent overeating; it's much harder to eat
when you're chopping firewood or exercising.

Exercise

There is no more beneficial substitute for problem behaviors than exercise. The cues for our problems are often physical urges; many successful self-changers learn to transform
these urges into cues for exercise. Instead of reaching for an
unwanted piece of chocolate cake, for instance, go for a
walk. You spare yourself the calories, *and* you gain the benefits of a good workout.

Omitting exercise from a self-change plan is like fighting
a foe with one hand tied behind your back. You may still
win, but the odds are against you. Inactive people are not
only in poor condition for dealing with physical problems,
they are frequently also in poor psychological condition for
coping with the distress that can accompany change. Still,
a majority of Americans—self-changers included—do not
engage in regular exercise.

If you are too busy to exercise, you are simply too busy.
You do not have to become a marathon runner to overcome
your problem. A sound program of routine aerobic exercise

takes as little as twenty minutes every other day. An aerobic exercise regimen produces a compelling list of benefits:

- Improved body image, self-image, and self-esteem
- Increased energy, metabolism, and heart function
- Increased endorphins (self-produced painkillers)
- Decreased anxiety and depression
- Decreased body fat and cholesterol
- Decreased physical and emotional pain

Although some of the rewards associated with aerobic exercise can be gained from nonaerobic exercises (such as walking, golf, or tennis), the maximum return on your time is achieved by exercising at your aerobic threshold for twenty minutes. The most popular methods are jogging, fast walking, aerobic dancing, swimming, bicycling, and rowing.

To determine your aerobic threshold, subtract your age from the number 220, then multiply the remainder by .7. The result is the heart rate that you should sustain for twenty minutes while exercising. If you are forty years old, for example, you should sustain a heart rate of 126 (220 − 40 = 180 × .7 = 126).

Be sure to consult your physician before beginning an exercise program. Work up gradually to your aerobic threshold. And do not confuse recreation with exercise. As much fun as they are, bowling, golf, and sex definitely do not qualify as aerobic exercise.

Relaxation

In many situations, there is no way to counter a problem cue with exercise. If the work day is tense, for instance, and you feel the need for a cigarette, you are unlikely to counter the urge with a quick jog. There are times, too, when a recent injury temporarily suspends exercise. Relaxation is one technique that can rescue you at a time like this.

In recent years, researchers have found that deep relaxation produces a mildly altered physical and mental state.

Ten to twenty minutes of deep relaxation each day can give you:

- Increased energy
- Increased rate of alpha (pleasurable) brain waves
- Decreased blood pressure and muscle tension
- Decreased anxiety
- Improved sleep
- Improved health
- Improved concentration

There are many popular and effective ways to evoke the deep relaxation response. Watching television is not among them! Transcendental meditation, prayer, autogenic training, yoga, and progressive muscle relaxation are the best-known methods, and all share these four elements:

- A quiet environment
- A comfortable position
- An internal focus
- A "letting go"

Police officers who have been trained to relax when rushing to emergency calls are better prepared to cope with physical turmoil or domestic violence. On the other hand, if they arrive at the scene with their adrenaline pumping, they are more likely to intensify the situation than pacify it.

You can give yourself the same advantage. When you practice deep relaxation regularly, you can call on a milder form of the response when you need it most. Instead of taking a cigarette or coffee break to relax, just sit back, breathe easy, let your muscles and mind go for a while, and tell yourself to be calm. Relax those muscles that you are not using. At a tense meeting, for example, you don't need your knees to bounce nervously. Thinking of a favorite, quiet place—perhaps the one you use for deep relaxation at home—can also help you to evoke the relaxation response.

Counterthinking

Freeing yourself from rigid behavior patterns often requires that you also free yourself from rigid thought patterns. Just as exercise substitutes healthy for unhealthy behavior, counterthinking replaces troubled thoughts with more positive ones. Successful self-changers often rely on counterthinking more than on relaxation because this technique is quick, covert, and takes relatively little energy. It can be used under almost all the conditions that trigger problem behaviors.

Many people make themselves anxious by allowing distressing thoughts such as "It will be awful if my dinner party doesn't go well," "It will be terrible if she gets the promotion instead of me," or "I will be crushed if he is angry at me" to get the better of them. The effective countering of irrational self-statements requires practice, since such statements tend to be automatic, subconscious, and compelling. Consciously practicing counterthinking prepares you to challenge the self-statements that trigger your problem.

Irrational thoughts are best countered with a dose of reality. An airplane crash is awful; the sinking of the *Titanic* was terrible. Although burning the dinner may be inconvenient, it is far from a disaster. An angry spouse is unpleasant, but not terrible. By counterthinking in this way, you become freer to cope with genuinely troubling situations. Molehills can remain molehills, instead of becoming mountains.

To counter other types of negative thoughts, first ask, "What am I telling myself that is getting me so upset?" A problem drinker, for example, might go through a thought process something like this:

What am I telling myself that makes me want to drink? If
I tell myself I can't stand going to a cocktail party without
drinking, then I have only two choices: Drink or don't go.

A more rational self-statement could help this person
counter these negative thoughts:

Realistically, there are very few things that I cannot stand
if I have to. If I tell myself, "It's harder to go to a cocktail
party without drinking, but I can stand it," then I can go to
the party without having to drink. I can respond to the
internal and social pressures to drink with relaxation and
counterthinking.

Counterthinking makes sense. Many of us could substitute healthier thoughts for some irrational self-statements*
such as these:

- I must have everyone like me.
- I can't stand it if someone doesn't approve of me.
- I should be thoroughly competent at everything I do.
- It's awful when I make a mistake.
- I can only feel good about myself when I am doing
  well.
- I can't control my anxiety (anger, despair, or other
  feelings).
- I can't resist the urge to smoke (drink, eat).
- I can't stand the tension and craving that occur when
  I am withdrawing.
- I can't stand it when the world doesn't treat me
  fairly.
- I need to drink (smoke, eat) in order to cope with
  life's stresses.

*These "irrationalities" were first codified by Albert Ellis, founder of rational-
emotive therapy.

Common to these self-statements is a mode of thinking that is absolutist, rigid, and closed to questioning. When you are *absolutely* sure of something, then you cannot question yourself. If you *must* do a thing, then there are no logical alternatives for you. This type of thinking is the equivalent of painting yourself into a corner. Although all humans have a propensity to think in absolutes, some do it more than others (especially individuals raised by dogmatic or overcontrolling parents).

To become more aware of your own tendency to think absolutely, take note of the number of times you say, "I have to . . ." or "I need . . ." or "I must . . ." in a day. How many of these declared needs are truly imperative? If we deny biological needs for sleep, nourishment, bodily relief, and protection from the elements, we can suffer irreversible harm. Otherwise, the vast majority of our "needs" are desires. Whenever a desire is expressed as a need, and it is not met, we become agitated, like a child who cries, "I need this toy." But if we recognize desires as desires—"I would *like* this toy"—our distress diminishes.

In *Slouching Towards Bethlehem*, Joan Didion puts the point more eloquently:

> Because when we start deceiving ourselves into thinking not that we want something . . . but that it is a moral imperative that we have it, then is when we join the fashionable madmen, and then is when the thin whine of hysteria is heard in the land, and then is when we are in bad trouble.

All human beings have the ability to think rationally and realistically. We all can realize, "Even if I am probably correct, there is still room for questioning." Thus we can allow discussion, disconfirmation, and new evidence to change our minds. Changing your mode of thinking isn't easy. But the very act of questioning and challenging absolutist thinking is a valuable start. And by repeatedly practicing counterthinking, you begin to increase your mental flexibility and your capacity for self-change.

Assertiveness

Problem behaviors can be expected, supported, and triggered by other people in your life as well as by internal forces. Self-changers sometimes feel despondent and helpless in the face of external pressures to maintain their problem behaviors. However, by being assertive, you are exercising your right to communicate your thoughts, feelings, wishes, and intentions clearly, thereby countering feelings of helplessness.

Unlike exercise and deep relaxation, assertiveness is not an activity that must be scheduled. It is a technique that you can use whenever you feel you are not being heard or respected. The benefits of exercising your right to be heard, and to change, are:

- Decreased anxiety, anger, and neuroses
- Increased self-respect, communication, and leadership abilities
- Increased satisfaction in all personal relationships

Most people can be assertive, but many become inhibited because they do not believe they have the right to be powerful. You may not realize that you have all of the following rights, and may be depriving yourself by not acting upon them:

- The right to be heard
- The right to influence other people
- The right to make mistakes
- The right to bring attention to yourself
- The right to change your mind
- The right to judge your own thoughts and feelings
- The right to resist other people's judgments
- The right not to have to justify yourself

- The right to have limits—limited knowledge, limited caring, limited responsibility for others, and limited time
- The right to have your limits respected

When you accept and act upon these rights, you are more likely to be assertive. And when you acknowledge that all people have the same rights as you, you will not confuse assertion with aggression. If nonassertive, passive behavior says that "you count, but I don't," and aggressive behavior says that "I count, and you don't," assertiveness respectfully communicates that "I count just as you do."

These are important but frequently overlooked distinctions. Assertion does not accomplish goals at the expense of another person, as aggression does, nor does it deny your own rights, as does passivity. Rather, assertiveness grants all parties their rights.

Whenever your response is more assertive than a situation warrants, it will probably be experienced as aggression, and it will generate counteraggression rather than compliance. If you are unsure whether your action is assertive or aggressive, complete the following mental checklist:

- Did I express my rights?
- Did I respect his or her rights?
- Was I specific about a behavior change?

Affirmative responses to these questions means that you were being assertive rather than aggressive. Of course, assertion doesn't guarantee that other people will honor your feelings or requests. What effective assertiveness does assure is that others will have an opportunity to understand your objectives, and hence you will have increased your chances of meeting them. If you don't make it clear how you want others to help you change, this pretty much guarantees that they won't do it.

Rhonda had always had a morbid dread of doctors. A critical situation was approaching; she had to enter the hospital for a minor operation. Rhonda was learning to be assertive about the process. Rhonda asked for a nurse who was willing to help her through her phobia of having blood samples taken, which were needed before the surgery. With the nurse's help Rhonda also found an understanding surgeon. In a pleasant but assertive style Rhonda set the following conditions:

- She was free to reschedule the surgery if her anxiety became too great;
- She would get to wear her own nightgown, rather than the standard hospital gown (the thought of wearing the kind that opened in the back made her feel vulnerable and exposed); and
- Her husband would be present to provide support.

While Rhonda's physician was unused to a patient setting the conditions of surgery, given the circumstances he welcomed her assertiveness. Fortunately, the operation went well, and Rhonda was able to function better both physically and psychologically.

Countering self-assessment

Here is a self-assessment to check your progress in using the process of countering. Be honest and realistic. Fill in the number that most closely reflects how frequently you have used the method in the past week to combat your problem.

1 = Never, 2 = Seldom, 3 = Occasionally, 4 = Often, 5 = Repeatedly

FREQUENCY:

_____ I engage in some physical activity when I am tempted to engage in my problem behavior.

_____ When I feel the onset of my problem, I try to relax.

_____ I find that other activities are a good substitute for my problem.

_____ When I feel my problem behavior coming on, I think about or do something else.

_____ = Score

A score less than 12 means that you have more work to do in countering. A score of 12 or more on this self-assessment indicates that you are ready to move into the maintenance stage, provided the other self-assessments in this chapter also indicate your readiness to proceed.

THE EIGHTH PROCESS:
ENVIRONMENT CONTROL

You can do all the countering in the world, but if you go out to a bar every night, you will not be able to control your drinking; if you head to a fancy restaurant when you get hungry, you will fail in your attempts to control your eating; if you say yes to every new project at the office, it will be difficult to avoid overworking. Unlike countering, which involves changing one's responses to a given situation, environment control involves changing the situation itself. Both are necessary for successful change.

Earlier in the twentieth century, behavioral psychologists demonstrated that much of our behavior depends upon our surroundings. Most of us, for example, are more on edge in noisy environments than in quiet ones, and more distressed when alone than when in the presence of supportive people. Behaviorists also discovered that to a considerable extent we can change our environment to control behavior, making and unmaking it so as to fit our needs and desires.

Environmental change involves restructuring your environment so that the likely occurrence of a problematic stimulus is significantly reduced. The changes can be quite simple. When I was a graduate student, I developed an anxiety about driving. It began after my car started shaking violently one day. Before long a universal joint broke with a startling noise, and luckily I managed to pull the car over to the shoulder. After I had the joint fixed, this event occurred two more times. A mechanic finally discovered and fixed the real problem (a bent drive shaft) but it was too late: I had developed a morbid dread of driving. I stopped driving, which did reduce my anxiety, but which made daily errands more difficult. Finally I used the environment control process and sold the car. And since my anxiety did not extend to the new car I purchased, the problem was solved.

Not every solution is quite so obvious. But there is always some way in which you can modify your environment. Like active diversion, control can take many forms, especially if you use your imagination. Spending time in a gym rather than at a bar is an example of control. I knew an eighty-five-year-old widow who devised a novel control technique. She would walk to a nearby funeral home whenever she felt alone. She would tell the deceased's family, "He was such a nice man," and help them as she helped herself!

Most of us already work hard to create a comfortable environment at home and at the workplace. Now it's time to put these environments to work for you. Here are some control techniques that will help you do so:

Avoidance

Many people believe that they must rely on willpower alone to resist temptation. However, avoidance, because it helps eliminate temptation, is a key technique of the control process. Avoidance is not a sign of weakness or poor self-control; in fact, effective self-control includes the ability to prevent a problem from starting.

Avoiding avoidance is foolhardy and dangerous. We have heard many unsuccessful changers say, "I need to have alcohol around for company," or "I need to have junk food around for the kids," or "I hate to throw a whole carton of cigarettes away." Such statements are self-defeating. If you are quitting drinking, it makes sense to avoid keeping liquor in the house. Smokers are equally smart to remove cigarettes or ashtrays from their homes, and overeaters to get rid of fattening foods.

Avoidance needn't be limited to objects. If you are an adult and your parents upset you, you may feel justified in avoiding them for a time. If being inactive depresses you, don't lie on the couch watching television. If going to rock concerts causes you to hanker for drugs, steer clear of those stressful situations.

Cues

Avoidance is not a permanent solution; eventually you will experience the cues that trigger your problem behavior. To prepare yourself to meet the challenge, you must gradually expose yourself to those cues as you progress through the action stage. Practicing cue exposure without responding in self-defeating ways will gradually increase your resistance.

Many successful self-changers have found that it helps to first confront problem cues in their imagination. For example, if your parents are a source of distress, imagine that you are visiting them, and the first thing they do is criticize you for avoiding them. Visualize yourself breathing deeply, relaxing, and saying, "I understand why you're upset, but I've needed more time to myself lately." Plan how long you are going to remain with them, under what conditions you will leave, and how you will continue to counter troubling cues.

As you successfully imagine your effective responses to problem cues, you will become better prepared to deal with problematic situations when you confront them in real life. It's a good thing, too—sooner or later you may want to visit your parents, attend a cocktail party, dine out on a special occasion . . . in short, engage in activities that have historically cued your problem behavior. But you will already have taken the necessary steps to counter whatever situation arises.

Reminders

Everyone uses clocks and calendars to help control their behavior. These simple tools remind us of how we are to respond next—when it's time to eat, go to work, take a break, or leave for vacation. We take these cues for granted; we find it natural to control our lives by reminders.

Reminders are equally important for people who are in the action stage. Put NO SMOKING signs in your office, STOP signs on your refrigerator door, or RELAX signs by the phone. These reminders may seem artificial and unnatural, but they are like stop signs at busy intersections, useful for controlling behavior.

One of the best reminders is a "To Do List." During periods when self-change is not a priority, this list might read:

1. Call John, 10 A.M.
2. Tennis, noon
3. Pick up milk on the way home
4. Put out trash, P.M.

Adding action goals is a natural extension. If, for example, you are working on losing weight, you might simply add Eat low-fat foods and Exercise to the list. If you are working to reduce anxiety, add:

5. Relax
6. Exercise
7. Counter thoughts

You can also use the list to reinforce yourself by scratching off the positive techniques you used during the day; checking something off a list is one of life's little pleasures.

Environment control self-assessment

This self-assessment measures your progress in using the environment control process. Once again, be honest and realistic. Fill in the number that most closely reflects how frequently you have used the method in the past week to combat your problem.

1 = Never, 2 = Seldom, 3 = Occasionally, 4 = Often, 5 = Repeatedly

FREQUENCY:

_____ I remove things from my home that remind me of my problem behavior.

_____ I leave places where other people are encouraging the problem behavior.

_____ I put things around my home or workplace that remind me not to engage in my problem behavior.

_____ I relate less often to people who contribute to my problem.

_____ = Score

A score of 8 or less means that you should concentrate more on your use of environmental controls. Taken in conjunction with the other self-assessments in this chapter, a score of 9 or higher indicates that you are ready to move into the maintenance stage.

THE NINTH PROCESS: REWARD

Environment control modifies the cues that precede and trigger problem behavior; reward modifies the consequences that follow and reinforce it. Historically, rewards have been used to reinforce desirable behaviors, and punishments to discourage undesirable ones. Since even the most ardent behavioral psychologists now believe that punishment tends only to suppress troubled behavior temporarily, we will concentrate on rewards.

We have met many unfortunate self-changers who argue that they should not reward themselves for changing problems, because they should not have been abusing alcohol, food, or tobacco in the first place. By failing to reinforce their positive self-change efforts, they are essentially punishing themselves. This is a mistake.

Reward would be unnecessary if resisting temptation were its own reward. If it felt good to decline fattening foods or avoid cocktails, self-change would require little effort. We need to be reinforced when we substitute carrots for chocolate, jogging for cigarettes, relaxation for anger, assertiveness for fear. Successful but naïve self-changers have learned the benefits of reward: They praise themselves for not getting angry, they buy themselves new outfits with the money saved from quitting smoking, they seek family recognition for losing weight.

There are three invaluable techniques for rewarding positive behavior:

Covert management

No matter what behavior you are changing, when cues arise, breathe deeply, tell yourself to be calm, and immediately follow your relaxation response with a private word of congratulations: "Nice job of relaxing," or "It feels good to be in control," or simply, "Way to go." These healthy self-administered pats on the back are examples of covert management.

If after relaxing or asserting yourself, you immediately begin to feel upset for not indulging your behavior, you are effectively punishing your resistance to temptation. Over time this will weaken your resistance and increase your risk of relapse. Substituting alternatives are self-change exercises that should be rewarded.

Suppose you slip and give in to temptation. Should you berate yourself? We think not. Although punishing yourself for slips may temporarily suppress undesired behavior, it does not alter it in the long run, because it does not offer suitable alternatives. Calling yourself a fool the morning after you drink is too long after the fact to be effective. Besides, you have already rewarded your slip by having a couple of favorite drinks. The same goes for overeating: If you say, "I shouldn't have eaten the whole thing," it's not only too late, but you have already reinforced yourself by eating the whole thing (and probably enjoying it). If delayed punishments worked, then hangovers and bellyaches would be natural cures for overindulgence.

Furthermore, covert punishments decrease self-esteem and increase emotional distress. Both of these are barriers to the change process. At this time, you need to believe in yourself, you need to be patient and calm; getting angry at yourself does no good.

When you correctly reinforce yourself, your self-statements will sound like echoes of positive role models from your past. Private kudos like "Nice going, pal," or "Good work" make you feel as though you are "reparenting" yourself to learn more mature behavior. Self-reinforcements such as "You can handle it," or "Don't give up; you can do it" are reminiscent of teachers or coaches who encouraged you to do your best and to feel good about yourself in the process.

If you had too much negative parenting, teaching, or coaching in the past, all the more reason to reinforce yourself in the present. Remember, you are in the process of changing your self-image and self-esteem, not just specific behaviors. It is important to feel good about the entire process of change, not just the planned outcome.

Contracting

Contracting, whether formal or informal, is used during the action stage. One teenage boy bets another one $10 that he's going to ask a girl out whom he likes, in order to pressure himself into it. A wealthy father promises his overweight teenage daughter that he will put $100 in an account for every pound she loses; if she loses twenty pounds, she will have enough to buy the horse she has always wanted. Some insurance companies offer $100 discounts to teenagers who make the honor roll; others grant $100 rebates to customers who quit smoking. With a fair contract, both parties gain from desirable changes.

Not everyone has an individual or company who is willing to contract for a change in problem behaviors, but anyone can make a contract with himself or herself. Written contracts tend to be more powerful than spoken ones, so write out your agreement. For example: "For every pound I lose I agree to put $10 [or whatever you can afford] into a shopping account." Whenever you need reinforcement, you can draw on your account and reimburse yourself.

It is important to remember the dual objectives here. You want to reinforce yourself for not engaging in problem behavior, and also reward yourself for substituting a healthier alternative. Consider adding another sentence to the contract in the last paragraph: "I will also deposit $5 for every 30 minutes I spend exercising." It is often easier to promote a new behavior than to eliminate an old one, and, as we have seen, countering is key to self-change.

A wealthy woman, who had plenty of extra money for shopping and vacations, wrote a contract stating that for every pound she lost she would donate $20 to CARE. It was a powerful reward for her to know that by doing this the food she did not eat might be used to support a starving child. When she felt tempted to indulge, she thought of how she could help someone besides herself by exercising self-control. This was a brilliant contract, and it truly helped this woman conquer her overeating.

One problem with contracts, of course, is that they can be unilaterally broken. No one is there to enforce them, so you must be unerringly honest with yourself when you enter such a contract. Although your honor may not be at stake, some of your self-esteem is on the line.

Shaping up

Overcoming problems requires that you *gradually* shape your behavior in a new, desirable direction. A person can't overcome agoraphobia, for example, all at once.* Using willpower to plan a vacation may be well intentioned, but panic reactions at the first bend in the road, or even the first step over the threshold can drive the agoraphobic back to the security of home. Setting yourself an immediate goal that is ambitious but unreasonable virtually guarantees failure.

A step-by-step approach, with reinforcement following each successive movement, is much more likely to be successful. A phobic person might begin by walking to the end of the block; the next step might be to walk part of the way around the block. Each step takes the person farther from the safety of home, each step is reinforced, and any feelings of anxiety are countered with relaxation.

The first step on your own personal path may seem simple and unworthy of being rewarded, and many people withhold rewards until they make more visible progress toward their goals. But the more difficult steps of the action stage must be built on a solid, well-reinforced foundation. When you slip (and most of us do), you want to ensure that you don't fall all the way. Well-practiced, well-rewarded earlier steps are good insurance that any slips will be brief lapses rather than complete relapses. Overcoming a prob-

---

*Agoraphobia refers to the persistent fear of leaving one's home.

lem is hard enough without depriving yourself of well-deserved reinforcements along the way.

Reward self-assessment

Here is a self-assessment to gauge your progress in using the reward process. Be honest and realistic. Fill in the number that most closely reflects how frequently you have used the method in the past week to combat your problem.

1 = Never, 2 = Seldom, 3 = Occasionally, 4 = Often, 5 = Repeatedly

FREQUENCY:

_____ I do something nice for myself in return for not giving in to my problem.

_____ I counter the temptation to punish myself with covert reinforcements.

_____ I reward myself for small self-change steps.

_____ Other people in my daily life try to make me feel good about changing.

_____ = Score

Taken in conjunction with the other self-assessments in this chapter, a score of 9 or higher on this self-assessment indicates that you are ready to move into the maintenance stage. A score of 8 or less means that you should devote more time to thinking of helpful rewards for yourself.

HELPING RELATIONSHIPS DURING ACTION

Action is the busiest period of change. Now more than ever, you need to depend on your helping relationships. Think of your problem as an old piano that needs to be carried down a flight of stairs. There is no way you would undertake such a task without calling on a few friends for assistance. Use the same strategy here and let several people help you to bear your problem away.

We hope that you began to share your burden by going public during the preparation stage, and by discussing your plans and goals with significant people in your life. We have heard countless self-changers complain about family members who did not care or support their change efforts. In many instances, however, the accused responds, quite honestly, that he or she was never told about the change. The changer then snaps, "Well, you should have known it!"— an overused variation on the if-you-really-loved-me-you-would-read-my-mind complaint.

Don't assume that your spouse or anyone else will intuit your plans; go public and do it clearly. Remember, too, that change is a life-saving operation; let people know that even if you become anxious, irritable, confused, and difficult, you want and need their support.

There are other ways in which helpers can assist with the change processes you will be using in the action stage:

Exercise together   Running, walking, aerobic dancing, even relaxing are easier and more fun with a loved one or a friend. Ask one or more of your helpers to join you in your countering techniques.

Buddy up   There are times when two people, working as a team, are able to change themselves more effectively than either can alone. John and Nancy Norcross, for example, are more successful maintaining a healthy diet together than separately.

Rearrange your home   An agreement with your family to ban high-fat foods, smoking materials, or alcohol from your home gives you a terrific advantage. Helpers can play an important role in controlling your environment so that you can avoid tempting cues.

Put it in writing As any lawyer will tell you, written contracts are the most binding. In order to bind yourself—and your helpers—to your self-change contract, write it down and distribute it to all concerned parties. The contract can specify your starting date, your goals, and the countering techniques and rewards you will be using. Make sure, too, to specify your helpers' commitments. This will not be an easy time for them either.

Roy, a bank auditor, constructed the following contract to control his angry outbursts:

1. Starting Saturday, December 4, I will do my best to keep from blowing up:
   a. I will talk with Becky about my frustrations and stresses before they get the better of me.
   b. I will let my daughter know if I'm in a bad mood.
   c. If I slip up, I will catch myself as soon as possible and apologize for any outburst.

2. In return, Becky will do her best to be more positive and less critical:
   a. She will let me know she appreciates it when I handle a frustrating situation without blowing up.
   b. She will try to be more supportive when I am having a bad day.
   c. She will help me to explain to our daughters that I am working on my temper.

Get "stroked" Many of our research participants complain of a lack of steady reinforcement. We encourage them—and you—to elicit rewards from helpers for even small amounts of progress. Tell your helpers that "strokes" come in many guises: Helpers can brag to others about your progress, or take on a dreaded chore for you. Verbal praise,

monetary rewards, extra hugs, small presents, back mas-
sages, and the like are all useful rewards.

Don't take guilt trips   Scolding, nagging, preaching, and embarrassing are not forms of support. Write in your contract
that helpers should not use these "methods," even if they
are well intentioned, because they increase distress and
eventually backfire on the helper.

Keep it positive   Many family members are mute supporters
for seven consecutive days of progress, but become vocal
critics the one day you slip. Tell them at the start that reinforcement is superior to punishment in behavior change,
and ask them to monitor the ratio of their positive to negative comments; we recommend at least three compliments
for every criticism.

Seek support for life   If you are short on significant others,
or if family and/or friends cannot give you the support you
need, find a local support group. People who are struggling
with the same problems can reinforce you, guide you
through the rough spots, and remind you of the benefits of
changing.

Group support need not come from formal organizations.
One of the most successful support groups I've ever known
involved seven women who worked in the same office.
They met twice a week to share their dieting concerns. They
ate a low-calorie lunch together on Tuesdays, and coffee (no
doughnuts) on Friday mornings. Successful as they were,
they resented being called a "group"; they were, they said,
"just a bunch of women talking."

Whatever the source of your helping relationships, they
are of vital importance during the action stage, and will remain extremely potent as you transform your short-term
changes into long-term revisions during the maintenance
stage.

GAIL TAKES ACTION

Once she started taking action, Gail's morale ran high for several weeks. She exercised regularly. She ate what she considered to be a low-fat diet. Gail felt good about focusing on being healthier and eating better rather than on looking better. She liked being more active and getting into shape. She hoped she would learn to like fat-free foods. She reminded herself that she had come to love skim milk and found that she disliked 2 percent milk, which to her tasted like coffee cream. By considering these positive feelings, Gail reinforced herself for the actions she was taking.

After about four weeks her morale fell when she discovered that she wasn't losing any weight. She found herself focusing too much on weight loss again, and knew she needed to do something to keep herself from relapsing to this old and narrow goal. So Gail determined to redo her decisional balance. She reevaluated how she was living and who she was becoming. Fortunately Gail was able to reaffirm the many values that her new lifestyle reflected: She had taken more responsible care of herself and was helping prevent a whole range of chronic diseases; she had more energy, was in better condition, and felt less sluggish; her stress level was lower; and she was becoming less preoccupied with her appearance.

Now she could counter defeating thoughts with the realization that regardless of what happened to her weight she was winning. She was feeling better and eating better even if she didn't weigh less. Gail also drew support from her helping relationships. Friends encouraged her to trust that her weight would soon respond to a healthier lifestyle. So Gail decided to reaffirm her commitment to her diet and exercise regimen.

It took her two months to lose her first pound. But it was

the most precious pound she had ever lost. It wasn't quick and easy. It didn't involve counting and cutting calories—an approach that had always given her immediate gratification but long-term demoralization. She lost the pound as a consequence of living healthier and living better.

This gave a tremendous boost to Gail's morale. She started exercising even more and eating even less fat. The pros of her new lifestyle were increasing the way she had hoped when she first shifted to her new strategy.

Gail found that she could cover the tennis court better than before. She was a little quicker, and had more stamina. Her moods were more stable, and she was continuing to lose weight, about a pound every one or two weeks. In the past she wouldn't have tolerated such slow progress. She would have cut calories drastically, stressing her body and herself, seeking a quick fix for a problem that had developed gradually. Now she was applying a sensible solution to her problem based on reasonable and responsible values, not on vanity and a poor self-image.

After Gail had lost about half of her excess weight, she reached a plateau. Her behavior change program was continuing but she was no longer enjoying the reinforcement that losing weight provided. Dan told her she looked better already, and that she should accept her body at this weight. Gail was tempted to adopt this rationalization (which might have come out of Dan's personal fears). Twenty-some extra pounds was better than forty, and if this was truly the best she could do then Gail felt she could accept the weight.

Before she shifted to acceptance, Gail wanted to be sure the modifications she had made were sufficient. She asked for an assessment at the cardiovascular rehabilitation clinic at her state university. The first thing she discovered was that her diet was not in fact as low-fat as she had thought. Her intake of 33 percent of calories from fat was lower than the national average, but it was only half the way to the national low-fat goal of 30 percent.

The exercise physiologist informed Gail that she could acquire further health benefits by increasing her exercise program, which might lead to additional weight loss.

Gail had discovered that her self-change plan was good but not good enough. She was moved to redouble her efforts. Not only did she want a fit and low-fat lifestyle, but society supported that lifestyle as well.

It wasn't always easy. There were times when Gail lapsed. When she felt unappreciated at work or at home, she was tempted to indulge in a late-night binge. And sometimes she gave in to the temptation. But she didn't sleep as well afterward, she didn't feel as well in the morning, and she never felt any more appreciated.

Gail decided to substitute bingeing with some social support by starting a group for menopausal women like herself. Gail organized the group around tennis. She invited four of her friends, all facing fifty. They could have fun together, they could exercise together, and they could share together some of the trials and tribulations of their changing bodies.

Gail also announced to Dan that she needed more from him emotionally, socially, and sexually. She told him that she wanted him to get into shape—and that she would help him if he wished. Dan's own journey through change is another story, but needless to say he greeted Gail's announcement with mixed emotions at first.

Gail is now many months into maintenance. She feels healthier and fitter than she has in fifteen years. Her morale is high. She is confident that this is the way she wants to live the rest of her life. And she is happily helping Dan progress through his stages of change.

CHAPTER 8

Maintainance— Staying There

WORKING IN THE YARD one hot summer day, Andrew, an accountant, had quite a scare. He felt flushed and overcome with heat; his heart beat rapidly and his chest hurt. He was only forty-two. Could he really be having a heart attack? He was frightened enough to go to the emergency room. Fortunately, the problem was nothing more than mild heatstroke. Wisely, however, his attending physician took the opportunity to advise Andrew to quit smoking and change his diet. Andrew's two-pack-a-day habit and his weight of 235 pounds were clear threats to his health; a real heart attack could be right down the road.

Andrew took the doctor's advice seriously. He did not touch a cigarette for nine months, and took off some weight. The initial months of quitting smoking were easy—his fear took care of that. But at tax season, when work stress increased dramatically, cigarettes started looking good to him again. On his way to the office one morning, he stopped at a convenience store, thinking that he would buy just one pack of cigarettes to get him through the weekend. After all, he reasoned, he had been successful for nine months. At this point, he could surely control his smoking . . .

Rudy hadn't touched cocaine or alcohol in five months.

His hospitalization was long past, he was attending Alcoholics Anonymous and Cocaine Anonymous regularly, things were beginning to level out at work, his social life was improving, and his relationships were the best they had ever been. Rudy no longer drank, and although at first he had worried that might put him in an awkward position with clients, he now felt they hardly noticed when he ordered ginger ale or Perrier as they enjoyed their scotch or beer.

On a business trip to New York City, Rudy and a client walked into a small, cozy bar in Greenwich Village. In a secluded booth, his client cut three lines of cocaine on the table in front of him; Rudy's heart started to beat fast and the sweat beaded on his forehead. His thoughts were racing. He began imagining that he could do a line or two and still maintain his sobriety. Since he lived in Atlanta, it occurred to him, even if he did some coke in New York, he would still be sober at home. His reactions surprised him, and momentarily he did not know what to do . . .

Annette was discouraged; it had been almost a year since she had felt this depressed. She was thirty-two, divorced after a brief marriage. She had long had trouble getting along with men, but was afraid of being alone. Several visits to a psychotherapist had helped her to become more assertive, both in her relationships and on the job. In the past year, she had been dating more, and getting to know men as people rather than as prospective mates. She had actually begun to like men—and herself.

All that now seemed light years away. About two months ago, she had met Tom. She was relaxed with him, she enjoyed being with him, and the attraction was mutual. But as their intimacy increased, Annette found that she became less assertive and more worried about what Tom thought of her. She was getting back into an old rut, of not liking herself and feeling that she was not good enough for Tom. Some problems at work compounded the difficulty. Annette felt as if she were back at square one.

The stories of Annette, Rudy, and Andrew illustrate the difficulties of maintaining change. No less important than action, maintenance is often far more difficult to achieve. Successful change means change that is sustained over time—not months, but years, decades, a lifetime. Maintenance is not a static stage in which you hold the line against unwanted behaviors. Rather, it is another busy, active period of change, one that requires you to learn new coping methods. Getting there is only half the battle.

As everyone knows, it's easy to slip back into old problems. Some popular sayings about maintenance—"You're a puff away from a pack a day"; "One drink, one drunk"—acknowledge the difficulties. The difference between the short, intense trip of the action stage and the long haul of maintenance is summarized by the facetious comment many smokers make: "Stopping is easy—I do it every day." Two factors are fundamental to successful maintenance: sustained, long-term effort, and a revised lifestyle.

This is tough work, but nothing else will do. For example, although many diets succeed in the short run, their long-run success rate is quite low. Many dieters lose weight quickly, but six months after beginning a diet, many people weigh more than they did when they started!

This is action without maintenance. New Year's resolutions also typify this phenomenon. About half of all American adults initiate self-change at the beginning of each new year. It is, after, all a traditional and socially reinforced time for changing behavior. Our research has found that a mere 77 percent of these resolutions are successful for one week. The success rate drops to 55 percent after one month, to 40 percent after six months, and to 19 percent after two years.

No one who has changed successfully, in or out of therapy, will deny that maintenance is difficult. As with the other stages, there are negative responses that lead to an erosion of commitment and failure. There are also basic strategies for long-term maintenance. Yes, staying there is tough; but it is possible and well worth the effort.

A STRATEGY FOR SUCCESS

All stages of change require a series of tasks, a stretch of time in which to try them, and a certain amount of energy and dedication. The action stage lasts for several months. The first month or two of this period is the most likely time for relapse. No wonder; just a glance back at the previous chapter will recall all the work involved in successful action.

Maintenance takes all that required work and builds on it. Difficult as it is, forsaking an undesirable behavior is not enough to overcome it for good. Almost all negative habits essentially become our friends—even, in many cases, our lovers. They play important, sometimes dominating roles in our lives. Andrew's smoking was his only way of coping with stress; Rudy's cocaine use kept his life from seeming boring; Annette's guarded relations with men resulted from her fears of intimacy. At some point, these behaviors aided Andrew, Rudy, and Annette in handling problems; for a time at least, they seemed under control. Eventually, however, our ill-considered strategies become our problems.

To overcome them fully, we must replace our problem behaviors with a new, healthier lifestyle. This strategy begins with the action-stage process of countering, but it doesn't end there. That is why the word "maintenance" can be misleading. Maintaining behavior change is not like maintaining a home, which often requires little more than a periodic coat of paint.

We *can* break old patterns by removing drugs from our lives, for example, or avoiding certain relationships. But those who do no more than remove an old habit condemn themselves to a life of longing and deprivation. Lifelong tolerance of this deprivation requires unceasing and powerful acts of will. The "dry drunks" of alcoholic treatment circles, the people who stop smoking but who would return to cigarettes tomorrow if they found out they had cancer may be *abstaining* but they still run a high risk of relapsing.

For all of us, former problems, especially addictive ones, will hold some attraction long after the habit is broken. To remain strong throughout maintenance requires that you acknowledge you are still vulnerable to the problem even while you're building a life in which the old behavior has no value. In our long-term follow-up of smokers who quit on their own, those who successfully maintained their change through to termination had learned to devalue the positive aspects of smoking; develop confidence in their ability to abstain from smoking; keep a healthy distance from cigarettes; and, through development of new, desirable habits, find few if any temptations to smoke.

Danger times, danger signs

The most common threats to maintenance are social pressures, internal challenges, and special situations. Social pressures come from those around you who either engage in the problem behavior themselves, or don't recognize its impact on you. Internal challenges usually result from overconfidence and other forms of defective thinking. Special situations arise when you are confronted by an unusual, intense temptation. While many of the more common temptations occur early in the action stage, you learn to deal with them before moving out of the stage. During maintenance, the relatively rarer temptations come into play. They are difficult to anticipate and pose serious threats to your confidence, convictions, and commitment.

Rudy's dilemma offers a good example of both social pressure and a special situation—the sudden and unexpected appearance of coke, offered by an important client. During the action stage, Rudy had used environment control a great deal, staying away from places and people associated with his cocaine use. He even agreed to keep clear of alcohol in order to avoid losing control while drinking and falling back to using cocaine.

Although environment control is an important strategy for breaking free of an addiction, it has its limitations. It is simply impossible to remain free of tempting cues forever. Faced with the opportunity to do coke and the encouragement of a drug-using "friend," Rudy faced a real challenge. The presence of the drug triggered an intense physical craving. And the situation was so charged that Rudy's old patterns of thinking—rationalization and minimization—returned. This is not uncommon: External dangers often trigger defective thinking, along with physical and psychological craving.

In Andrew's case, defective thinking posed the greatest threat to his smoking abstinence. Faced with escalating stress—with which he used to cope by smoking—Andrew engaged in denial and indulged a false sense of confidence. Andrew's thoughts on his way to the convenience store eroded his commitment and any efforts at environment control. Buying a pack of cigarettes signaled the second step toward the collapse of maintenance efforts and a relapse to regular smoking.

By becoming more assertive, Annette was able to change how she related to men. And everything seemed to work well, as long as her involvements remained casual. But old patterns, as we know, die hard. When she began to develop a more intimate relationship, intense fears were triggered and earlier patterns reemerged. Such situations, though dangerous, are signs of success, not failure—they can be experienced only after significant and sustained changes have been made.

In a study of smokers who abstained for months, we

found that one group returned to smoking after visiting hospital emergency rooms. Serious illness to a family member created a level of stress that had not been reckoned with in the earlier action stage. While these individuals had previously handled many diverse stresses without smoking, they were overwhelmed by the sudden anxiety created by the emergency room visit. Once again, extreme stress enabled them to justify a return to smoking—"just for the moment"—that ultimately led to relapse.

It is difficult to prepare for the extreme, the accidental, and the unexpected. This is what makes maintenance such a great challenge.

Courting relapse

There are three common internal challenges that are closely related to slips, or brief lapses: overconfidence, daily temptation, and self-blame. Each is a mind game, played by people who are subconsciously courting relapse. Awareness of these responses, and vigilance against them, are important in successful maintenance.

Several years ago, one of our clients remarked that maintenance reminded her of Charles Dickens's opening line in *A Tale of Two Cities*. "It was the best of times, it was the worst of times." Her successful weight loss and slimmer self made her feel great. But times were tough because she was beginning to feel complacent and cocky about her hard-earned svelte appearance. She feared the prospect of overconfidence.

A statement such as "I've got this beat forever" is a telltale sign of overconfidence. Such self-changers sometimes brush aside the concerns of their friends, insisting, "I can handle one." However, the sad truth of addictive problems, borne out by scientific research and clinical experience, is that most people *cannot* handle "one" of any problem product. Remaining mindful of this natural propensity toward overconfidence can prevent you from taking those first few steps down the road to relapse.

Overconfidence can also beget daily temptation, to which you intentionally and unnecessarily subject yourself regularly. Overconfident alcoholics keep a bottle of booze in their desk drawer, to "remind" themselves. Ex-smokers stash a pack or two at home to "test willpower." Dieters buy high-calorie goodies "just in case company drops in." Intentionally exposing yourself to substances or situations you are trying to avoid is not a sign of strength, a measure of willpower, or a positive reminder. Sooner or later temptation wins and you lose. We have yet to meet a self-changer who played the daily temptation game early in maintenance and won.

Beyond overconfidence and daily temptation is the final pitfall, self-blame. In several studies, including our own, the severity of misplaced self-blame is one of the best predictors of failed maintenance. Ironically, occasional and appropriate self-blame may actually rekindle your commitment to change. Frequent, inappropriate self-blame backfires. Far from being the motivator or activator it is held to be, self-blame is demoralizing and it stymies commitment.

PROCESSES FOR MAINTAINING CHANGE

As you move through the maintenance stage, you won't need to use the processes of change quite as much as you did during contemplation, preparation, or action. In a very real way, maintenance refers not only to maintaining change but also to maintaining the use of the change processes. During the action stage, for example, you relied on self-liberation to help you use the strategies necessary to break a problem habit; in maintenance you must continue to use them.

You must keep up your commitment. Challenges make it not only easy but natural to let your guard down. The erosion of commitment is subtle. Since threats to maintenance occur infrequently (unlike threats during action, which occur almost constantly), complacency can easily take hold. Humans have the ability to forget painful passages in their lives. Usually, this is a blessing, but selective memory is detrimental to maintaining change.

If you forget the tremendous effort it took to change, everything begins to look easier than it was and all arguments against indulging "just for the weekend" fail. Why not taste a little of that forbidden fruit, when you can change right back again on Monday?

Many people find success difficult to accept, and their tendency to attribute success to others—God, a spouse, a therapist—challenges their commitment. Giving credit to others is admirable to a degree, but it has its dangers. By not accepting responsibility and credit for liberating yourself, you undermine your self-confidence, your self-esteem, and your commitment. If you think others are responsible for your success, how can you maintain it yourself?

Self-changers often don't give themselves credit because they don't know just what they did to change. Many people we have interviewed first tell us, "I just woke up one morning and quit." When we ask more detailed questions, they begin to remember. They remember the weeks prior to that fateful morning, when perhaps they switched brands and became increasingly disgusted with smoking. They remember earlier attempts to quit smoking. They remember when they avoided people and the places that were filled with smoke during the two weeks after quitting. They remember enlisting the aid of several friends at work by announcing their attempts to quit smoking. Remembering your own efforts to change will reinforce your commitment.

Change is often associated with a new way of life. A diet is successful when it is combined with more exercise, healthier foods, and revised eating patterns. In maintaining weight loss, overeating may not be the first danger sign. Instead, the early warning signs may involve a lessening of commitment to the new lifestyle. Maybe you and your family return to sitting in front of the TV, and suddenly it becomes "too late" or "too hard" to exercise. The loss of these valuable new supports undermines your commitment and makes it almost inevitable that you will gain weight again. Once you abandon exercise in favor of watching TV, how far are you from grabbing a bag of chips?

How, then, can you maintain your commitment? First, jot down the difficulties you encountered in your early change efforts. Review the list you made from months ago of the negative aspects of your problem behavior. Keep both lists in a safe place, look at them periodically, and refer to them at the first sign of slipping. During the maintenance stage, they can act as psychic booster shots.

Second, take credit for your accomplishment. Maintenance is not the time for criticizing yourself for having had problems, but for taking both credit and responsibility for change. Use the new year, your birthday, or the anniversary of your change (it need not be a year—celebrate a month!) to reflect on the success you have had and to renew your commitment.

Renewing your commitment is especially important when you are trying to modify regularly occurring behaviors. Maintaining weight loss is a constant issue for people with weight problems, and requires frequent boosts of commitment. Similarly, timidity and passivity in interpersonal relationships require that you make special efforts with a variety of people. With these problems and many others, redoubling commitment is a critical part of maintaining change.

Keep a healthy distance

In maintenance as in action, commitment is not enough; environment control remains a necessary ingredient for success. As you progress through the months of maintenance, you will find your self-confidence increasing and temptation decreasing. Gradually, you will be comfortable in the presence of certain temptations or situations. But you may not become completely immune to them. Too many times, situations arise that can trigger a relapse.

Especially during the early months of maintenance, it's best to continue to avoid people, places, or things that could seriously compromise your change. Hanging out at a bar in order to be close to a group of friends may maintain friendships but endangers your sobriety. Staying "friends" with your former spouse may feel familiar, but it can threaten your independence. And stopping at the bakery because your kids are coming over for dinner is a generous but ultimately self-defeating gesture. Controlling your environment never signifies weakness but, rather, intelligence, health, and foresight.

Create a new lifestyle

In maintenance as in action, countering is an important partner to environment control. Since stress often triggers problems, from weight gain to marital discord, it is invaluable to develop ways to cope with stress. Chief among stress-reduction techniques, as always, are exercise and relaxation.

Working to create alternative behaviors is one of the most important and rewarding challenges of maintenance. Individuals with drinking problems, for example, are frequently amazed at the number of activities open to them that do not revolve around alcohol. Make time for something that you've always wanted to do, and you will find you like yourself more and more.

Check your thinking

What you think and say to yourself has profound effects on your behavior; negative thinking can pose serious problems. Your attitudes toward a problem remain as important in the maintenance stage as your ability to deal with that problem, the quality of your life without it, and the consequences of possible relapse.

When you moved from precontemplation and contemplation to preparation and action, the positive aspects of changing became more prominent, and the negative aspects began to dwindle. If you are in the midst of a major change, no doubt you remember how your pros and cons charts changed as you drew closer and closer to action. Health matters, family pressures, and personal concerns all contribute to a decision to take action. Eventually the positives clearly outweigh the negatives.

Problems may now seem far away and less threatening as you move into the maintenance stage. Being at this distance now may lead you to minimize the dangers and risks of your unwanted behavior, and maximize its appeal. Again, the process of forgetting is involved. You may tell yourself that your drinking wasn't that bad; that smoking is better than gaining weight; that the difficulties your shyness created were never major. Denial, distortion, and rationalization are the enemies of maintenance.

To prevent these negative thoughts from gaining a solid foothold, check your thinking periodically to see if you are being consistent and honest with yourself. Review your reasons for changing. Ask one of your helpers to remind you just how serious your problem was. Go back to the pros and cons exercise in Chapter 6. Be honest with yourself. When it comes to your problem, you are as capable of distorting the truth as anyone. The smarter you are, the better you are at rationalizing.

SELF-EFFICACY—A MEASURE OF SUCCESS

Self-efficacy* refers to how you rate your ability to perform specific tasks related to your problem. Related to self-esteem and self-confidence, self-efficacy can be an aid to evaluating how you see yourself. As you change, your confidence will grow, and your self-efficacy level will rise.

In order to assess your level of self-efficacy, first choose a behavior pattern that you want to follow. Then make a list of situations that tempt you to abandon the behavior. For each situation, evaluate just how confident you are that you could still behave the way you want. For example, you may be completely sure that you will not drink at a church social, but your efficacy may wane when it comes to the annual company party. Use a scale from 1 (not at all confident) to 10 (extremely confident). Following is a sample self-efficacy chart, from the point of view of someone trying to stop drinking in social situations:

1. When I am on vacation and want to relax	9
2. When I am under work-related stress	6
3. When I am lonely	8
4. When I see others drinking at a bar or party	9
5. When I am depressed	7
6. When I am craving a drink	8
7. When I am hassled by others	5
8. When I am offered a drink in a social situation	10
9. When I feel I need a drink to help cope with life	6
10. When I want to test my willpower over drinking	8
Total confidence	76
Total number of situations	10

*Self-efficacy is a concept developed by Albert Bandura, a well-known psychologist at Stanford University.

Average level of confidence	7.6
Highest confidence Situation	#8
Lowest confidence Situation	#7

You must be brutally honest with yourself in filling out a self-efficacy form. In one of our studies, a male smoker who was attempting to quit gave himself a string of 10s after barely reading each situation. He did not want to confront situations that might shake his confidence. His efficacy evaluation was more fantasy than reality, and wishing didn't do the trick for him. Another individual, who didn't expect too much from herself, rated herself low in every situation; that did her no good. Bear in mind that the self-efficacy assessment is not a test, but a tool that can help you manage your maintenance.

Once you have made a self-efficacy evaluation, examine your scores. In which situations are you least confident? Is there a pattern to them? Are certain situations especially challenging? You can use this newfound knowledge to develop your own relapse prevention plan. Rather than wishing you were supremely confident, develop a strategy to cope with difficult situations. Use environment control to avoid the most difficult ones, and countering to handle less threatening temptations.

Guarding against slips

The goal of maintenance is nothing short of a permanent change that becomes part of your personality. Permanent change is a high ideal, rarely attained without false starts or mistakes. Most people slip along the way—go off their diets, fail to be assertive with a boss or lover, or take a drink. How do you keep these momentary slips from turning into major relapses?

Slips are usually the result of overwhelming stress or insufficient coping skills. Although slips are far from admirable, you can recover from them, learn from them, and continue toward your goal of permanent change. First, you must take responsibility for your slips and realize that they indicate vulnerability. Check high-risk situations—they should be on your self-efficacy evaluation—and develop a plan of attack against them. Then you must combat the absolutist thinking that equates a single lapse with total relapse.

Life without problem behavior is undeniably different, especially when you have given up a substance or a way of life that was once your best friend. Quite often, the euphoria of an initial change gives way to a sense of loss and deprivation, which in turn may wear down your resolve.

When we work with people who have given up drugs or alcohol, we encourage them to go through a mourning process. To maintain abstinence, it's important that they say good-bye to their old friend and trusted companion. Yes, alcohol causes broken marriages, DWI arrests, lost jobs, but for many alcohol is a constant companion and sturdy crutch over the years.

Regardless of your problem behavior, regardless of your level of disgust when you enter the action stage, don't be surprised if you wake up one day missing your old habits. Don't think, however, that this means you cannot live without your old behavior; you are in the process of making a new self that does not need your old problems.

HELPING RELATIONSHIPS DURING MAINTENANCE

People around you are often extremely supportive while you are in the action stage. Soon they take your change for granted. One person who recently kicked his habit complained to me: "I wish they would keep up the congratulations for as long as they kept giving me grief about my drug use. How soon they forget!"

It's not unusual for self-changers to complain about the difficulties of continuing with helping relationships during the maintenance stage. But it is more important than ever to have an understanding person nearby during maintenance, especially when you are experiencing a crisis that could lead to a relapse. One of the most valuable functions of organizations such as Alcoholics Anonymous is the support they provide their members during maintenance. Having someone to call on who has been where you are, who can understand, and who can help is invaluable.

There are many ways in which you can help your helpers to be supportive during maintenance:

Revise your contract   Expand your initial contract with your helpers. Give them the permission and even the responsibility to confront you if you start reverting to old behavior or express overconfidence and expose yourself repeatedly to tempting situations.

Put your helper on call   Make a "crisis card" to put in your wallet or pocketbook. On this card write a list of the negative aspects of your problem, as well as a set of instructions to follow when you are seriously tempted to slip. The instructions could read like this:

1. Review the problem list.
2. Substitute positive thinking for negative statements.
3. Remember the benefits of changing.
4. Engage in vigorous distraction or exercise.
5. Call [support person's name and number].

Practice new behavior   Strongly supportive friends can help you practice confronting temptations before they actually occur. This can be accomplished through role playing, which serves to generate realistic situations while you try out new, adaptive responses to them.

Helpers should remember that they are not drama critics, but supportive resources; they can help the self-changer to say no clearly, both verbally and nonverbally. Therapists who teach "drink refusal skills" like to suggest alternative behaviors. A helper can encourage the self-changer to ask for a club soda, a second helping of salad, or a piece of gum. Helpers can assist you in practicing assertion skills by having you insist that they stop tempting you. Above all, they can discourage you from making temporary excuses—"Not tonight," "I have a cold," "I'm on medication." These devices may work for a night or two, but delay the inevitable and firm no. These excuses also imply that the self-changer may be willing to accept an offer to go drinking in the future— another night, when he or she is healthier or off medication.

Help someone else The last step of the Alcoholics Anonymous program, called the Twelfth Step, involves helping others with similar problems. This has become an integral part of many alcohol and drug programs. Although it may seem contrary to getting support for yourself, many people report that helping others is a key to helping themselves maintain change. The psychiatrist Karl Menninger liked to say, "Love cures people—both the ones who give it and the ones who receive it." It is a refreshing, esteem-boosting experience to discover that you can not only help yourself but others too.

Patience and persistence

Many behaviors that we wish to change become problems because of our tendency to take a short-term perspective. We have become accustomed to the instant fix: fast food, instant coffee, quick pleasures. We can no longer wait for gratification. But short-term ecstasies—eating, drinking, or taking drugs—create long-term agonies. And a short-term perspective is counterproductive during the maintenance stage, where there is no such thing as a quick. Difficult as it may be, a shift in perspective can help yo transform your life.

Patience and persistence are the hallmarks of mainte-nance. Time can be an ally as you progress across the stages of change. One comforting thought, as you struggle with maintenance, is that the process is a lengthy one. You don't have to get everything right all at once. Recalling how long you spent in the precontemplation and contemplation stages can provide an important reality check. However long it takes to change, consider how many years you may be adding to your life, and how improved the quality of that life will be in the years to come.

CHAPTER 9

ycling—Learning from Relapse

GINNY WAS IN the depths of depression for the fourth time. Although she thought she had overcome her fears of failure, her new job was not going well and her emotions were out of control. She was drinking and eating too much, but her top priority was coping with her depression, and compulsive consumption seemed to help. In past depressive episodes, Ginny had felt that she was not herself and would never be again. This time, as painful as the depression was, she felt confident that it would pass. Meanwhile, she was trying to keep it from disrupting her life any more than necessary.

Molly was disappointed and surprised when she went back to drinking. She had done without alcohol for nearly five years. Despite an occasional temptation, she honestly believed that she would never again turn to drink. She was sure that she had dealt with every tough situation, but when her youngest son left home she found herself alone with a bottle. She knew she had to take action soon; she just wasn't sure she was ready.

Ginny and Molly have both experienced relapses. They both made excellent progress on their problems and maintained their changes for years. Eventually, however, they fell back to earlier stages of change. Ginny is contemplating her problem, trying to understand how she became so dis-tressed by the prospect of temporary failure. Molly is feeling down but not out. She is preparing to get back into action, to resume her battle with the bottle.

Fortunately, the vast majority of relapsers do not give up on themselves and their ability to change. Like Ginny and Molly, most return to the contemplation or preparation stage and get ready to take action again. And our research shows that they have reason to be hopeful. Experience with change strengthens people, and relapses most often take them not to precontemplation, but to contemplation or preparation, relatively close to making commitments to re-newed action.

There are exceptions. For example, after losing many pounds, Steve, found to his dismay that he was gaining it back again. He had developed control over his once con-stant trips to the kitchen, and he was able to go out to eat without overindulging. But he was having a difficult time dealing with his anxiety, anger, and depression. Al-though Steve had learned how to cope with his environ-ment, he hadn't yet learned how to cope effectively with his emotions. And when he became angry and distressed, he began to overeat.

Steve became so demoralized by his relapse that he lost all energy for change. He showed all the signs of a precon-templator on the verge of giving up. Some self-changers look on themselves as total failures after relapsing. Guilt, shame, or embarrassment makes them feel that the struggle is not worth continuing. They become defensive and try to avoid or ignore the problem.

Although relapse is never desirable, our view is that change is often circular and difficult. The spiral cycle of change (page 49) shows how contemplation, preparation, and action usually follow relapse. Relapsers most often take one step backward in order to take two steps forward.

THE TEN LESSONS
OF RELAPSE

After relapse, before committing to another round of action, most people benefit from a period of self-reevaluation in which they learn from their recent mistakes. To strengthen subsequent self-change efforts, there are ten important lessons to be learned from relapse.

Few changers terminate the first time around

It's rare to overcome a problem on your first attempt. Clinical research indicates that only about 20 percent of the population permanently conquers long-standing problems on the first try. This means that the vast majority of self-changers relapse.

We do not fully understand why, but it is clear that few people have had any help or instruction in applying psychological methods to their problems. They are unaware of the relationship between processes and stages (and quite frequently, of the existence of either). Yet, despite this lack of experience or training, many people expect to get it right the first time. This is an unrealistic expectation.

Without the help of a professional or a book such as this one, a change regimen is necessarily developed by trial and error.

Trial and error is inefficient

After discovering that many self-changers eventually succeed at overcoming problems of weight control and smoking, one leading psychologist observed: "That's what self-changers do. They rely on trial-and-error learning—but with more errors than learning."

It's tremendously frustrating to set out to change only to relapse in spite of your best efforts. What do you do the second time around? That is a major dilemma facing professionals, who say, "We gave our clients our best effort the first time. If we knew anything better to do, we would have tried it. So what do we do with the relapsers?"

The answer is, help them learn from their relapse experiences but encourage them to rely on guided learning rather than on trial and error. It is inefficient, not to mention frustrating, painful, and unhealthy, for smokers to make four attempts at quitting over ten years before finally succeeding. Most people want to move to a smoke-free life much sooner than that.

Using relapse as a guide to effective learning can help you benefit not only from your own experiences but from those of other people. For example, just by reading this book you can take advantage of the combined wisdom of thousands of self-changers, laypeople, and psychotherapists. You can learn to apply the appropriate change process to each stage of change, a lesson that would take years of trial and error to master.

Change costs more than you budgeted.

Few self-changers realize how much change costs, and consequently fail to budget enough time, energy, or money. You may recognize that it took years to establish your problem behavior, but believe unrealistically that you can reverse this deeply embedded pattern in a few weeks. In reality, it takes an average of about six months of concerted action before you may be ready to move into maintenance.

Nor is time the only issue. Few self-changers are prepared to use five different change processes during action. Even those who are aware of the variety of processes at their disposal believe, at least the first time around, that willpower alone can overcome their problem. As a result, they have developed no substitutes for behaviors that have served an important function in their lives. How will they replace 30 cigarettes a day, 210 a week, or over 10,000 a year? How will they counter 8,000 temptations during six months of action? What reinforcements will they use to make up for all the instant gratification?

Sheer willpower is not enough. What is needed is a commitment over time to an action plan that exploits all that the processes have to offer. The lack of such a commitment leads to insufficient effort, an attempt to move into maintenance too soon and eventually and predictably, relapse.

Professional state-of-the-art weight-control programs have learned this from experience. These action-oriented programs, which once lasted for ten weeks at most, have in many cases been extended to twenty-two weeks or more. Because this reinforces clients during most or all of the action stage of a weight-control program, a higher percentage of participants successfully reach the maintenance stage.

Using the wrong processes at the wrong time

Many people blithely apply powerful psychological processes with little forethought. The result can be mistreatment. Here are three major ways in which the basic processes of change are often used incorrectly:

Becoming misinformed   When information on self-change is scarce or inaccurate, consciousness-raising techniques may backfire. Self-help information can be partisan or outdated. A generation ago, many men read marriage manuals to gather information about overcoming premature ejaculation. These manuals taught men that they were becoming too aroused during intercourse and needed to distract themselves (by thinking about work or by chewing on the inside of their cheeks). Later research has shown that overcoming premature ejaculation actually requires learning to tolerate more arousal, not less. Distraction prolongs the problem.

You need accurate information to avoid misguided strategies.

Misusing willpower When people attempt to change and fail, they frequently conclude that they have not used enough willpower. We have already discussed how excessive reliance on willpower at the expense of other change processes can lead to failure and frustration. Willpower can be misapplied in other ways. Many people try to will the unwillable—to change what happened in the past, for example. This is an excellent way to produce anger, anxiety, or depression, but is quite ineffective as a strategy for change.

There are problems that do not respond to direct applications of willpower—impotence, for example. When Stan tried to command an erection—clenching his fists, tightening his muscles, and saying to himself, "Come on baby, get it up"—he had no success. As we tense up, blood is drawn back to the heart, where it can be pumped to the muscles involved in voluntary activity. The blood comes from the involuntary parasympathetic nervous system, which controls areas like the stomach and the genitals. By misplacing his willpower, Stan wound up with hard muscles and soft genitals. He was powerless to will an erection.

You cannot will every change. You must turn to more effective change processes.

Substituting one bad behavior for another By mistreating themselves, people frequently wind up substituting one problem for another. This occurs most often with people who counter anxiety by taking a drink, thus transforming an anxiety problem into a drinking problem. People who use eating as a countering technique for smoking often end up with a weight problem when they quit smoking. And many people would rather return to smoking than face extra weight.

Although problem substitution does not occur automatically, it does occur frequently. Good countering and environment control techniques are essential during the action and maintenance stages in order to prevent it.

Be prepared for complications

It would be pleasant if change were so simple that you could work out each individual problem at your own pace. But change seldom involves only one problem at a time. Problems often coexist; changing one can exacerbate another.

The encouraging news is that our research shows that common problems have common solutions; the techniques may vary but the processes remain the same. The processes used to solve smoking problems can be used simultaneously to solve eating problems. The processes for coping with external social pressures can be applied to internal emotional pressures. If you have learned to use relaxation, exercise, assertion, and countering thoughts techniques, you are prepared to counter not only the temptation to relapse but also the emotional distress and social pressures that often accompany major change.

The path to change is rarely a straight one

Self-motivated behavior change follows a cyclical pattern similar to that of developmental change. For example, many young people in the United States leave home "permanently"—and return—an average of three times before they are truly ready to live on their own. They go off for a time to practice independence, then come back to the security of home. With the support of their families, they further prepare themselves to meet the challenges of adulthood. When they return home, all that was gained from their forays into the world is not lost; normal development means that they are not going in circles but, rather, progressing up the spiral staircase of change.

A lapse is not a relapse

If one swallow does not make a summer, one slip does not make a fall. In changing your problem behavior, you are likely to slip at times and lapse into old ways. A lapse does not mean that you have failed, or that a complete relapse is inevitable; you may still win the battle the next time around.

Many people do give up as soon as they lapse, because of how they view the event.* They have an almost religious belief that abstinence is an absolute state that can never be broken. If they lapse even once—by having a single cigarette, dessert, or drink—this means that they have fallen from grace. A corollary belief is that if abstinence is ever broken, willfully or not, the change attempt has been a total failure. Guilt and recrimination are then in order; any new change attempt must begin again at the start.

Guilt and self-blame are actually very ineffective change processes. They tend to cripple change efforts, not stimulate them. We regularly encounter clients whose guilt turns a lapse into a relapse. Darla sought psychotherapy for assistance with her weight problem and her resultant social isolation. She had repeated the identical diet cycle six or seven times without learning from her failures. She would take effective action for one or two weeks, then suffer a relapse brought on by binge eating junk food while watching television. After the first few cheese puffs, she told herself, "I've failed. It's hopeless. I'll never be able to lose weight. I might as well pig out now." Once Darla learned not to equate a lapse with a relapse, and to avoid "catastrophizing" her slip, she was able to resume dieting and exercising the next morning. Ultimately, she conquered her weight problem.

---

*Marlatt and Gordon term this phenomenon the Abstinence Violation Effect (AVE).

Every relapse begins with a slip. But it is foolish to give up hope after relapsing. We can recover from our slips, learn from them, and continue toward our goal of permanent change. Take lapses as signs that you must redouble your self-change efforts.

Mini-decisions lead to maxi-decisions

Few relapses are conscious. The stated intent of all changers is to take action and maintain their gains until they are free from their problem. But change teaches you how easy it is to fool yourself. You may make any number of what we call "mini-decisions" that ultimately have negative consequences.* We mentioned some of these earlier: deciding to keep some beer in the house in case company drops by; buying some of your favorite cookies for the kids; easing up on your exercise program because you feel so good.

Such mini-decisions can lead you to begin shifting direction away from maintenance and toward relapse. Before you know it, you may find you've gone back to your old ways, never having made a conscious maxi-decision to relapse.

Distress precipitates relapse

The most common cause of relapse is distress. Researchers consistently find that distress (including anger, anxiety, depression, loneliness, and other emotional problems) is involved in 60 to 70 percent of relapses in alcohol, drug, smoking, and eating problems.

What makes emotional distress such a high-risk factor in relapse? For one thing, you cannot avoid your emotions the way you can avoid bars, restaurants, and in-laws. Also, emotional distress weakens you psychologically, in much the same way a fever weakens you physically. During times

*Marlatt and Gordon call them Apparently Irrelevant Decisions.

of high distress, you are likely to regress to less mature and rational ways of thinking and behaving. Distressing emotions speak in an absolute language until you tell yourself that you must do whatever it takes to overcome them.

Few people have learned healthy ways of coping with intense feelings. As youngsters, many of us are taught to suppress our emotions in order to be considered "good" kids; we haven't had adequate opportunities at home, school, or work to learn to talk about our distressing feelings. The outcome is that, as adults, we cope with distress by having affairs, smoking, spending, eating, drinking, avoiding close relationships, or in other frequently unhealthy behaviors.

Social pressure is the other major cause of relapse. If your social network contains mainly people who share your problem, you are likely to experience intense pressures against changing. Self-changers threaten precontemplators who are not ready to confront their problematic behaviors. Change also threatens people who contemplate changing but have put it off.

During periods of active change, you may feel that you not only have to change yourself, but you must change your social network as well. And if your social network values the status quo, it may reject you for violating its rules. Conversely, if your friends, colleagues, and family value individual differences and personal growth, you are less likely to feel pressure to stay the same; in fact, you may count these people among your helping relationships.

Since distress and social pressure trigger the vast majority of relapses, it is important for you to include coping with these formidable forces when you create your action plan. This is especially true if you are in a cycle of change where you have already suffered a lapse due to distress or social pressure. Your plan should include a judicious mixture of relaxation, exercise, assertion, and countering techniques.

You may find some old friends are stubbornly unsupportive; if so, your plan might include steering clear of certain social groups, and making new friends.

Learning translates into action

It won't do you much good to have excellent ideas if you don't put them to work. As someone once said, "Good ideas eventually deteriorate into hard work." If you think about what you have been learning without acting on it, you are in danger of becoming a chronic contemplator. One of the crucial lessons we have learned is that far too many people get stuck in the contemplation stage. The strength of re-lapsers is that they usually are willing to risk taking action again in the near future; their initial action gives them strength and courage.

Have you learned from relapse, and used your experience to prepare you for later success? Are you ready to base your next action attempt on informed change principles? You can find out the answers to these questions by responding to the following simple self-assessment:

- Have you identified the major causes of your previous relapse(s)?
- Do you have specific, action-oriented processes to counter the situations and emotions that induced your relapse?
- Are you more informed about the cycle of change and how it relates specifically to your problem?
- Can you tolerate a slip (lapse) without a total fall (relapse)?
- Are you planning to make change one of your highest priorities for the next three to six months?
- Have you prepared yourself for the possibility of complications and for more than one change at a time?
- Can you put your newfound learning into action?

If you can honestly answer yes to all of the above, you are well prepared to recycle through the action and maintenance stages. However, if one or more of your responses is no, you may not be ready for renewed action quite yet. Instead of despairing or becoming apathetic, recognize that you have more to learn. Draw energy from the knowledge that you have not yet given the problem your best effort. A more active and informed change attempt awaits you.

SEEKING PROFESSIONAL HELP

After a number of relapses, or a particularly distressing one, you may decide that self-change is not working for you and consider turning to professional help. This section will help you determine what sort of help to seek.

Increasingly, Americans are availing themselves of mental health services at a rate that has more than doubled over the past generation. In 1957, approximately 14 percent of American adults had sought professional help for mental health problems sometime during their lives.[*] By 1976, this number had risen to 26 percent,[†] and current estimates place it higher still. But even with this dramatic increase in mental health treatment, the fact remains that the vast majority of people still grapple with their problems on their own. We have begun to treat our emotional well-being with respect, and to recognize the transformational power of psychotherapy in our lives. Yet, there is a stigma attached to psychotherapy, based on some persistent myths:

"You have to be crazy to see a shrink."   The majority of psychotherapy clients suffer from depression, anxiety, and in-

[*]Gurin et al., 1960.
[†]Veroff et al., 1981

terpersonal problems. Sound familiar? Marital problems
and work conflicts are two primary reasons for seeking help,
and surely these do not make a person "crazy." A good
argument can be made for the reverse. If you suffer from a
pressing and continuing problem even after you have made
sincere attempts to change, then perhaps you have to be
crazy *not* to seek help.

"All psychiatric patients are hospitalized." This was the case
up until the 1950s. Nowadays, however, fewer than 20 percent of people with mental disorders ever require hospitalization.

"If not hospitalized, I'll be in psychotherapy for years." This is
possible but not probable. The average number of visits to
a psychotherapist ranges from three (public clinics) to four-
teen (private offices). Most psychotherapy treatment tends
to be brief, pragmatic, and problem-oriented. Intensive,
long-term psychotherapy is the exception rather than the
rule.

Knowing what to do

The question remains: How do you know when you need
professional help? We have found five factors that distinguish people who rely on self-change alone from those who
try psychotherapy after unsuccessful attempts at self-
change.

Ineffective self-change Many people seek professional help
when their self-change efforts are not effective. In studies
of college students' use of psychological services, for instance, it was discovered that most students decided to enter
psychotherapy only after trying unsuccessfully to cope with
the problem alone or with the help of a close friend or relative. Our own research has found that psychotherapists

give the same reason for their entering therapy.

Although we encourage relapsers to learn from their setbacks and to prepare to recycle through the stages of change, there are times when self-change is insufficient or when people become stuck or frustrated. Few self-change efforts are "wasted." At the least, most reduce the severity of the problem and assist therapists in understanding what has been accomplished and what remains to be tackled.

Long-term problems If your problem persists indefinitely despite your efforts, it might be time for professional help.

Recurring problems All changers require helping relationships. If your emotional distress has been prolonged or severe, you may profit from enlisting a professional helper. Many problems, such as weight management and emotional distress, are lifetime challenges rather than short-term difficulties. Some people find themselves recycling through the same problem month after month, year after year, never learning more about the process or improving their chances at success.

The key question then becomes: How many times should you recycle through a problem without improvement before seeking professional assistance? There is, of course, no single answer to this question. This self-assessment, however, can help you address it yourself. Answer yes or no to the following questions:

- Do you feel you have given self-change your best effort?
- Have you tried to learn from your previous self-change efforts?
- Is your problem important enough for you to seek professional help?

If your honest answer to all these questions is yes, you should seriously consider professional assistance. If, like many people, you respond to the first two questions with a begrudging no, then you should consider a more serious, sophisticated self-change attempt, following the guidelines in this book.

Negative coping Strategies of negative coping—especially wishful thinking and self-blame—make it much more difficult to change, and our research has found that people who use these strategies excessively often seek psychotherapy. Wishing a problem would change by itself instead of actively taking charge of it leads to prolonged contemplation and inactivity. Intense self-denunciation may paralyze your adaptive resources and add distress to your original problem.

No helping relationships Professional assistance is especially valuable if there are few helping relationships in your life. Few of us have as many satisfying relationships as we would like, but most of us receive enough support to go on about our lives. Others do not have supportive friends and family, or are involved in relationships that when it comes to change are unsupportive or even downright hostile.

This is where psychotherapy can be extremely helpful. After all, it is basically an interpersonal, helping relationship. Many prospective clients enter treatment yearning for technical expertise—information, methods, and guidance. But the most highly rated curative factor in psychotherapy is the therapeutic relationship, a natural and effective remedy for a scarcity of supportive friends and family.

The "Three Unables"

There are inherent limitations in self-change books, including this one, about which you should be aware when considering professional help. We call these limitations the "Three Unables":

Unable to understand   No matter how clearly we present the stages and processes of change, and how they can be used by self-changers, some people will distort or misunderstand that information. In a minority of cases this is due to intellectual, visual, or memory limitations, but most usually, it results from selective perception. Most people understand what they want to understand and vice versa. Professionals can help remove these perceptual blinders, although unfortunately you might not be aware of having them.

Unable to apply   The interpersonal nature of psychotherapy virtually guarantees an ongoing check on whether the message is being understood and applied. No self-change book can accomplish this. Although we have made every effort to make our guidelines broad enough to apply to all self-change situations, while making them specific to the most common problems, it is possible that you can come away with a conceptual understanding that is not the same as an ability to apply the information in a practical fashion. Your individual difficulties may require more detail and assistance than a book intended for thousands of people can provide. Under these circumstances, psychotherapy is a good option. Be honest with yourself, though. "This self-change stuff sounds great, but it'll never work for me" is an all too frequent rationalization.

Unable to comply   Perhaps you understand our self-change methods, and even begin to apply them tentatively. But then, as quickly as you began, you stop. You have achieved awareness but have problems with action. As you know, awareness is only the beginning of change, not the end point. If insight was all it took to change, there would be fewer cases of obesity, anxiety, and other maladaptive behaviors. It is not easy to translate awareness into sustained action. Psychotherapy has the advantage of repetitive and monitored practice. You are provided with a guide who can restate points, repeat methods, and personally shepherd you through action.

If you have decided to change, and none of the exceptions noted in Chapter 3 apply to you, consider first the sophisticated self-change methods described in this chapter. If, however, you honestly believe that self-change alone is insufficient, then it is would be wise to supplement it with professional treatment.

WHERE TO SEEK HELP

After having decided to consult a professional, how do you find the one that is best for you? The advice you receive from friends will probably be vocal and conflicting: "See Dr. X, he's the best!" "Anyone but Dr. X; I've heard bad things about him." "I think you need an experienced female counselor." "I'd only go to a psychologist [or psychiatrist or social worker]." And so on.

In order to rank the importance of sixteen factors in choosing a therapist, we asked more than five hundred psychologists, psychiatrists, and social workers what criteria they followed when they chose a therapist. We found that among the most important factors were:

- Competence
- Clinical experience
- Professional reputation
- Warmth and caring
- Openness

The five least important were:

- Specific profession
- Being outside of the client's social network
- Success with similar patients
- Cost per session
- Research productivity

For us, a therapist's clinical expertise and interpersonal skills are the two most important factors. Keep these two characteristics foremost in your mind when searching for a psychotherapist. Although cost per session was not judged to be a decisive factor by psychotherapists entering therapy, this was probably due in part to their relatively high incomes. Your budget may be much tighter. However, health insurance covers at least half the cost of therapy for many people, and a majority of therapists use a sliding scale to benefit less affluent clients.

We agree that the specific profession of the psychotherapist should not be a major influence in deciding where to seek treatment. Be careful of people who claim to be a "counselor" or "psychotherapist"; in most states, anyone can call himself or herself counselor or psychotherapist (neither is a legally protected title). In contrast, clinical psychologists, psychiatrists, clinical social workers, and psychiatric nurses are all licensed practitioners. Yet, there are considerable differences among them.

Psychologists generally have had the most formal psychotherapy training, have doctoral degrees in clinical or counseling psychology, and have spent one or two years as interns. They alone provide psychological assessment and testing. Look for a psychologist who has a doctorate in psychology, not in a "related" field.

Psychiatrists are physicians with residencies in psychiatry. They alone may prescribe medication and, compared with other mental health professionals, specialize in organic and biological treatments. Look for a psychiatrist who has completed a psychiatric residency and is board certified; ap-

proximately half of those listing themselves as psychiatrists
do not have this certification.

Clinical social workers typically have a master's degree in
social work or social sciences, followed by two years of full-
time, supervised experience leading to inclusion in the
Academy of Certified Social Workers (ACSW). Clinical social workers offer psychotherapy and, compared with other
mental health professionals, are specialists in community
work. Look for a social worker who was extensively trained
in psychotherapy, not in social services or administration.

Psychiatric nurses are registered nurses (R.N.s) who have
obtained a master's of science degree in nursing (M.S.N.).
Psychiatric nurses practice psychotherapy and have the advantage of offering an integrated medical-psychological
model of practice. Look for a psychiatric nurse who spe-
cializes in psychotherapy, rather than one who operates as
an administrative aide.

What about theoretical orientation—the conceptual approach that the clinician uses to formulate cases and pri-
oritize therapeutic methods—which those we surveyed
believed to be of moderate importance? Today, the most
popular theory is eclectic, or integrative, combining a number of diverse approaches to fit the needs of the particular
client. Integrative theories are followed in popularity by
psychodynamic, cognitive, behavioral, humanistic, and sys-
tems/family approaches. We recommend two routes to get
through this psychotherapeutic maze.

Since different therapies emphasize different processes of
change, your first option is to find a psychotherapist with
an orientation that matches your stage of change. Self-
reevaluation and consciousness-raising, instrumental
during contemplation, are most frequently used by psychodynamic, psychoanalytic, and humanistic-existential
therapists. Once into the action stage, where countering,
control, and reward are very important, you might be most

comfortable with a cognitive, behavioral, or systems therapist.

The second option is to select an integrative psychotherapist who can guide you through all of the stages of change,
helping you choose the right processes for each one.

Take the case of Arthur, who consulted John Norcross,
complaining of depression. Arthur's wife was responsible
for the appointment; Arthur, quite reluctantly, "came along
for the ride"—a typical precontemplator. However, with
the supportive urging of his wife, children, and psychologist, Arthur began to recognize the existence of his depression and the negative impact it had on himself and his
family. During this early contemplation stage, John joined
with Arthur's family in repeatedly stressing his choices as
well as the benefits of elevating his mood. After five or six
sessions, Arthur began to initiate antidepressive behaviors.

Eight or nine weeks into treatment, Arthur made the
decision to enter the action stage. He started exercising,
socializing on a regular basis, and countering his self-
defeating thoughts. At three months, Arthur's mood was
improved and his marital relationship was revitalized. He
and his wife began to wonder how these gains could be
consolidated and maintained over time, a sure tip-off that
Arthur was about to enter the maintenance stage. Eager
and motivated to institute long-term changes in their lifestyles, Arthur and his family have maintained improvement for several years now.

Arthur's progress was swift and sure, in part at least because of John's willingness to follow his client's stage of
change. If Arthur had chosen a therapist who was determined to explore interminably the impact of his client's
childhood upon his current depression, Arthur's self-
described "action program" would have been stalled. If the
therapist had pushed Arthur into specific behavioral tasks
at the beginning of treatment, the client, by his own ad-

mission, would not have returned for his next session. By using the processes drawn from multiple theories at the right time, John successfully led Arthur through the stages of change.

How can you avoid therapists who will take you in unsuitable directions? How can you find one who will suit the treatment to you and not try to fit you into a predetermined mold? By assertively asking friends, workmates, physicians, clergy, school personnel, and mental health professionals. Ask as many people as you can so as to receive a balance of opinions. Once you have narrowed the field to two or three choices, arrange for a single appointment with each therapist. It is our conviction—and clinical experience bears this out—that most psychotherapists welcome assertive and well-informed consumers.

CHAPTER 10

A Changer's Manual

BECAUSE OUR MODEL of the stages of change applies to a wide range of problematic behaviors, we have provided examples of a variety of self-change experiences. Individuals and health professionals alike should understand that our model has proven to be effective with every behavior we have studied thus far, not simply with one or two specific problems. Still, there is a virtue in examining in detail how to change a few of the more common problems.

In this chapter, we track what you need to do to overcome three specific problems—smoking, drinking, and psychological distress. Even if you do not have any of these problems, read on. This chapter describes in some depth the methods for applying many of the theoretical principles we have discussed earlier. While some approaches are specific to a given problem, many of them can be generalized to your own behaviors. And although this chapter is designed as supplemental guides for those who wish to overcome one or another of these three problems, we recommend that you read the rest of the book to help you prepare for successful termination.

SMOKING—THE NUMBER ONE
HEALTH PROBLEM

If you want to quit smoking, you are not alone. Smoking is the world's most prevalent and recognizable health risk and modifiable behavior problem. Thirty million Americans have quit smoking since the first Surgeon General's report appeared in 1969, but fifty million are still smoking today. If you are among them, you have undoubtedly thought about quitting and probably tried to. You bought this book out of frustration, out of desire, and out of a willingness to change—and you want to know what to do.

We will hit you with the hard facts in a moment. These provide the most useful information available to move you through the stages of change and quit smoking once and for all. If you can resist running from the facts, and can effectively implement our recommendations, your chances of defeating humankind's deadliest habit will be greatly increased.

Until recently, smoking was so acceptable that, with the exception of adolescents, everyone knew who smoked and who didn't. In contrast, many smokers now hide their addiction—from their loved ones and even themselves—just as troubled drinkers do. Increasingly, we see spouses who don't know that their partners smoke; young and adult children who don't know that their parents smoke; and friends and co-workers who don't know about their colleagues' smoking habits.

Many smokers deny their habit to themselves. Many minimize not only the threats that smoking poses to their health, but the actual amount they smoke; some even deny that they are smokers. But you are a smoker if you have smoked at least one hundred times in your lifetime and if you smoke regularly, even monthly, now. If you typically smoke your first cigarette within thirty minutes of awakening, or if you smoke twenty or more cigarettes a day, you are addicted to nicotine.

Stage of change self-assessment

This self-assessment establishes your stage of change in the struggle to quit smoking. The more work you have already accomplished, the better your chances for success in the near future. Success will also depend on how conscientiously you apply the processes of change as you move through the stages. Give honest answers to the following questions:

1. Do you seriously intend to quit smoking in the next six months?
2. Do you plan to quit in the next thirty days?

You can determine your stage by the combination of answers you gave to these two questions (see chart).

Question 1	No	Yes	Yes
Question 2	No	No	Yes
Your Stage	Precontemplation	Contemplation	Preparation

If you quit smoking within the past six months, you are in the action stage. If you quit smoking more than six months ago and are still tempted to smoke, even occasionally, you are in the maintenance stage. If you quit, and are free of the temptation to smoke, congratulations.

The remainder of this section concerns the change processes, described earlier, that can help you quit smoking.

Precontemplation

Precontemplators rely heavily upon minimization and rationalization, both of which must be countered by con-

TABLE 11. CHRONIC DISEASES ASSOCIATED WITH TOBACCO USE

1. Lung cancer	10. Coronary heart disease
2. Cancer of the mouth	11. Stroke
3. Cancer of the esophagus	12. Atherosclerosis of peripheral vessels
4. Cancer of the larynx	13. Atherosclerotic aortic aneurysm
5. Bladder cancer	14. Emphysema
6. Kidney cancer	15. Chronic bronchitis
7. Cancer of the pancreas	16. Other chronic obstructive pulmonary diseases
8. Cancer of the cervix	17. Low-birthweight babies
9. Peptic ulcer	18. Facial wrinkles

sciousness-raising. Rationalization provides smokers with various and spurious "good" reasons for continuing their habit. Minimization similarly allows smokers to discount the overwhelming evidence that smoking is a destructive habit.

Table 11 lists some of the diseases and disorders caused by tobacco use. Smoking increases your level of risk for most of the major killers of our time. The good news is that, as a former smoker, you will dramatically decrease your level of risk for almost all of the same problems.

Most people cannot name even ten of the above diseases that result directly from smoking. That is because in this country, despite the well-intended but underfunded attempts of public health officials, the majority of "information" available about tobacco comes from advertising. And of course corporate ads feed fantasy rather than reality. In Australia, highway billboards spell out the facts: More people will die from smoking this year than from automobile accidents, homicides, suicides, and AIDS combined. What is true in Australia is true here.

Information about the disease-causing aspects of smoking will make it tougher to minimize the effects of your habit, but if you are like most smokers, you can still rationalize your addiction. You can tell yourself that by the time you develop lung cancer or emphysema, there will undoubtedly be cures for them. The fact is that scientists have already discovered a cure for most lung cancer and emphysema—quitting smoking.

You may say, "We all have to die from something—why not smoking?" Smoking not only causes death, it causes premature death. Tobacco use is presently the single most preventable cause of disease and premature death in the world. Of all the people alive today, five hundred million will die as a result of using tobacco, and half this number will die well before their natural time, losing an average of twenty years of life. If you consider this unequivocal evidence, you must seriously contemplate quitting.

It is important that you allow yourself to become emotional as you progress through the precontemplation stage. The chilling fact that almost one in ten of the world's citizens will die before his or her time as a result of tobacco addiction *should* arouse feelings. We should get angry at an industry that glamorizes carcinogens and other disease-causing chemicals, and makes literally billions of dollars doing so. Cigarette manufacturers have been rightly called merchants of death.

After emotion, an inclination to blame yourself may follow. I've heard many clients say, "I never should have started in the first place." Remember, virtually no one who is fully adult chooses to start smoking. You were seduced into the habit as a teenager or as a young adult. You wanted to look older; you wanted to be a sophisticated woman or an attractive, rugged man. You were led to associate cigarettes with socializing, fun, coolness, calmness, and sexual attractiveness. Now, five, ten, twenty or more years later, as a result of smoking, you are likely to look older than average, not sexier. Your risk of all the diseases listed in the chart is greater than if you had never smoked (and greater than it will be a year from now if you stop).

Social liberation can also help you make the commitment

to quit. Society is intent on making it much easier for individuals to be free from cigarette smoke—their own and
other people's. The Environmental Protection Agency has
ruled that secondary smoke is a Class A carcinogen, and the
rights of everyone to be free from this smoke are going to
increase as the years go by. Smoking will be banned in more
and more work areas and public places, and liability insurance rates will rise for employers and owners who do not
cooperate with regulations.

How will this affect you as a smoker? The longer you
remain in the precontemplation stage, the more hassles and
pressures you will experience. You can fight the forces of
social liberation, or you can let them free you from smoking.

Remember to ask who is on your side before you scoff at
external pressure; the answers are not so simple. Whose
side are medical societies on when they support smoke-free
public and workplaces? Whose side are the tobacco companies on when they spend tens of millions of dollars to
fight policies designed to free nonsmokers and those who
struggle to become former smokers?

If you could help other people not to smoke, would you
use that power? If you were fully free of your dependence,
would you rather support the American Cancer Society or
the American tobacco industry? Would you rather be part
of a social movement to prevent unnecessary death and disease, or support tobacco industries that profit at the expense
of the world's health? Use your answers to these questions
to help move yourself into the contemplation stage.

Contemplation

Outside influences will not *make* you quit smoking. But
they can *help* you quit smoking, if you allow them to. If you
have begun to drop your defenses and have lowered your
resistance, you are beginning to be guided by knowledge,

influenced by facts, and moved by emotional and social forces into contemplation.

Next, you must become more aware of the ABC's—Antecedents, Behaviors, and Consequences—of your habit. What makes you smoke? What does it do for you? What are the results of all the cigarettes you smoke each week?

Typical reasons people give for smoking include:

- To cope with stress
- To cope with emotions (anger, anxiety, boredom, or depression)
- To cope with social situations
- To enhance an image
- To reduce nicotine craving
- To satisfy a long-standing habit

Monitor your smoking for just a couple of days. You will become aware of how often you smoke for each of these reasons. Just monitoring your habit helps to raise your consciousness. It makes you ask yourself, "Why?" each time you light up; it identifies which cigarettes you smoke out of sheer habit, which will be the first you give up once you enter the preparation stage; and it will increase your awareness of the conditions you will need to counter when you take action.

Once the social, emotional, and informational forces are flowing favorably, you will find that you are reevaluating yourself. If you take a look at the real reasons why you smoke, it becomes difficult to view yourself as a rational smoker. You may become upset or even disgusted for continuing to smoke.

Eventually, you will reject the image of the sophisticated smoker, let go of the media-induced image that puts smokers in the social spotlight. You will become aware that smokers are now regarded as not very smart, not socially acceptable, and not glamorous.

As you reevaluate your self-image, you become freer to create a new persona. Imagine how you will feel when you are no longer a smoker, free from the fear you are causing your own death and disease, free from being hooked on a poisonous substance, free from pressures not to smoke in public places, and free from smelly cigarette butts, bad breath, burned clothing, dead taste buds, and stained teeth and fingers. Visualize the tremendous sense of accomplishment you will have in overcoming one of the toughest addictions in the world.

Preparation

In the preparation stage, continue to draw on what you have gained from the two earlier stages. When you are ready to make the commitment to quit, throw your whole self into the process. Rely on your rational side, which is now acutely conscious of the dire consequences of smoking. Allow your emotions to prevail; think perhaps of someone you know who has suffered from emphysema or other disease caused by smoking. At this stage, you can be encouraged by your evaluative skills, which will provide you with a commitment to healthier values for your future life. And you can join with your social self in identifying with those forces that are trying to persuade you to become free of smoking.

You also will need to rely on the responsible part of you that makes commitments, for becoming the kind of person you want to be. It's not necessary to take responsibility for having been a smoker; that decision perhaps was made in adolescence. Now that you are an adult, you must take responsibility for becoming a former smoker.

You don't have to do it alone; in fact, you shouldn't. Let your interpersonal self accept the social support that comes from helping relationships. Go public with your commitment to quit and announce to others that you are going to take action and would like their help.

Tell your family, friends, and colleagues that you are planning life-saving psychic surgery and will not be your usual self for a while. Tell them that, like all major surgeries, the process may be painful and distressing, and may not even be successful, but that the chances of success will be greatly increased if they support you. Make sure, too, that they understand that your recovery will be measured in weeks or months rather than in days. As time goes on, you will need their support less frequently, but that support will remain a critical part of your recovery.

If you don't have helping relationships, join a self-help group. Call your state or local lung association or cancer society to find out about appropriate groups in your area.

Action

As you get ready for action, prepare to counter the conditioning that currently controls your cigarette consumption. Especially in the short run, these conditions include the intense urges you may experience as you withdraw from nicotine. You can counter these urges by chewing sugarless gum, taking deep relaxing breaths, and reminding yourself that urges are like waves in the ocean—they peak quickly and then subside.

If you are highly addicted to cigarettes, and have never been able to quit for more than a few days, a nicotine patch or nicotine gum can satisfy your physical cravings. Just remember that nicotine replacements are not a long-term solution. They are effective with highly addicted smokers only when they are part of a more comprehensive approach to behavior change.

If smoking has helped you cope with stress, you will need to rely heavily on healthy substitute behaviors, especially relaxation and exercise. If you have used cigarettes to cope with distressing feelings, you will have to assert yourself and express your feelings verbally in order to manage your emotions.

In the past you were reinforced countless times for smoking. Now you need to reward yourself frequently for not smoking. Covert or silent praise is often sufficient, although it can be satisfying to receive public acknowledgment of what you have accomplished. Don't fall into the trap of rewarding yourself with sweets, alcohol, or other unnecessary substances—there's no reason to substitute a new problem for the old. But do give yourself appropriate rewards. Many people use the money they save by not smoking to buy themselves some long-desired present.

Maintenance

You may slip, take one cigarette or more, and find you are back in situations associated with smoking. If so, you must take action quickly. It is much easier to prevent a single lapse from becoming a relapse than it is to recycle through all the stages of change. You have made it this far: Commit yourself to limiting a lapse to a slip, rather than giving up and allowing it to become a relapse.

Think about your ABC's, and examine why you are craving a cigarette. Review the long-term benefits of becoming a nonsmoker and the long-term hazards of relapsing. Renew your commitment to throw your whole self into action. If at all possible, get rid of those stimuli that are tempting you to smoke, even if it means avoiding your friends for a while. Rely on the most powerful countering controls you have to get you through this trying time.

Reach out to others you trust. Don't keep your lapse a secret; share it so that others can give you a helping hand. But be selective about whom you share your lapses with, especially since you will be feeling so vulnerable. Tell friends or relatives who are fully aware of your struggles, who sympathize and are likely to help you back to a positive course.

Remember, as you counter internal and external temptations to smoke, you strengthen your sense of self-efficacy, not only to cope with quitting smoking, but to change yourself into the kind of person you want to be.

ALCOHOL—PRECONTEMPLATIVE HELL

The fact that alcohol is legal makes it no less potent or dangerous than many illicit drugs. Seventeen million Americans either abuse alcohol or are dependent upon it. As many as 50 percent of all emergency room admissions are alcohol-related, as are one hundred thousand deaths each year. Problems caused by alcohol cost this country $136 billion yearly in lost productivity, accidents, health care, and court and criminal justice system expenses. Problems related to alcohol affect one of every four American families.

These figures are staggering. Yet few people admit to having problems with alcohol. You may have heard excuses like these:

> I have no such problem. Yes, I drink, but it isn't a problem for me or my family; my drinking in under control. The way I drink, it could never become a problem, even if I get soused every once in a while. Anyway, most of my friends drink in the same way—we couldn't all have problems! And talk about problems! My dad had a real problem with alcohol, and I promised myself that I would never become like that.

Such statements are typical of individuals with drinking problems who are in the precontemplation stage of change. And there are a lot of precontemplative drinkers. Although now there is a stigma associated with smoking where one didn't exist before, moderate drinking remains an integral part of our society. From the wedding toast to the dinner party, liquor consumption is not only accepted but encouraged. This is not a threat to moderate drinkers, but it may be to you. Because national attitudes toward drinking are not clear-cut, few problems are as difficult to own up to as alcohol abuse.

Part of this is due to a lack of education. You have probably heard, or perhaps have made, one or more of the following statements:

- I only drink beer; you can't become an alcoholic by drinking beer.
- One sure sign of alcoholism is early-morning drinking, and I never drink before noon.
- I only drink with meals; you can't get intoxicated if you eat while you drink.
- I always have a cup of coffee before I drive home from a party so I'm not intoxicated.
- Having two or three drinks after work doesn't pose any problems. The attitude-adjustment hour at the local bar is just what I need to handle the stress of my work.
- I only drink at home, so I won't get into trouble with alcohol.

Some of these statements are completely false; others contain half-truths. All protect the drinking habit, and make it difficult or impossible to recognize the problem. Alcoholism is often called the disease of denial, and indeed denial is a major aspect of the precontemplation stage in which drinkers so often remain.

Precontemplation

There are many reasons to use alcohol. Its sedative effect leads to pleasant physical reactions, reducing arousal and influencing thinking and feeling. For many, the effects are so powerful that they cannot find anything wrong with their drinking: "It can't be bad for me if it feels so good."

Alcohol, if ingested frequently enough and in sufficient

quantity, creates a physical addiction. Once addicted to alcohol, you suffer harsh withdrawal effects when you stop drinking. The physical addiction is abetted by psychological dependence. People rely on alcohol to cope with anxiety or act as a "social lubricant." Physical addiction, psychological dependency, and conditioning effects—"Five o'clock, time for a drink"—create a steady, secure habit of alcohol consumption.

When there are such positive reasons to drink, and so many negative aspects to quitting, it is difficult for most people to admit, or even recognize, that they have a problem. The result for them is a lifetime of precontemplation.

There are ways to break through, however. It always helps to ask someone else for feedback. This is not always easy. First of all, the question is a difficult and potentially embarrassing one. Second, how others evaluate your alcohol consumption depends greatly on their own consumption levels. Heavy drinkers tend to keep company with other heavy drinkers; most teetotalers are uncomfortable with any level of drinking.

What can you do to evaluate accurately whether you have a problem? As with any self-change strategy, it's best to begin with awareness and consciousness-raising. Start keeping a record of the amount you drink, not just individual drinks, since they can vary in size and in alcohol content. Twelve ounces of beer, four ounces of wine, and an ounce and a half (a shot) of 80-proof spirits all contain the same amount of ethanol; a double therefore counts as two drinks, and a pint of beer as one and a half. Don't let the numbers or types of alcoholic beverages deceive you. Also, don't overestimate the buffering effect your body weight has, or how slowly it takes you to down your drinks.

Then take a look at the problems caused by your drinking—for you or others. They are the surest indicators of abuse. To do this effectively, you must be honest and persistent, persistently exploring the possibilities and asking questions. For instance, most drinkers claim not to experience withdrawal symptoms. However, there are many stages of withdrawal that fall short of the DTs (delirium tremens), the worst case. Hangovers, even mild ones, are a form of withdrawal (which is why "the hair of the dog" works so well), as are memory loss and blackouts. Answer these questions:

- Do you have frequent morning-after headaches, nausea, and cotton mouth?
- Have you experienced blackouts?
- Have you forgotten how you got home from a party, dinner, or bar?
- Has your drinking caused you any social embarrassment?
- Do you come home later than expected because of drinking?
- Do you argue with your spouse when you drink?
- Do you argue about drinking?
- Has your work suffered, or have you been late or absent frequently?

Be honest when answering these questions. A hangover is the consequence of drinking; calling in sick after a night out is an indication that drinking is affecting your work.

Being stopped by the police and charged with DUI (driving under the influence) or DWI (driving while intoxicated) is a sure sign that you have an alcohol problem. Many people drink and drive without being apprehended, so they continue to believe that their drinking practices are safe, and that they have committed no crime. Answer these questions:

- Do you drive after a party where you drank heavily?
- Do you have a few drinks before going out on a date or to a party?

• Do you use a designated driver when you go out drinking with friends?

Examine your own view of alcohol's impact on our society. Do you tend to downplay its role in family violence and abuse, in sexually transmitted diseases and lost productivity, in auto and household accidents? Finally, take a look at the role alcohol plays in your life. Can you imagine your life without it? Could you go to a party or a bar and order juice? Does the image of a can of beer or a mixed drink appear whenever you imagine yourself relaxing or having fun? If so, drinking may be an integral part of your self-image.

Even when confronted with strong evidence, many problem drinkers remain evasive. If you are not sure if you are a problem drinker, but suspect that you may be, you may choose to consult a professional for objective feedback. Many employee assistance programs offer a confidential two- or three-session evaluation; the evaluator may refer you to a different program if you have a problem that requires extensive treatment.

Shorter evaluations exist as well. At the University of Houston's psychology clinic, for example, a program called Drinker Checkup offers a two-hour assessment. Quick checks such as these, which offer written and verbal feedback about drinking levels, patterns, benefits, and problems, are becoming increasingly available.

You must be careful when you seek professional help. Some programs offer feedback simply as a way to drum up business. And certain addiction specialists believe that your concern about your drinking is prima facie evidence. The fact that you have showed up is enough for them to diagnose a drinking problem. Investigate the evaluator before making an appointment.

If you candidly and honestly answered the questions on the previous pages, or if you have seen a professional evaluator, you know if you have a problem with alcohol and that awareness is not enough. The challenge is in making the decision to change.

Contemplation

The decision to change drinking behavior is difficult. In addition to the formidable physical challenge of quitting, there are countless emotional difficulties that make this decision a frightening one. When you decide to tackle your problem drinking, there will be no choice except to go public, since everyone who knows you will become aware of it. If you used alcohol as a social stimulant, you will have trouble socializing; if drinking was your way of letting off steam, you will be uptight. Many people never change their drinking patterns because they believe they will have to give up too much.

Even your spouse may not encourage you. One woman, who was genuinely upset about her husband's drinking binges, declared that she really hoped he was not an alcoholic who had to quit drinking. The effect on their social life, she felt, would be chilling.

Many problem drinkers decide that their problem is not so bad, and can be solved with minor behavioral adjustments or a little self-control. In some cases, this is possible. Perhaps a minor change in your drinking habits is all you need. Or perhaps that would be the equivalent of trying to change you car tires with a pair of needle-nose pliers.

Fierce debates rage throughout the professional community over the appropriate goal for people with drinking problems. In general, therapists view abstinence as the best and safest goal for individuals considered to be "alcoholic" or "alcohol dependent." Restraint and self-control are looked upon as responsible goals for "alcohol abusers" or "problem drinkers." The problem, of course, is in how you define who is "alcohol dependent" and who is an "alcohol abuser."

We believe the argument is moot. No one is diagnosed as alcohol dependent until they have tried to use restraint to solve their drinking problem. This is a key dimension of the definition of dependence: The individual drinks more than intended or has tried, unsuccessfully, to stop. Once restraint has been eliminated as a possibility, abstinence is the logical goal. In many ways, it is easier to achieve success at abstinence than restraint. Once you have started drinking, it begins to affect the evaluation and judgment centers of the brain, and it becomes more difficult to maintain your commitment to moderation.

Preparation

Whether your goal is restraint or abstinence, you must first develop a realistic plan and make a firm commitment to follow through on it. The secret is not simply to work harder but to work smarter to implement the plan. Seize upon an opportunity—a particularly embarrassing or inspirational event—to gain extra motivation. Listen to the frequent, forceful verbal commitments you are making, and gird them with a continuing commitment and a solid time frame for action.

Action means stopping some behaviors and beginning others; in the beginning, for days and even weeks, not drinking is the central focus. This may seem obvious, but to succeed in this abstinence (or restraint, if you choose that path), you must develop "behavioral refusal skills" the skill to refuse offers and pressures to drink, the skill to order nonalcoholic beverages, the skill to know when the urge to drink nearly overwhelms you, and the skill to avoid or walk away from tempting situations.

A good action plan starts with environment and stimulus control. Limit availability of alcohol, avoid places where drinking is encouraged, shun contact with other drinkers. If alleviating frustration and controlling anger have been important reasons for drinking, relaxation is an important countering method. Physical exercise and assertiveness training are also beneficial, as are anger management techniques. Seek solutions to depression and anxiety problems, and work to create healthier personal relationships and a positive lifestyle. All of these techniques are needed to avoid becoming what A.A. members call a "dry drunk," someone who is not drinking but who has not changed his or her lifestyle.

Maintenance

As you move from action into maintenance, remember that a lapse is not a relapse. You can eat one potato chip without finishing the bag; you can have one drink without reneging on your total commitment. Don't assume that taking a single drink means that you have lost control—unless you give up and give in. A relapse means a full-fledged return to your old pattern of drinking, not one evening's slip-up.

Rather than undermining your self-confidence with multiple slips and self-defeating statements, reward yourself regularly. Give yourself credit each time you encounter a situation in which you used to drink but avoid it now. Your family and friends will take your abstinence for granted quite rapidly, and their praise will die down long before the struggle is over. For this reason, it becomes even more important to keep giving yourself positive reinforcement, both in words and deeds.

A big challenge is in the long haul. Many individuals find that they must recycle through the stages several times before they are successful in controlling their drinking. You must employ active change strategies over months and years in order to achieve long-term sobriety or nonproblematic drinking.

Remain active and vigilant during maintenance, and continue to use your refusal skills. Do not become overconfident. A big danger sometimes lies in the belief that you are free to return to risky situations. Keep reviewing the reasons you have for not drinking, and stay alert for signs of trouble—increasingly frequent urges or temptations to drink, returning to the old haunts, and generally putting yourself in harm's way.

You may be acutely aware of the difficulties and sacrifices you have made by giving up drinking; now make an effort to focus on the long-term benefits. Your liver, central nervous system, and overall well-being will improve dramatically; your family's lives will improve as well.

The road from precontemplation to maintenance is filled with problems and possibilities. Alcohol is an addictive substance, and giving it up requires courage, patience, and persistence. To be successful, take each stage a step at a time; work hard to overcome urges; have the courage to make a commitment and follow through on your decision; show persistence in taking action; and learn to navigate the cycle of change. Many others affected with alcohol problems have been able to gain safe passage.

DISTRESS—THE FEVER OF MENTAL HEALTH

If you suffer from psychological or emotional distress, rest assured that you are not alone. Distress is the country's most prevalent and recognizable psychological problem. According to the 1978 President's Commission on Mental Health, distress affects as much as one quarter of the adult population at any given time. A national household survey found that a third of all women and nearly a fifth of all men admitted to being troubled by distress in the previous year.* Because it is so common but does not localize the disorder, psychological distress is known as the fever of mental health.

The vast majority of distressed people confront their prob-

*Mellinger et al., 1978.

lems without professional treatment. They overcome the problem by themselves or with the help of friends, family, clergy, or others. Although most individuals eventually overcome their distress, they do not do so as quickly or efficiently as they would have had they followed a systematic guide for behavior change. A large number of self-changers mistreat themselves by using alcohol or food to alleviate the blues. Drinking and overeating often exacerbates distress. This makes it doubly important that you relieve emotional distress by the careful application of change processes, and not by overindulgence.

Psychological distress self-assessment

The self-assessment shown here measures the severity of your present level of distress. What it does not do is establish a specific diagnosis or explain the reasons for your distress. Please indicate how much you have been bothered by these problems during the past month, putting the appropriate number (0, 1, or 2) in the space provided beside each sentence.

0 = not bothered at all, 1 = not bothered much,
2 = bothered a lot

1. Not having much interest in
   things   ___
2. Feeling too tired to do things   ___
3. Feeling afraid or scared
   without good reason   ___
4. Having trouble remembering
   things   ___
5. Feeling hopeless about the
   future   ___
6. Having trouble getting up in
   the morning and facing the
   day, even when I've had
   enough sleep   ___

7. Worrying too much   —
8. Having trouble making up my
   mind   —
9. Feeling sad or crying without
   good reason   —
10. Having trouble getting myself
    going   —
11. Feeling nervous, fidgety, tense   —
12. Being so restless I can't sit still   —
13. Being bothered by some
    unimportant thought that
    keeps running through my
    mind   —
14. Feeling blue or down in the
    dumps or depressed   —
15. Losing my appetite or losing
    weight without trying   —
16. Feeling keyed-up or
    overexcited   —
17. Avoiding certain places,
    people, or things because they
    frighten me   —

☐ ☐ ☐ ☐
D   L   A   I

Add the numbers in each column separately and record the total score in the box at the bottom of the column. The result will be four scores; double-check your arithmetic. If your score on D—for Depression—is 3 or higher, then write "high" next to the box labeled D. If it is 2 or less, write "average." If your score on L—for Lowered Energy—is 3 or higher, then write "high" next to that box. If it is 2 or less, write "average." If your score on A—for Anxiety—is 5 or higher, then write "high" next to the box. If it is 4 or less, write "average." And if your score on I—for Inefficient Cognitive Functioning—is 2 or higher, write "high" next to it. If it is 1 or 0, write "average."

If you scored high on two or more of the four scales, with at least one of the high scores being depression or anxiety, then you may well be suffering from high distress. If the self-assessment reveals this, it probably indicates the presence of psychological pressure and the need for change, whether on your own or with professional assistance.* A high score on any one scale is still cause for concern, but you might be able to address the problem within the context of helping relationships. Average scores on all four scales, assuming that you responded honestly, indicates that there is currently no need for you to be concerned about emotional distress.

There are widespread misunderstandings about the meanings of depression, lowered energy, anxiety, and inefficient cognitive functioning. The term "depression" may conjure up a picture of a tiny, elderly woman shuffling around a hospital ward in paper shoes. You may imagine someone in the throes of a panic attack when thinking of "anxiety." These stereotypes are widespread but unfortunate; each represents an extreme case. Much more typical are milder and less disruptive forms of distress.

Although we all experience distress differently, most of the following elements are usually present:

Depression Unlike everyday hassles and occasional disappointments, depression is a pervasive state. You may feel

---

*If your score is high on three or more of these scales, then we recommend that you consult a mental health professional, after reading the section in Chapter 9 about finding a good psychotherapist. In addition, go to your physician for a checkup to rule out diseases such as anemia, diabetes, thyroid condition, and mitral valve prolapse, all of which may cause or mimic the distress syndrome.

sad, discouraged, and hopeless, have a diminished interest in life, and derive little pleasure from anything.

Lowered energy   The technical term for this condition is *anergia,* which literally means "lack of energy." You may have trouble initiating projects, or experience decreased appetite and weight loss, general fatigue, or difficulty in getting started in the morning.

Anxiety   More than occasional nervousness, anxiety is a frequent feeling of nervousness and tension, excessive worrying, unrealistic fears of specific places or situations, general fears, and restlessness.

Inefficient cognitive functioning   Your cognitive abilities— memory, decision making, and concentration—are lower than usual. You may find yourself distracted, in a haze, or with a shortened attention span.

Stage of change self-assessment

The first step in any cycle of self-change is to recognize what stage of change you are in. This brief self-assessment will pinpoint your stage for psychological distress; complete it only if you had one or more high scores on the chart on pages 260–261.

1. Are you seriously considering overcoming your distress within the next six months?
2. Are you planning to overcome distress in the next thirty days (and perhaps taking small steps to do so)?
3. Are you now actively overcoming your distress?

You can determine your particular stage through the combination of answers you give to these three questions.

Question 1	No	Yes	Yes	Yes
Question 2	No	No	Yes	Yes
Question 3	No	No	No	Yes
Your Stage	Precontemplation	Contemplation	Preparation	Action

The remainder of this section will help you apply the change processes to psychological distress. We will cover each stage and recommend techniques to invoke each process in breaking the fever of mental health.

Precontemplation

Although distress is both common and recognizable, many people do not view it as a problem, thanks either to apathy, overt defenses, or ignorance. There are people who have been chronically distressed for years, and don't realize that alternative states of being exist. They accept their psychological condition as normal, or "just how I've always been."

Distress may go unnoticed because it is masked by other behavioral problems that receive all the attention—physical aggression, for example, abusive drinking, or loneliness. Understandably, people respond most quickly to visible problems like getting into fights, being fired from work, coming home drunk, or not leaving the house for days, while neglecting the underlying but less obvious distress.

More women than men acknowledge distress. Because of sex-role socialization and cultural expectations, women are generally both more aware and more expressive of their internal turmoil. In private moments or public surveys, they admit distress and label it as such; they are disinclined to mask it. Men are less receptive to this so-called wimpish problem, and rarely express distress verbally. They may become verbally abusive, develop hypertension, or increase their substance abuse. One recent study found that fully half of drug users have a depressive disorder. Whether you are male or female, substance abuse may reduce your distress, but only temporarily. Distress returns with a vengeance along with the increased substance use.

Sooner or later, distress becomes so unbearable that recognition and change are necessary. The good news is that most distressed people do overcome the problem successfully.

Contemplation

Psychological distress is an outrageous liar. It makes us think, feel, and behave in self-defeating and self-perpetuating ways. If you suffer from distress, chances are at least one of these statements is only too familiar:

> "It's all my fault."
> "I'll never get better!"
> "I'm a shit."
> "I'm too afraid to do that."
> "I can't do it—I'm helpless and incompetent."
> "That's too hard—it makes me feel scared. I won't do it."

A crucial step for distressed contemplators is to develop an awareness of the implicit, dysfunctional thoughts that reinforce their unhappiness. Cognitive therapists recommend making a daily log of these thoughts. Initially, the thoughts can be difficult to uncover. Start by logging instances of distressed behavior:

DAILY LOG—SATURDAY

1. Told Fred I can't come to his party tonight.
2. Spent evening sitting home, watching television, and feeling upset.
3. Gave up on cleaning the house.
4. Began to drink.

Eventually, you will become adept at identifying the automatic thoughts underlying your behaviors. The client who began this log was able, on reflection, to remember the thoughts that triggered his behaviors:

DAILY LOG—SATURDAY (with the thoughts underlying my behaviors)

1. Told Fred I can't come to his party tonight:
   "I won't have a good time." "Nobody likes me."
2. Spent evening sitting home, watching television, and feeling upset:
   "Nothing I do makes a difference." "Maybe I'm going crazy."
3. Gave up on cleaning the house:
   "My mind just won't cooperate." "I don't have the energy."
4. Began to drink:
   "Maybe this will make me feel better." "Nothing else is working."

Even a simple daily log can provide you with lots of essential information. Your own list will reveal the number of times your distress is associated with negative consequences. If you record your log on a daily basis, factual incidents, not distorted recollections, will provide you with the reasons you need for changing. These jottings can form the basis for a pros and cons assessment (discussed in detail in Chapter 5).

In addition, you will begin to see the pattern of your elusive thought processes. For example, the preceding log reveals indifference, helplessness, and low self-esteem. Information such as this will be essential when you try to alter your thought processes during the action stage.

It is also useful at this stage to gather factual information about distress and its ramifications. Few distressed people realize just how universal their problem is. Do some reading about your type of distress. Ask your loved ones how they experience your distress. Does it influence your behavior toward them and your children, co-workers, and neighbors? The answers may make you uncomfortable, but self-awareness will lead to incisive self-reevaluation. How long are you willing to remain distressed?

Action

Chronic distress can operate in a vicious cycle. The causes of distress give rise to effects that can in turn cause further distress. A failure at work, for example, can cause distress. The effects of anxiety, depression, lowered self-esteem, and cognitive impairment can cause further failures at work, which leads to more distress, and the cycle continues.

Yet you can disrupt your own cycle by understanding the circular and self-perpetuating relationship of all the parts, and by intervening at one or more points. You do this by using the three change processes that are most effective during the action stage—countering, environmental control, and reward—and applying them to at least two, and preferably more, points on the circle of distress.

Countering techniques   These can take the form of exercise, relaxation, assertion, countering thoughts, and active diversion. As long as you are physically able, you should exercise, for both the psychological and physiological benefits. Daily aerobic exercise is the simplest popular therapy for depression.

You might also consider "pleasant event scheduling." Create a list of pleasurable activities, and make sure that you partake in at least some of them every day. Many of these activities, such as gardening, dancing, playing a musical instrument, crocheting, or social engagements, combine relaxation and activity or recreation. The list is endless; the important thing is to tailor the activity to your own interests.

Progressive muscle relaxation was originally developed to counteract anxiety. The relaxation state is incompatible with anxiety; you cannot be anxious as long as you are relaxed. Learn and practice the relaxation techniques described in Chapter 7.

Clinicians recognize that passive, dependent personalities often repress their frustrations; over time, this can result in pent-up anger or depression. Assertiveness training is frequently used in treating psychological distress. Assertiveness affects many parts of the distress cycle, helping you to correct thoughts, alter relationships, improve interpersonal behavior, and feel more capable and vital.

The most thoroughly researched professional treatment for distress is cognitive therapy, which combines the above methods, emphasizing the countering of dysfunctional thoughts. Regardless of the origin of distressing feelings, behaviors, and relationships—countering maladaptive beliefs can stop the vicious cycle cold. The objective of cognitive methods is deceptively simple: Identify dysfunctional thoughts, dispute them, and replace them with realistic, healthy ones. You have already learned to identify underlying thoughts by keeping a daily log. Here is a method to counter those thoughts, using a triple-column diary.

In the first column of the diary, record your "Automatic Thought," what you tell yourself when you are distressed. In the second column, indicate whether there is solid, scientific evidence in support of your thought. Ask yourself: Is this thought a realistic appraisal of the situation? Or have I fallen for the lies of distress?

The third column is reserved for balanced, realistic thought. When your first, automatic thought is realistic—a minority of cases—there will be nothing to enter in this

TABLE 12. SAMPLE DIARY

Automatic Thought	Evidence for It	Substitute Thought
I won't have a good time.	None. Always had a good time before.	When I'm distressed I tend to withdraw from others. But I'll probably have a good time and it would help me to go.
Nobody likes me.	None.	Another lie told by distress. I could have more friends of course, but Louise, Joyce, and Fred are my friends when I allow them to be.
Nothing I do makes a difference.	None.	I can't control everything, but I do run most things in my own life.
I don't have the energy.	Some. It's true that I have less energy when I'm distressed.	I can decide to go whether or not I have energy. I don't really need a lot of energy just to be at a party.

column. Most times, however, your distressed thoughts are not grounded in evidence or reality. In these instances, you will actively dispute the original thought and replace it with a realistic and healthier self-statement. Table 12 is a sample diary, filled out by the client who decided against going to a party.

In the face of active, rational thinking, most automatic thoughts turn out to be falsehoods. Dispassionate examination allows you to see that there is very little evidence to support these thoughts. Your task then becomes to replace them with balanced and logical thoughts. As you practice countering many times, day in and day out, dysfunctional thoughts begin to fade and realistic replacements take their place. Your distress will fade, too.

Environment control   While restructuring thought processes, you can also restructure your environment so that it works for you rather than against you. The most important action you can take is to avoid those relationships, places, and situations that prompt your distress and replace them with supportive and healing contexts.

Take the example of Lisa, a thirty-four-year-old chef, who went days without distress despite work conflicts, single-parent pressures, and omnipresent financial woes. Her commitment to change and countering techniques were exemplary—until she visited her parents. Lisa's religiously intolerant mother and father belittled her and were unaccepting of her as a person, a mother, and a worker. A weekend of parental rejection overwhelmed weeks of self-change; Lisa quickly reverted to self-depreciation. It took her some time and effort to resolve the initial guilt involved in temporarily avoiding this degrading interpersonal contact, since it essentially meant staying away from her parents. But once she did, Lisa was able to consolidate her change and build her assertion skills. This accomplished, she was able to gradually reintroduce herself to her parents' home without prompting a relapse.

Reward   Reinforce even small steps in your progress. Treat yourself to a movie for completing a triple-column diary, or give yourself an hour of rest for exercising; solicit a kiss from someone for confronting fear or congratulations for assertiveness. Use whatever reward works for you. Contract with another person for pleasant-event scheduling, exercise, or relaxation. And contract with yourself to avoid the guilt and recrimination that accompanies psychological distress. Reward, not punishment, is the most effective catalyst for change.

Used simultaneously, countering, environment control, and reward can disrupt the vicious cycle of psychological distress. These change processes are complementary rather than contradictory. If you substitute healthy responses for distress by using countering techniques, rearrange distress-inducing situations by employing environmental control, and reinforce recovery by rewarding yourself appropriately, then you can deal with all potential sources of distress—behaviors, cognitions, feelings, relationships, and family interactions.

Maintenance

Pulling out of individual distress episodes is indeed a major accomplishment. The goal, however, is maintaining a distress-free life. Having said that, it is worth pointing out that no one's life is actually "distress free"; as food will always be necessary to the overeater, so anxiety and depression are, in the words of one self-changer, "part of the cost of being alive." But when you reach the maintenance stage, your life can be free from clinically significant distress. You should be able to prevent inevitable losses and disappointments from leading to a full-blown disorder.

Begin the maintenance stage by honestly recognizing the possibility of relapse. Although it may seem paradoxical, the acknowledgment of this possibility will help you to firm up your commitment, maintain a healthy distance from distressing situations, and impress upon you the necessity of creating a new lifestyle. All of these ingredients are essential to successful, long-term maintenance, and to the recognition that a lapse is not a relapse, a slip is not a fall.

People who are distressed can change, but distressful situations can always arise. Life simply cannot be free of psychological distress, as the triple-column-diary entry on the next page demonstrates.

Automatic Thought	Evidence for It	Substitute Thought
Once I have recovered from distress, I should never experience it again.	None. This is a wish, not a fact.	Difficult as it is to accept, my distress will probably return. However, I am now better equipped to recognize it, alleviate it, and prevent it from getting too severe or going on for too long.

Maintenance strategies prevent ordinary distress from becoming neurotic misery. All of the processes used during the action stage should be used in maintenance, and there are some further strategies to employ. One of the major allies of psychological distress is unstructured time. Empty hours, goalless days, and languid weeks conspire to elevate anxiety and compound depression. Exercise, activity, and diversion can fill the void in the short run, and relaxation training can help you tolerate unstructured time, and even to learn to use it for regeneration. But in the long run, these strategies may not suffice. You need to develop an assertive lifestyle, personal commitments, and a goal-directed life plan.

A very important strategy in strengthening your commitment involves interpersonal relationships, which bring meaning and context to all our behavior. Most satisfying lives include satisfying relationships, and many people see family and friends as a primary source of gratification in life. Emerging research shows that helping relationships can serve as a buffer against future distress episodes by diminishing the severity of the harsh realities of the world and their negative impact. This buffer is one hypothesis for the repeated finding that married people live longer and more happily than single people.

The hard facts of life—sadness, disappointment, tragedy—cannot be avoided. But your reaction to the needn't be distress; if you successfully navigate the cycle of change, you can learn to react to even the severest blows with appropriate, healthy behavior.

...ination—Exiting the ...ycle of Change

IDEALLY, YOU WILL proceed systematically through the cycle of change, moving out of the resistance of precontemplation and into the acknowledgment of contemplation, then entering the anticipation of preparation, the flurry of action, and, last, the consolidation of maintenance. Few changers actually follow the path so directly; most become sidetracked at one stage or another. However, with persistence, knowledge, and experience, you may arrive at the point where you consider that you are now free from a long-standing problem. This is called "termination," the exit from the spiraling cycle of change.

There are professionals who believe that termination is impossible, that the most anyone can hope for is a lifetime of maintenance. In his 1937 paper *Analysis Terminable and Interminable*, Sigmund Freud asked, "Is there such a thing as a natural end to analysis?" His conclusion was that meaningful change was a lifelong pursuit, and that even psychoanalysis—the most intensive and extensive treatment then available—could not provide a complete resolution of all conflicts.

This is a realistic approach. Personal growth is an open-ended enterprise. In the course of our work, we have met people who have maintained behavior change for five or even ten years before returning to an old maladaptive habit.

Usually the return is triggered by a personal disaster, such as the death of a spouse. No program of behavior change can possibly anticipate and prepare you for tragedies that are decades away.

Do not, however, overlook the benefits of overcoming a problem. With experience, you can identify its early warning signs: lethargy, overconfidence, and renewed temptations. Even if a problem is never terminated, it becomes less of a threat as the years go by. Vigilance can safely decrease over time.

As for true termination, there is little consensus among the experts. We believe that it can occur, depending on the nature of the problem. While you may hope to terminate certain problems, others appear to be interminable. Experts often disagree as to which problems belong in which camp.

Alcoholism, for example, is usually seen as a lifelong disease; Alcoholics Anonymous refers to abstinent drinkers as "recovering" alcoholics, never "recovered." An increasing number of behavioral scientists, however, view alcohol abuse as a disorder that is subject to the same controls and contingencies as any other dysfunctional behavior. They chart the progression from abuse to dependence to addiction along a continuum, and resist the oversimplified classification of "alcoholic." Our goal, whenever possible, is to help people be recovered rather than spend a lifetime in recovery.

Age factors into the question of termination. With problems like smoking and substance abuse, the older you get, the more likely you are to lose your taste for the habit and quit. People have a greater potential to bring to termination those problems that tend to disappear with age. With other problems, like being inactive or obese, age works against you. People tend to become more sedentary and heavier with age. Problems that naturally worsen with age are more likely to require a lifetime of maintenance.

DEFINING TERMINATION FOR YOUR PROBLEM

How far and how long must you go before you consider your problem to be terminated? How do you determine when you have been vigilant long enough? How can you distinguish the real signs of termination from the rationalizations that will cause your problem behavior to return?

Our research and clinical experiences indicate that there are at least four defining criteria. These approximate standards divide terminators from lifetime maintainers:

A new self-image   Short-term change may be transitory, or it may result from temporary but unsustained action, developmental events, or just plain luck. However, if a significant revision in your attitude and self-image takes place during the maintenance stage, there is a good chance you will approach termination.

Clients in maintenance frequently tell their psychotherapists that, while they have mastered their problem, they do not yet feel that the change is "theirs." Their old self-image is inconsistent with their new behavior, but they have not yet developed a new one. As the new behavior takes hold, a new self-image, one that feels consistent with the healthier behavior, gradually develops. This development is a promising sign of termination.

No temptation in any situation   To terminate for good, you must experience no temptation to return to your old behavior, regardless of the situation. If you no longer feel any desire to smoke, abuse food or alcohol, spend money, or engage in any other type of problem behavior, no matter where you are or how you are feeling, you may have terminated the change process for that particular problem. The ability to enter restaurants, stores, bars, or parties without being tempted to lapse is a clear sign of termination. When you can feel sad, angry, depressed, or anxious without being tempted to counter these feelings with problematic behaviors, you should be encouraged. When you no longer dream or daydream about eating, smoking, or drinking, those problem desires are becoming extinct.

Obviously, this does not happen overnight. We believe that it takes smokers an average of thirty-six to forty-eight months of maintenance before they feel little or no temptation to smoke. Some never pass the maintenance stage, reporting significant longings for cigarettes in certain situations even after fifteen years of abstinence. Some former smokers appear to use no conscious change processes to control their behavior because they experience no temptations that need to be controlled. They experience themselves in the same way as individuals who never smoked.

Solid self-efficacy Terminators transfer their "center of gravity" from their problems to themselves. They look, think, feel, and act not with false bravado but with genuine confidence. They are convinced that they can function well without ever again engaging in their former problem behaviors.

It takes an average of twelve months before many people who ultimately terminate smoking become fully confident that they can cope with tempting situations without lapsing. Confidence peaks one year after action begins, but temptation does not bottom out until two or three years later.

Solid self-efficacy is never guaranteed. Again, certain people who have not smoked for ten years still lack the confidence to say they will never smoke again. Such "lifers" must continue to counter the temptation to smoke; some stave it off by promising themselves that if they ever develop a fatal disease, they will begin smoking again.

Using the criteria of 100 percent self-efficacy and zero

temptation across all high-risk situations, we have found that 16 percent of former smokers and 17 percent of former alcoholics have reached the termination stage. These people are not in recovery; they have recovered. This does not only mean that these former alcoholics will never have a drink again. It also means that they will have no temptation to drink and are fully confident that no matter what situations they encounter—whether they are angry, anxious, bored, depressed, celebrating, or socializing—they will never again rely on alcohol as a way of coping.

Many others still have to use some change processes in certain situations to keep from relapsing. Those who still experience some temptation and lack of confidence in certain situations continue in the maintenance stage. This doesn't mean that they will necessarily relapse. It just means that they still have to make some efforts to control tempting situations.

A healthier lifestyle   Life changes are essential for maintenance; a new lifestyle is essential for termination. The difference is in the permanence of the change. In maintenance, you modify parts of your life—social contacts, daily schedules, behavior patterns—to overcome your problem. In termination, you institute a healthier lifestyle as a means of preserving your gains and promoting new growth.

Two approaches to abstinence from alcohol illustrate the difference. Robert has alternated between action and maintenance for twenty years, staying sober 90 percent of the time. When he lapses or relapses, he puts his action plan back into gear; he cuts out parties, goes back to A.A., works out three times a week, and rewards himself for each week and month of sobriety. After months of success, he quits going to A.A. and to his health club. He puts himself back in tempting situations and he expresses resentment over always having to control his temptation to drink.

Shawna, on the other hand, learned early that staying

sober was much easier when it was part of a healthier lifestyle. After quitting drinking, she quit smoking for good measure. She sees herself as a health advocate—one who has integrated exercise, not smoking, and a low-fat diet into her life. She loves to socialize, but in healthy settings, not in smoke-filled bars and clubs.

Shawna does not spend her energies on struggling to stay sober or free from smoking. She spends her time on activities that are healthy and enlivening.

The real solution

Creating a healthier lifestyle involves altering more than your problem. Recent studies of people who successfully overcame troubled drinking on their own showed that half of those individuals also quit smoking on their own. Smokers in relationships with other smokers have little chance of successful termination unless they develop new relationships that support their changing selves. It is simply naïve to believe that you can go on living the way you did before and have the consequences be different.

Although you can never be problem free, you can live in ways that reduce the recurrence of self-defeating behaviors. Just as being in top physical shape is the best way to prevent injury and disease, being in top psychological shape makes it less likely that you will engage in self-destructive behaviors.

If you believe that life is passing you by, you will find it easy to give up on yourself. Spend your time and energies on self-enhancing activities instead. You will be less tempted to indulge in self-defeating behaviors. Pursue your dreams of being a student or a teacher, a parent or a lover, an adventurer or a traveler, and in this way commit to live life to its fullest while preventing behaviors that short-circuit your endeavors. As long as you act on your potential to change, you will discover that even the darkest days will end and the most tempting situations will pass.

As you progress through the stages of change, you will appreciate the major accomplishment you have achieved in moving from precontemplation to termination. By acting on your potential for change you not only resolve a problem, but create a happier and healthier self.

Foolish Freedom

IT REMAINS DIFFICULT to believe that many otherwise intelligent human beings actively resist becoming aware of the ways in which they are endangering, damaging, or even destroying their lives. You have no doubt heard the slogans of people who maintain their right to just such a foolish freedom. They go something like this: "No one can tell me how to live my life." "I'll pull my own strings even if they hang me." "They're my children—I'll spoil them [or beat them] if I want to." "No one is going to tell me how to manage my money—even if I am going broke."

Often those who have grown up with an overcontrolling parent are especially vulnerable to this all-consuming need for control. These people seem to have vowed to themselves, "Never again will I let anyone control me. If anyone is going to be in control, it will be me."

Maria had a tyrannical father who insisted on knowing and controlling every detail of her life. He chose her clothes, her friends, and her college. When she went out on a date, he waited up for her and pumped her with questions as soon as she walked in the door. Maria seethed inside, but never dared stand up to her father. At the age of thirty-three she found that she had total control over her husband. She determined what they did, when they did it, what they bought, and whom they socialized with. She was in such control during sex that she was unable to let go and enjoy herself.

Even people who do not have an overwhelming need to control their lives can be vehement about continuing their self-destructive behaviors unimpeded. A partial explanation can be found in the laboratory research of a zoologist named Calhoun. Unlike most researchers, Calhoun studied wild mice (instead of domesticated white mice and rats) to learn how they strive to control their own behavior.

Calhoun provided his wild mice with an electric switch with which they could choose bright light, dim light, or no light in their cages. The mice consistently threw the switch that turned on the dim lights, avoiding bright lights and darkness. But when the experimenter turned on the dim light, the mice ran over to turn it off, substituting bright light or no light. In another experiment, Calhoun gave the mice control of a switch that turned a revolving wheel on and off. Running in the wheel was their only source of exercise. To stay healthy, caged mice need to run about eight hours a day, so, as you might expect, the mice periodically turned on the switch and ran. But every time the experimenter turned on the wheel, the mice immediately switched it off, even though they needed and wanted to run.

This is *foolish freedom*. The mice preferred mastering the switch to running. They demanded control over their behavior, even if it meant sacrificing their own health. White mice, bred to be easily handled and manipulated, are too tame to exhibit this kind of behavior. Many of the research psychologists, like B. F. Skinner, who studied domesticated animals, concluded that human beings can be easily controlled by external conditioning. Sigmund Freud, on the other hand, believed that human beings are more like wild animals, controlled by internal biological drives.

In the industrial age in which Freud lived, much of life consisted of boring routines, and an individual's defenses served to control internal impulses that threatened to master the psyche. In those days, inhibitions were strong because internal impulses were correspondingly powerful. Today inhibitions are weaker. In our information age, it is the external not the internal messages that threaten to overwhelm us. Humanity's very same psychological defenses now seek to control the demands society and the media make on us—to just do it, to choose the real thing, because what you want is what you get. Too many people cannot control their media-fueled desires. We smoke, drink, overeat, and overspend. We seek fulfillment in external objects.

Internal impulses can keep us from attending to the tasks at hand. Similarly, external messages can captivate our minds and keep us from concentrating on what is most important to us. Unfortunately, we have trouble distinguishing helpful messages from harmful ones. It seems the only freedom we can achieve is negative—freedom from the demands of others. It is certainly true that many of us have such a strong desire to be in control that we resist beneficial changes.

People who, like the wild mice, insist on being in control at all costs are out of balance. They are rebellious precontemplators, equating freedom with control and resisting the most well-intentioned external influences that could free them from self-destructive behavior. Such people maintain closed lives, filtering out all information that might help them change, regardless of the source. As a result, they are often surprisingly uninformed about the very behaviors that others see as problematic.

Under what conditions are we likely to be open to the developmental processes within us or the environmental processes outside us as freeing influences that enable us to change our lives intentionally? Under what conditions do we experience these same processes as coercive forces imposing change on us that we must resist with our best defenses?

To respond to these issues adequately would require an adequate theory of personal freedom. Unfortunately, such a theory does not yet exist, mainly because psychologists and other social scientists have not taken personal freedom seriously. But the existentialist philosopher Bergmann does point the way to a model of personal determinism.

First, let us be clear that the assumption that people can be free is not a tender-minded position that contradicts the tenets of tough-minded scientists. Freedom is not incompatible with determinism. Freedom and determinism have all too long been paired as polar opposites. Personal freedom requires a deterministic world which is predictable and controllable. One of the most terrifying problems is to experience our lives as being unpredictable and uncontrollable.

By opposing determinism to freedom, we are left with the untenable notion that we can be free only when our behavior is entirely uninfluenced. According to this notion, only acts of sheer caprice, performed in total independence of advantage or reason, can be free. Freedom becomes limited to actions that are truly spontaneous and unpredictable, totally unbounded, and yielding to no authority—not even reason. Freedom thus must materialize out of nothing, like the irrational but apparently spontaneous acts of rock bands who end up smashing their instruments for the sheer sake of being free from encumbrances.

Before I can experience this chaos as freedom, I must experience my reason as something other than myself. If I feel coerced when obeying my reason, then my reason is not an intimate part of myself. I experience my thoughts as alien and unfree when I am obsessing, when I cannot get *that* thought out of my mind. I don't identify with the thought. The thought is intrusive, oppressive, and obsessive.

The primary prerequisite of freedom is a sense of self that

is possessed by something that wants to be acted out. If I identify myself as essentially a reasonable person, for example, then I experience myself as most free when I act in harmony with reason. Reason is not alien to my sense of self but rather is an essential part of it. If the environment provides new evidence for quitting smoking, I can freely begin to contemplate quitting smoking if I identify the evidence as reasonable. From this perspective, I am not free when I am coerced into acting irrationally. As a reasonable person I might prefer not to smoke, but I may feel compelled to smoke by irrational forces within me. Thus, I experience my problems as due to coercion or compulsion, not to free choices.

If I identify myself with all my internal impulses, all actions that flow from within are free. From this perspective, I may continue to smoke unreasonably but feel guilty rather than coerced. This sense of self denies any psychological compulsion but at a cost of considerable guilt. The only true coercion occurs when forces literally external to me compel me to action. If my family pressures me into psychotherapy to work on my drinking, I may go, but out of a sense of coercion, not choice, because they were the prime movers of my action.

An act is free if I identify with the elements that generate it. An act is coerced if I feel dissociated from the elements. Thus, identification is logically prior to independence. Freedom is not a primary, but a derivative, experience. A sense of self is logically prior to self-control. Personal freedom is the acting out of our identity, our self.

Self-reevaluation is an important change process for preparing for liberating action. Through this process you come to think and feel differently about yourself (as a drinker, smoker, or whatever). You are preparing to give up and grieve for an important part of your identity—not just for now but forever.

Our research shows that increases in self-reevaluation

lead to the greatest increases in the pros of changing. As you look to a future free from compulsions, addictions, or depressions, you can imagine a growing number of good reasons to shed your old sense of self.

Some of the reasons can be surprising. In a study with the Centers for Disease Control and Prevention, I was surprised by the number one reason our research participants gave for practicing safer sex. These were IV drug users, prostitutes, and street youth in five of the toughest cities in the United States. You might expect that the only reason to always use condoms would be to keep from contracting AIDS. This was the second most important pro. The first was to be a more responsible person.

Responsible freedom is when you choose to change for the best of reasons, regardless of what you were conditioned to do, what you feel compelled to do, or what is most immediately gratifying to do. Our fullest freedom emerges when we have the opportunity to choose that which would enhance our life, our sense of self, and our society.

Foolish freedom is reactive—reacting just to keep from being controlled or reacting to immediate consequences. Responsible freedom is interactive—interacting with feedback and information about how changing our behavior can be beneficial to ourselves and to others. You don't have to resist if someone is trying to change you for good reasons. You can interact with the person and his or her reasons. If that person influences you to change for good, so much the better for both of you.

A New Paradigm

OUR WORK ON the stages of change represents a new paradigm of behavior change. Health officials will be especially interested in how this paradigm fares in health promotion programs. Some of the comprehensive data that support this paradigm are:

1. The stages of change approach has been cited as being perhaps the most important development in the past decade of research on smoking cessation specifically (*JCCP*, 1992) and health behavior change generally (*Diabetes Spectrum*, 1993).
2. The stages of change approach is being used for all of the HIV and AIDS prevention programs directed by the Centers for Disease Control in the United States. It is also implemented in all health promotion programs for dieting and for countering smoking and substance abuse in the National Health Service of Great Britain.
3. Our work is not just another action-oriented intervention. It is a new approach to understanding, studying, and optimizing how people change high-risk behaviors.
4. We have demonstrated with a dozen different problem behaviors that change involves progress

through a series of stages, not just a progression from high risk to no risk.

5. Our work is producing principles of change that were hitherto unknown. It matches the most powerful processes of change to the needs of individuals at each stage of change.

6. Our approach is designed to match people's self-change efforts at each and every stage of change. It is designed to work in harmony with how people change naturally.

7. Our approach is appropriate for individuals at every stage of change, and not just the 20 percent or fewer who are prepared to take action.

8. Action-oriented health promotion programs typically generate 1 to 5 percent participation rates. Programs based on the new paradigm typically generate 50 to 85 percent participation.

9. Action-oriented programs (aimed, for example, at smoking) typically reduce the rates of risk by 1 to 2 percent. Programs based on the new paradigm typically reduce the rates by 12 to 18 percent.

10. Action-oriented programs typically produce high initial success rates followed by dramatic declines in success over time. Programs based on the new paradigm typically produce lower initial success rates followed by dramatic increases in success over time.

11. Action-oriented programs typically place high demands on both health promotion professionals and participants. The new paradigm can provide high-intensity, interactive programs that demand much less of both professionals and participants.

12. Our approach produces realistic goals that can maximize the benefits of brief or low-intensity interventions.

13. Programs based on the new paradigm can effectively complement current action-oriented programs in two ways:
    a. Stage-based programs are excellent for people who do not participate in traditional action-oriented programs.
    b. Stage-based programs are promising alternatives for people who do not succeed in traditional action-oriented programs.

14. Our approach is appropriate for high-risk populations with multiple behavioral risk factors.
15. The most effective action-oriented programs typically cannot be delivered in a cost-effective manner to remote sites. The most effective programs based on the new paradigm can deliver high-quality services to remote sites.

Bibliography

Bergmann, F. (1977). *On Being Free.* South Bend, Ind.: University of Notre Dame Press.

Cohen, S., E. Lichtenstein, J. O. Prochaska, et al. (1989). "Debunking Myths About Self-Quitting: Evidence from 10 Prospective Studies of Persons Quitting Smoking by Themselves." *American Psychologist, 44,* 1355–1365.

DiClemente, C. C. (1985). Antonio—More Than Anxiety: A Transtheoretical Approach. *Casebook of Eclectic Psychotherapy.* New York: Brunner/Mazel.

DiClemente, C. C. (1991). "Motivational Interviewing and the Stages of Change." In W. R. Miller and S. Rollnick, eds. *Motivational Interviewing: Preparing People to Change Addictive Behavior.* New York: Guilford.

DiClemente, C. C. (1993). Alcoholics Anonymous and the Structure of Change. In W. R. Miller and B. S. McCready, eds., *Research on Alcoholics Anonymous: Opportunities and Alternatives.* Newark, N.J.: Rutgers University Press.

DiClemente, C. C. (1993). Changing Addictive Behaviors: A Process Perspective. *Current Directions in Psychological Science, 2,* 101–106.

DiClemente, C. C., J. P. Carbonari, and M. M. Velasquez (1992). Alcoholism Treatment Mismatching from a Process of Change Perspective. In E. R. R. Watson, *Drug and Alcohol Abuse Reviews, Vol. 3: Alcohol Abuse Treatment.* Totowa, N.J.: Humana.

DiClemente, C. C., and S. O. Hughes (1990). "Stages of Change Profiles in Alcoholism Treatment." *Journal of Substance Abuse, 2,* 217–235.

DiClemente, C. C., E. A. McConnaughy, J. C. Norcross, and J. O. Prochaska (1986). "Integrative Dimensions for Psychotherapy." *International Journal of Eclectic Psychotherapy, 5,* 256–274.

DiClemente, C. C., and J. O. Prochaska (1982). "Self-change and Therapy Change of Smoking Behavior: A Comparison of Processes of Change in Cessation and Maintenance." *Addictive Behaviors, 7,* 133–142.

DiClemente, C. C., and J. O. Prochaska (1985). "Processes and Stages of Change: Coping and Competence in Smoking Behavior Change." In

S. Shiffman and T. A. Wills, eds. *Coping and Substance Abuse*. San Diego: Academic Press.

DiClemente, C. C., J. O. Prochaska, S. K. Fairhurst, W. F. Velicer, M. M. Velasquez, and J. S. Rossi (1991). "The Process of Smoking Cessation: An Analysis of Precontemplation, Contemplation, and Preparation Stages of Change." *Journal of Consulting and Clinical Psychology, 59,* 295–304.

DiClemente, C. C., J. O. Prochaska, and M. Gilbertini (1985). "Self-efficacy and the Stages of Self-change of Smoking." *Cognitive Therapy and Research, 9,* 181–200.

Farber, B. A., and J. D. Geller (1977). "Student Attitudes Toward Psychotherapy." *Journal of the American Health Association, 25,* 301–307.

Gleser, G. C., and D. Ihilevich (1969). "An Objective Instrument for Measuring Defense Mechanisms." *Journal of Consulting and Clinical Psychology, 33,* 51–60.

Gurin G., J., Veroff and S. Feld (1960). *Americans View Their Mental Health.* New York: Basic Books.

Luborsky, L., B. Singer, and L. Luborsky (1975). "Comparative Studies of Psychotherapies: Is it True That Everybody Has Won and All Must Have Prizes?" *Archives of General Psychiatry, 32,* 995–1008.

McConnaughy, E. A., C. C. DiClemente, J. O. Prochaska, and W. F. Velicer (1989). "Stages of Change in Psychotherapy: A Follow-up Report." *Psychotherapy, 26,* 494–503.

McConnaughy, E. A., J. O. Prochaska, and W. F. Velicer (1983). "Stages of Change in Psychotherapy: Measurement and Sample Profiles." *Psychotherapy, 20,* 368–375.

Marlatt, G. A., and J. R. Gordon (1985). *Relapse Prevention.* New York: Guilford.

Mechanic, D. (1962). *Students Under Stress.* New York: Free Press.

Mellinger, G. D., M. B. Balter, E. H. Uhlenhuth, I. H. Cisin, and H. J. Parry (1978). "Psychic Distress, Life Crisis, and Use of Psychotherapeutic Medications: National Household Survey Data. *Archives of General Psychiatry, 35,* 1045–1052.

Munroe, S. M., D. J. Rohsenow, J. C. Norcross, and P. M. Monti (1993). "Coping Strategies and the Maintenance of Change After Inpatient Alcoholism Treatment." *Social Work Research and Abstracts, 29,* 18–22.

Norcross, J. C., ed. (1991). "Prescriptive Matching in Psychotherapy: Psychoanalysis for Simple Phobias?" *Psychotherapy, 28,* 439–472.

Norcross, J. C., B. A. Alford, and J. T. DeMichele (1992). "The Future of Psychotherapy: Delphi Data and Concluding Observations." *Psychotherapy, 29,* 150–158.

Norcross, J. C., and D. C. Aboyoun (1994). "Self-change Experiences of Psychotherapists." In T. M. Brinthaupt and R. P. Lipka, eds. *Changing the Self.* Albany: State University of New York Press.

Norcross, J. C., and M. R. Goldfried, eds. (1992). *Handbook of Psychotherapy Integration.* New York: Basic Books.

Norcross, J. C., and P. R. Magaletta (1990). "Concurrent Validation of the Levels of Attribution and Change (LAC) Scale." *Journal of Clinical Psychology, 46*, 618–622.

Norcross, J. C., and J. O. Prochaska (1986). "Psychotherapist Heal Thyself I: The Psychological Distress and Self-change of Psychologists, Counselors, and Laypersons." *Psychotherapy, 23*, 102–114.

Norcross, J. C., and J. O. Prochaska (1986). "Psychotherapist Heal Thyself II: The Self-Initiated and Therapy-Facilitated Change of Psychological Distress." *Psychotherapy, 23*, 345–356.

Norcross, J. C., J. O. Prochaska, and C. C. DiClemente (1986). "Self-change of Psychological Distress: Laypersons' vs Psychologists' Coping Strategies." *Journal of Clinical Psychology, 42*, 834–840.

Norcross, J. C., J. O. Prochaska, and C. C. DiClemente (1991). "Helping Clients Stick to It." *IDEA Today, 9* (6), 23–26.

Norcross, J. C., J. O. Prochaska, and C. C. DiClemente (in press). "The Stages and Processes of Weight Control: Two Replications." In A. Kutscher et al., eds. *Obesity and Weight Control.* Philadelphia: Charles Press.

Norcross, J. C., J. O. Prochaska, and M. Hambrecht (1985). "Levels of Attribution and Change (LAC) Scale: Development and Measurement." *Cognitive Therapy and Research, 9*, 631–649.

Norcross, J. C., J. O. Prochaska, and M. Hambrecht (1991). "Treating Ourselves vs. Treating Our Clients: A Replication with Alcohol Abuse." *Journal of Substance Abuse, 3*, 123–129.

Norcross, J. C., A. C. Ratzin, and D. Payne (1989). "Ringing In the New Year: The Change Process and Reported Outcomes of Resolutions." *Addictive Behaviors, 14*, 205–212.

Norcross, J. C., D. J. Strausser, and F. J. Faltus (1988). "The Therapist's Therapist." *American Journal of Psychotherapy, 42*, 53–66.

Norcross, J. C., and D. J. Vangarelli (1989). "The Resolution Solution: Longitudinal Examination of New Year's Change Attempts." *Journal of Substance Abuse, 1*, 127–134.

Orleans, C. T., and others (1988, November). *Effectiveness of Self-Help Quit Smoking Strategies.* Symposium presented at the annual meeting of the Association for the Advancement of Behavior Therapy, New York, N.Y.

Prochaska, J. O. (1991). "Prescribing to the Stages and Levels of Change." *Psychotherapy, 28*, 463–468.

Prochaska, J. O., and C. C. DiClemente (1982). "Transtheoretical Therapy: Toward a More Integrative Model of Change." *Psychotherapy, 20*, 161–173.

Prochaska, J. O., and C. C. DiClemente (1983). "Stages and Processes of Self-Change in Smoking: Toward an Integrative Model of Change." *Journal of Consulting and Clinical Psychology, 5*, 390–395.

Prochaska, J. O., and C. C. DiClemente (1984). *The Transtheoretical Approach: Crossing Traditional Boundaries of Therapy.* Melbourne, Fla.: Krieger.

Prochaska, J. O., and C. C. DiClemente (1985). "Common Processes of

Change in Smoking, Weight Control, and Psychological Distress." In S. Shiffman and T. Wills, eds. *Coping and Substance Abuse.* San Diego: Academic Press.

Prochaska, J. O., and C. C. DiClemente (1986). "Toward a Comprehensive Model of Change." In W. R. Miller and N. Heather, eds. *Treating Addictive Behaviors: Processes of Change.* New York: Plenum.

Prochaska, J. O., and C. C. DiClemente (1992). "Stages of Change in the Modification of Problem Behaviors. In M. Hersen, R. M. Eisler, and P. M. Miller, eds. *Progress in Behavior Modification.* Sycamore, Ill. Sycamore Press.

Prochaska, J. O., and C. C. DiClemente (1992). The Transtheoretical Approach. In J. C. Norcross and M. R. Goldfried, eds., *Handbook of Psychotherapy Integration.* New York: Basic Books.

Prochaska, J. O., C. C. DiClemente, and J. C. Norcross (1992). "In Search of the Structure of Behavior Change." In Y. Klar et al., eds. *Self-Change: Social-Psychological and Clinical Perspectives.* New York: Springer-Verlag.

Prochaska, J. O., C. C. DiClemente, and J. C. Norcross (1992). "In Search of How People Change: Applications to Addictive Behaviors." *American Psychologist, 47,* 1102–1114.

Prochaska, J. O., C. C. DiClemente, W. F. Velicer, S. Ginpil, and J. C. Norcross (1985). "Predicting Change in Smoking Status for Self-changers." *Addictive Behaviors, 10,* 395–406.

Prochaska, J. O., and J. C. Norcross (1983). "Psychotherapists' Perspectives on Treating Themselves and Their Clients for Psychic Distress." *Professional Psychology, 14,* 642–655.

Prochaska, J. O., and J. C. Norcross (1994). *Systems of Psychotherapy: A Transtheoretical Analysis,* 3d. ed. Pacific Grove, Calif.: Brooks/Cole.

Prochaska, J. O., J. C. Norcross, J. L. Fowler, M. J. Follick, and D. B. Abrams (1992). "Attendance and Outcome in a Work Site Weight Control Program: Processes and Stages of Change As Process and Predictor Variables." *Addictive Behaviors, 17,* 35–45.

Prochaska, J. O., W. F. Velicer, C. C. DiClemente, and J. S. Fava (1988). "Measuring Processes of Change: Applications to the Cessation of Smoking. *Journal of Consulting and Clinical Psychology, 56,* 520–528.

Velicer, W. F., C. C. DiClemente, J. O. Prochaska, and N. Brandenburg (1985). "A Decisional Balance Measure for Assessing and Predicting Smoking Status. *Journal of Personality and Social Psychology, 48,* 1279–1289.

Veroff, J., E. Douvan, and R. A. Kulka (1981). *Mental Health in America.* New York: Basic Books.

Watzlawick, P. (1983). *The Situation Is Hopeless but Not Serious.* New York: Norton.

Wilcox, N., J. O. Prochaska, W. F. Velicer, and C. C. DiClemente (1985). "Client Characteristics As Predictors of Self-change in Smoking Cessation." *Addictive Behaviors, 40,* 407–412.

Index

Page numbers in *italics* refer to tables and figures.